Other Books and Series by Jeff Bowen

Applications for Enrollment of Chickasaw Newborn Act of 1905
Volumes I thru VII

Cherokee Intermarried White 1906 Volume I thru X

Applications for Enrollment of Creek Newborn Act of 1905
Volumes I thru XIV

Applications for Enrollment of Choctaw Newborn Act of 1905
Volume I, II, III & IV

Visit our website at **www.nativestudy.com** to learn more about these and other books and series by Jeff Bowen

APPLICATIONS FOR ENROLLMENT OF CHOCTAW NEWBORN ACT OF 1905

VOLUME V

TRANSCRIBED BY
JEFF BOWEN

NATIVE STUDY
Gallipolis, Ohio
USA

Other Books and Series by Jeff Bowen

1901-1907 Native American Census Seneca, Eastern Shawnee, Miami, Modoc, Ottawa, Peoria, Quapaw, and Wyandotte Indians (Under Seneca School, Indian Territory)

1932 Census of The Standing Rock Sioux Reservation with Births And Deaths 1924-1932

Census of The Blackfeet, Montana, 1897- 1901 Expanded Edition

Eastern Cherokee by Blood, 1906-1910, Volumes I thru XIII

Choctaw of Mississippi Indian Census 1929-1932 with Births and Deaths 1924-1931 Volume I
Choctaw of Mississippi Indian Census 1933, 1934 & 1937, Supplemental Rolls to 1934 & 1935 with Births and Deaths 1932-1938, and Marriages 1936-1938 Volume II

Eastern Cherokee Census Cherokee, North Carolina 1930-1939 Census 1930-1931 with Births And Deaths 1924-1931 Taken By Agent L. W. Page Volume I
Eastern Cherokee Census Cherokee, North Carolina 1930-1939 Census 1932-1933 with Births And Deaths 1930-1932 Taken By Agent R. L. Spalsbury Volume II
Eastern Cherokee Census Cherokee, North Carolina 1930-1939 Census 1934-1937 with Births and Deaths 1925-1938 and Marriages 1936 & 1938 Taken by Agents R. L. Spalsbury And Harold W. Foght Volume III

Seminole of Florida Indian Census, 1930-1940 with Birth and Death Records, 1930-1938

Texas Cherokees 1820-1839 A Document For Litigation 1921

Choctaw By Blood Enrollment Cards 1898-1914 Volumes I thru XVII

Starr Roll 1894 (Cherokee Payment Rolls) Districts: Canadian, Cooweescoowee, and Delaware Volume One
Starr Roll 1894 (Cherokee Payment Rolls) Districts: Flint, Going Snake, and Illinois Volume Two
Starr Roll 1894 (Cherokee Payment Rolls) Districts: Saline, Sequoyah, and Tahlequah; Including Orphan Roll Volume Three

Cherokee Intruder Cases Dockets of Hearings 1901-1909 Volumes I & II

Indian Wills, 1911-1921 Records of the Bureau of Indian Affairs Books One thru Seven;
 Native American Wills & Probate Records 1911-1921

Other Books and Series by Jeff Bowen

Turtle Mountain Reservation Chippewa Indians 1932 Census with Births & Deaths, 1924-1932

Chickasaw By Blood Enrollment Cards 1898-1914 Volume I thru V

Cherokee Descendants East An Index to the Guion Miller Applications Volume I
Cherokee Descendants West An Index to the Guion Miller Applications Volume II (A-M)
Cherokee Descendants West An Index to the Guion Miller Applications Volume III (N-Z)

Applications for Enrollment of Seminole Newborn Freedmen, Act of 1905

Eastern Cherokee Census, Cherokee, North Carolina, 1915-1922, Taken by Agent James E. Henderson   Volume I (1915-1916)
Volume II (1917-1918)
Volume III (1919-1920)
Volume IV (1921-1922)

Complete Delaware Roll of 1898

Eastern Cherokee Census, Cherokee, North Carolina, 1923-1929, Taken by Agent James E. Henderson   Volume I (1923-1924)
Volume II (1925-1926)
Volume III (1927-1929)

Applications for Enrollment of Seminole Newborn Act of 1905 Volumes I & II

North Carolina Eastern Cherokee Indian Census 1898-1899, 1904, 1906, 1909-1912, 1914 Revised and Expanded Edition

1932 Hopi and Navajo Native American Census with Birth & Death Rolls (1925-1931) Volume 1 - Hopi
1932 Hopi and Navajo Native American Census with Birth & Death Rolls (1930-1932) Volume 2 - Navajo

Western Navajo Reservation Navajo, Hopi and Paiute 1933 Census with Birth & Death Rolls 1925-1933

Cherokee Citizenship Commission Dockets 1880-1884 and 1887-1889 Volumes I thru V

Copyright © 2013
by Jeff Bowen

ALL RIGHTS RESERVED
No part of this publication may be reproduced
or used in any form or manner whatsoever
without previous written permission from the
copyright holder or publisher.

Originally published:
Baltimore, Maryland
2012

Reprinted by:

Native Study LLC
Gallipolis, OH
www.nativestudy.com
2020

Library of Congress Control Number: 2020918113

ISBN: 978-1-64968-098-3

Made in the United States of America.

This series is dedicated to the descendants of the Choctaw newborn listed in these applications.

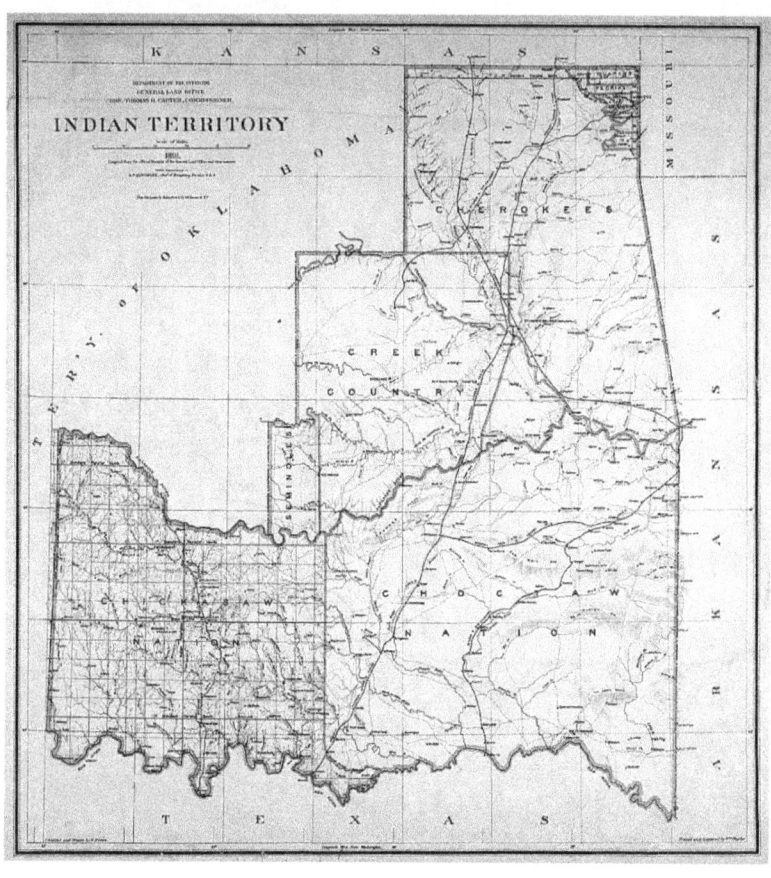

This map of Indian Territory shows how large the Choctaw and Chickasaw Nations' land base was that contained huge deposits of asphalt and coal. Just the size and territory involved was flooded with the "Grafters".

DEPARTMENT OF THE INTERIOR.

Commissioner to the Five Civilized Tribes.

NOTICE.

Opening of Land Office at Wewoka,
IN THE SEMINOLE NATION, INDIAN TERRITORY.

Notice is hereby given that on Monday, September 4, 1905, the Commissioner to the Five Civilized Tribes will establish a land office at Wewoka, in the Seminole Nation, Indian Territory, for the purpose of allowing citizens and freedmen of the Seminole Nation to select allotments of land for their minor children enrolled under the Act of Congress approved March 3, 1905 (33 Stat. L 1060), and for the further purpose of allowing citizens and freedmen of the Seminole Nation, whose allotments are incomplete, to select additional land in order to bring the value of their allotments up to the standard of $309.09, as nearly as may be practicable.

Each child whose enrollment in accordance with the Act of March 3, 1905, has been duly approved by the Secretary of the Interior, is entitled to receive an alllotment of forty acres without regard to the character or value of the land selected.

Selection of allotments for minor children must be made by their citizen or freedmen parents or by a duly appointed guardian, or curator, or by a duly appointed administrator.

TAMS BIXBY,
Commissioner.

Muskogee, Indian Territory,
July 29, 1905.

This particular notice for the Seminole and Creek Newborn makes mention of the Act of 1905. It is likely that a similar notice was posted in the Choctaw and Chickasaw Nations for the registration of newborn children.

DEPARTMENT OF THE INTERIOR,
Commission to the Five Civilized Tribes.

Rules and Regulations Governing the Selection of Allotments and the Designation of Homesteads in the Choctaw and Chickasaw Nations.

1. Selections of allotments and designations of homesteads for adult citizens and selections of allotments for adult freedmen must be made in person except as herein otherwise provided.

2. Applications to have land set apart and homesteads designated for duly identified Mississippi Choctaws must be made personally before the Commission to the Five Civilized Tribes. Fathers may apply for their minor children and if the father be dead the mother may apply. Husbands may apply for wives. Applications for orphans, insane persons and persons of unsound mind may be made by duly appointed guardian or curator, and for aged and infirm persons and prisoners by agents duly authorized thereunto by power of attorney, in the discretion of said Commission.

3. At the time of the selection of allotment each citizen and duly identified Mississippi Choctaw shall designate as a homestead out of said selection land equal in value to one hundred and sixty acres of the average allottable land of the Choctaw and Chickasaw Nations, as nearly as may be.

4. Each Choctaw and Chickasaw freedman, at the time of selection shall designate as his or her allotment of the lands of the Choctaw and Chickasaw Nations, land equal in value to forty acres of the average allottable land of the Choctaw and Chickasaw Nations.

5. Citizens, freedmen and identified Mississippi Choctaws who are married, whether they have attained their majority or not, will be regarded as of age for the purpose of making selections.

6. Selections may be made by citizen and freedman parents for unmarried male children under twenty-one years of age and for unmarried female children under eighteen years of age, and a male citizen or freedman may make selection for his wife, if she is entitled to make selection, unless she shall, at the time or previously thereto, protest in writing.

7. Where the father of an unmarried minor citizen, freedman or identified Mississippi Choctaw is a non-citizen, the citizen, freedman or identified Mississippi Choctaw mother of such children must make selection in person in behalf of said children.

8. Selections of allotments and designations of homesteads for minor citizens and selections of allotments for minor freedmen may be made by the citizen father or freedman father or mother, as the case may be, or by a guardian, curator, or an administrator having charge of their estate, in the order named.

9. Selections of allotments and designations of homesteads for citizen, and selections of allotment for freedmen, prisoners, convicts, aged and infirm persons and soldiers and sailors of the United States on duty outside of Indian Territory, may be made by duly appointed agents under power of attorney, and for incompetents by guardians, curators, or other suitable person akin to them.

10. Selections may be made and homesteads designated by duly identified Mississippi Choctaws, who have, within one year after the date of their identification as such, made satisfactory proof of bona fide settlement within the Choctaw-Chickasaw country, at any time within six months after the date of their said identification,

11. Persons authorized to make selections by power of attorney, as provided in rules 2 and 9 hereof, must be the husband or wife, or a relative not further removed than a cousin of the first degree of the person for whom such selection is made.

12. It shall be the duty of the Commission to the Five Civilized Tribes to see that selections of allotments and designations of homesteads for the classes of persons mentioned in rules 2, 6, 7, 8 and 9 hereof, are made for the best interests of such persons.

13. Selections of allotments for citizens, freedmen and identified Mississippi Choctaws who have died subsequent to September 25, 1902, and before making a selection of allotment, shall be made by a duly appointed administrator or executor. If, however, such administrator or executor be not duly and expeditiously appointed, or fails to act promptly when appointed, or for any other cause such selections be not so made within a reasonable and practicable time, the Commission to the Five Civilized Tribes shall designate the lands thus to be allotted.

14. In determining the value of a selection the appraised value of the land selected shall be increased by the appraised value of such pine timber on such land as has heretofore been estimated by the Commission to the Five Civilized Tribes.

15. Selections of allotments may be made only by citizens and freedmen whose enrollment has been approved by the Secretary of the Interior, and by persons duly identified by the Commission to the Five Civilized Tribes as Mississippi Choctaws, and by none others.

16. When a selection of land has been made by a citizen, freedman or identified Mississippi Choctaw, and the land so selected is claimed by a person whose rights as a citizen or freedman have not been finally determined, contest for the land so selected may be instituted by the person claiming the land, formal application for the land being first made as is required by the Rules of Practice in Choctaw and Chickasaw allotment contest cases.

THE COMMISSION TO THE FIVE CIVILIZED TRIBES.
TAMS BIXBY, Chairman.

Muskogee, Indian Territory, March 24, 1903.

The above statement published prior to 1905, was established for what was supposed to be a set of guidelines when it came to allotments. But with supplemental agreements and Congressional legislation, time frames as well as rules and regulations often changed and were not the same for every tribe.

INTRODUCTION

The *Applications for Enrollment of Choctaw Newborn Act of 1905*, National Archive film M-1301, Rolls 50-57, are found under the heading of Applications for Enrollment of the Commission to the Five Civilized Tribes. For this series, I have transcribed the application forms filled out by individuals applying for enrollment in the Five Civilized Tribes under the Dawes Commission. These applications contain considerably more information than stated on the census cards found in series M-1186. M-1301 possesses its own numerical sequence, separate from M-1186. To find each party's roll number you would have to reference M-1186.

The Choctaw as well as the Chickasaw allotments were likely some of the most sought after properties in Indian Territory. There was supposed to be a 25-year restriction on the sale or lease of any Indian lands so as to insure that the owners wouldn't be swindled, but that isn't what happened. This fact is borne out in the Dawes Commission General Allotment Act, of February 8, 1887, Section 5, which "Provides that after an Indian person is allotted land, the United States will hold the land 'in trust [1] for the sole use and benefit of the Indian' (or his heirs if the Indian landowner dies) for a period of 25 years. (Land held in trust by the United States government cannot be sold or in anyway alienated by the Indian landowner, since the United States government considers the underlying ownership of the land held by itself and not the tribe. After the period of trust ends, the Indian landowner is free to sell the land and is free from any encumbrance from the United States.)"[1] Instead, Native Americans were exploited by the devious. The Choctaw and Chickasaw Districts both had huge asphalt and coal deposits, so there was pressure from outsiders to acquire them from the minute they were discovered. After repeated attacks throughout the years and many legislative changes, President "Roosevelt finally signed the Five Tribes Bill at noon on April 26, 1906, the forces seeking to end all restrictions were disappointed. Section 19 removed restrictions from the sale of all inherited land but directed that no full-bloods could sell their land for twenty-five years. The Act also prohibited leases for more than one year without the approval of the Secretary of the Interior."[2]

Angie Debo described the opportunists that wanted these Native American allotments as, "Grafters". The parents of the newborns enumerated within this series would no sooner receive the approval for their child's allotment than there would be someone there with cash in hand holding a new deed or lease for the parents to sign their child's birthright away. Angie Debo said it best, "As the business incapacity of the allottees became apparent, a horde of despoilers fastened themselves upon their property." According to Debo, "The term 'grafter' was applied as a matter of course to dealers in Indian land, and was frankly accepted by them. The speculative fever also affected Government employees so that it was almost impossible to prevent them from making personal investments."[3]

---

[1] General Allotment Act, Act of Feb. 8, 1887 (24 Stat. 388, ch. 119, 25 USCA 331)
[2] The Dawes Commission and the Allotment of the Five Civilized Tribes, 1893-1914 by Kent Carter, pg. 173
[3] And Still the Waters Run, Angie Debo, p. 92.

INTRODUCTION

According to the Department of Interior in 1905, "It is estimated that there will be added to the final rolls of the citizens and freedmen of the Choctaw and Chickasaw nations the names of 2,000 persons, including 1,500 new-born children to be enrolled under the provisions of the act of Congress approved March 3, 1905."[4]

The quote below explains, in detail, the requirements for qualifying as a newborn Choctaw, "By the act of Congress approved March 3, 1905 (H.R. 17474), entitled 'An act making appropriations for the current and contingent expenses of the Indian Department and for fulfilling treaty stipulations with various Indian tribes for the fiscal year ending June 30, 1906, and for other purposes,' it was provided as follows:

'That the Commission to the Five Civilized Tribes is hereby authorized for sixty days after the date of the approval of this act to receive and consider applications for enrollment of infant children born prior to September twenty-fifth, nineteen hundred and two, and who were living on said date, to citizens by blood of the Choctaw and Chickasaw tribes of Indians whose enrollment has been approved by the Secretary of the Interior prior to the date of the approval of this act; and to enroll and make allotments to such children.'

'That the Commission to the Five Civilized Tribes is authorized for sixty days after the date of the approval of this act to receive and consider applications for enrollment of children born subsequent to September twenty-fifth, nineteen hundred and two, and prior to March fourth, nineteen hundred and five, and who were living on said latter date, to citizens by blood of the Choctaw and Chickasaw tribes of Indians whose enrollment has been approved by the Secretary of the Interior prior to the date of the approval of this act; and to enroll and make allotments to such children.'

"Notice is hereby given that the Commission to the Five Civilized Tribes will, up to and inclusive of midnight, May 2, 1905, receive applications for the enrollment of infant children born prior to September 25, 1902, and who were living on said date, to citizens by blood of the Choctaw and Chickasaw tribes of Indians whose enrollment has been approved by the Secretary of the Interior prior to March 3, 1905."[5]

Following is the scope of these transcriptions: Besides the applications themselves, researchers will find the identities of other individuals within these applications -- doctors, lawyers, mid-wives, and other relatives -- that may help with you genealogical research.

Jeff Bowen
Gallipolis, Ohio
NativeStudy.com

---

[4] Annual Reports of the Department of the Interior For the Fiscal Year Ended June 30, 1905, p. 609.
[5] Annual Reports of the Department of the Interior For the Fiscal Year Ended June 30, 1905, p. 593.

Applications for Enrollment of Choctaw Newborn
Act of 1905 Volume V

Choc New Born 247
>   May Sophina Seeley
>   (Born Oct. 8, 1903)
>   Ralph Whitfield Seeley
>   (Born Jan. 26, 1905)

NEW-BORN AFFIDAVIT.

Number..................

Choctaw Enrolling Commission.

IN THE MATTER OF THE APPLICATION FOR ENROLLMENT, as a citizen of the Choctaw   Nation, of   May Sofina[sic] Seeley

born on the 8   day of   October   190 3

Name of father   George W. Seeley   a citizen of   Marriage
Nation final enrollment No   779
Name of mother   Birdie Seeley   a citizen of   Choctaw
Nation final enrollment No   10020

Postoffice   Durant I.T.

AFFIDAVIT OF MOTHER.

UNITED STATES OF AMERICA, ⎫
   INDIAN TERRITORY,   ⎬
   Central   DISTRICT   ⎭

I   Birdie Seeley   , on oath state that I am   25   years of age and a citizen by   blood   of the   Choctaw Nation, and as such have been placed upon the final roll of the   Choctaw Nation, by the Honorable Secretary of the Interior my final enrollment number being   10020 ; that I am the lawful wife of   George W. Seeley   , who is a citizen of the   Choctaw Nation, and as such has been placed upon the final roll of said Nation by the Honorable Secretary of the Interior, his final enrollment number being   779   and that a   female   child was born to me on the   8   day of   October   190 3; that said child has been named   May Sofina Seeley   , and is now living.

WITNESSETH: Birdie Seeley
  Must be two   ⎱ Mrs Sophina Veach
  Witnesses who ⎰
  are Citizens.   Isaac Duer

1

Applications for Enrollment of Choctaw Newborn
Act of 1905   Volume V

Subscribed and sworn to before me this   14   day of   January   190 5

                 B.F. Moreman
                         Notary Public.

My commission expires   Nov 11th 1907

AFFIDAVIT OF ATTENDING PHYSICIAN OR MIDWIFE

UNITED STATES OF AMERICA
INDIAN TERRITORY
   Central   DISTRICT

     I,   J.F. Park   a   Practicing Physician
on oath state that I attended on Mrs.   Birdie Seeley   wife of   George W Seeley
on the   8   day of   October   , 190 3, that there was born to her on said date a   female
child, that said child is now living, and is said to have been named   May Sofina[sic] Seeley

                         J. F. Park   M.D.
Subscribed and sworn to before me this, the   14   day of   January   190 5

                 B.F. Moreman
                         Notary Public.

WITNESSETH:
   Must be two witnesses { Isaac Duer
   who are citizens and
   know the child.   A Frank Ross

     We hereby certify that we are well acquainted with   J.F. Park
a   Practicing Physician   and know   him   to be reputable and of good standing in
the community.

                 Isaac Duer

                 A Frank Ross

Applications for Enrollment of Choctaw Newborn
Act of 1905 Volume V

NEW-BORN AFFIDAVIT.

Number..............

Choctaw Enrolling Commission.

IN THE MATTER OF THE APPLICATION FOR ENROLLMENT, as a citizen of the Choctaw Nation, of Ralph W Seeley

born on the 26th day of January 190 5

Name of father   George W Seeley   a citizen of   Choctaw Nation
Nation final enrollment No 779
Name of mother   Birdie Seeley   a citizen of   Choctaw Nation
Nation final enrollment No 10020

Postoffice   Durant I.T.

AFFIDAVIT OF MOTHER.

UNITED STATES OF AMERICA,
   INDIAN TERRITORY,
  Central   DISTRICT

I   Birdie Seeley   , on oath state that I am   23   years of age and a citizen by   blood   of the   Choctaw Nation, and as such have been placed upon the final roll of the   Choctaw Nation, by the Honorable Secretary of the Interior my final enrollment number being 10020 ; that I am the lawful wife of   George W Seeley   , who is a citizen of the   Choctaw Nation, and as such has been placed upon the final roll of said Nation by the Honorable Secretary of the Interior, his final enrollment number being   779   and that a male   child was born to me on the   26th   day of   January   190 5 ; that said child has been named   Ralph W Seeley   , and is now living.

WITNESSETH: Birdie Seeley
  Must be two ⎱ Mary *(Illegible)*
  Witnesses who ⎰
  are Citizens.   C Veach

Subscribed and sworn to before me this   31st   day of   January   190 5

B. F. Moreman
                Notary Public.

My commission expires   Nov 11th 1907

Applications for Enrollment of Choctaw Newborn
Act of 1905   Volume V

AFFIDAVIT OF ATTENDING PHYSICIAN OR MIDWIFE

UNITED STATES OF AMERICA
INDIAN TERRITORY
Central   DISTRICT

I,   J. F. Park   a   Physician on oath state that I attended on Mrs.   Birdie Seeley   wife of   George W. Seeley   on the   26th   day of   January , 1905 , that there was born to her on said date a Male   child, that said child is now living, and is said to have been named   Ralph W Seeley

J. F. Park   M.D.

Subscribed and sworn to before me this, the   31st   day of   January   190 5

B. F. Moreman
Notary Public.

WITNESSETH:

Must be two witnesses who are citizens and know the child.

Mary *(Illegible)*
C Veach

We hereby certify that we are well acquainted with   Dr J. F. Park   a   Physician   and know   him   to be reputable and of good standing in the community.

Mary *(Illegible)*
C Veach

BIRTH AFFIDAVIT.

DEPARTMENT OF THE INTERIOR.
COMMISSION TO THE FIVE CIVILIZED TRIBES.

IN RE APPLICATION FOR ENROLLMENT, as a citizen of the   Choctaw   Nation, of May Sophina Seeley   , born on the 8th   day of   October   , 1903

Intermarried

Name of Father: George W Seeley   a citizen of the   Choctaw   Nation.
Name of Mother: Birdie Seeley   a citizen of the   Choctaw   Nation.

Postoffice   Durant, Indian Territory

Applications for Enrollment of Choctaw Newborn
Act of 1905   Volume V

AFFIDAVIT OF MOTHER.

UNITED STATES OF AMERICA, Indian Territory,
Central DISTRICT.

I, Birdie Seeley, on oath state that I am twenty three years of age and a citizen by blood, of the Choctaw Nation; that I am the lawful wife of George W Seeley, who is a citizen, by Intermarriage of the Choctaw Nation; that a female child was born to me on Eighth day of October, 1903; that said child has been named May Sophina Seeley, and was living March 4, 1905.

Birdie Seeley

Witnesses To Mark:
{

Subscribed and sworn to before me this 25th day of March, 1905

Com Ex
Feb 8th 1908

Charles A Phillips
Notary Public.

AFFIDAVIT OF ATTENDING PHYSICIAN OR MID-WIFE.

UNITED STATES OF AMERICA, Indian Territory,
.... DISTRICT.

I, J. F. Park, MD, a Physician, on oath state that I attended on Mrs. Birdie Seeley, wife of George W Seeley on the 8th day of October, 1903; that there was born to her on said date a female child; that said child was living March 4, 1905, and is said to have been named May Sophina Seeley

J. F. Park, M.D.

Witnesses To Mark:
{

Subscribed and sworn to before me this 25th day of March, 1905

Com Ex
Feb 8th 1908

Charles A Phillips
Notary Public.

Applications for Enrollment of Choctaw Newborn
Act of 1905   Volume V

BIRTH AFFIDAVIT.

DEPARTMENT OF THE INTERIOR.
COMMISSION TO THE FIVE CIVILIZED TRIBES.

IN RE APPLICATION FOR ENROLLMENT, as a citizen of the Choctaw Nation, of Ralph Whitfield Seeley, born on the 26th day of January, 1905 by Intermarriage

Name of Father: George W Seeley   a citizen of the Choctaw Nation.
Name of Mother: Birdie Seeley   a citizen of the Choctaw Nation.

Postoffice   Durant, Indian Territory

AFFIDAVIT OF MOTHER.

UNITED STATES OF AMERICA, Indian Territory,
   Central   **DISTRICT.**

I, Birdie Seeley, on oath state that I am twenty three years of age and a citizen by blood, of the Choctaw Nation; that I am the lawful wife of George W Seeley, who is a citizen, by Intermarriage of the Choctaw Nation; that a Male child was born to me on 26th day of January, 1905; that said child has been named Ralph Whitfield Seeley, and was living March 4, 1905.

                              Birdie Seeley

Witnesses To Mark:
{

Subscribed and sworn to before me this 25th day of March, 1905.

Com Ex   Charles A Phillips
Feb 8th 1908   Notary Public.

AFFIDAVIT OF ATTENDING PHYSICIAN OR MID-WIFE.

UNITED STATES OF AMERICA, Indian Territory,
.... **DISTRICT.**

I, J. F. Park, MD, a Physician, on oath state that I attended on Mrs. Birdie Seeley, wife of George W Seeley on the 26th day of January, 1905; that there was born to her on said date a male child; that said child was living March 4, 1905, and is said to have been named Ralph Whitfield Seeley

                              J. F. Park, M.D.

Witnesses To Mark:
{

Applications for Enrollment of Choctaw Newborn
Act of 1905   Volume V

Subscribed and sworn to before me this 25th day of   March   , 1905

Com Ex
Feb 8th 1908

Charles A Phillips
Notary Public.

Choctaw 3527

Muskogee, Indian Territory, March 30, 1905.

George W. Seeley,
    Durant, Indian Territory.

Dear Sir:

    Receipt is hereby acknowledged of the affidavits of Birdie Seeley and J. F. Park to the birth of May Sophina Seeley and Ralph Whitfield Seeley, children of George W. and Birdie Seeley, October 8, 1903 and January 26, 1905, respectively, and the same have been filed with our records as an application for the enrollment of said children.

Respectfully,

Chairman.

Choc New Born 248
    Hunter Dwight
    (Born Sep. 2, 1903)

BIRTH AFFIDAVIT.

DEPARTMENT OF THE INTERIOR.
COMMISSION TO THE FIVE CIVILIZED TRIBES.

IN RE APPLICATION FOR ENROLLMENT, as a citizen of the   Choctaw   Nation, of Hunter Dwight   , born on the 2 day of Sept , 1903

Name of Father: Edwin Dwight   a citizen of the Choctaw Nation.
Name of Mother: Emma Dwight   a citizen of the Choctaw Nation.

Postoffice   Boswell, I.T.

Applications for Enrollment of Choctaw Newborn
Act of 1905   Volume V

AFFIDAVIT OF MOTHER.

UNITED STATES OF AMERICA, Indian Territory,
Central   DISTRICT.

I, Emma Dwight , on oath state that I am 29 years of age and a citizen by blood , of the Choctaw Nation; that I am the lawful wife of Edwin Dwight , who is a citizen, by blood of the Choctaw Nation; that a male child was born to me on 2 day of Sept , 1903; that said child has been named Hunter Dwight , and was living March 4, 1905.

                               Emma Dwight

Witnesses To Mark:

     Subscribed and sworn to before me this 27 day of April , 1905

                               Thos W. Hunter
                                 Notary Public.

AFFIDAVIT OF ATTENDING PHYSICIAN OR MID-WIFE.

UNITED STATES OF AMERICA, Indian Territory,
Central   DISTRICT.

I, Belle Vinson , a Female , on oath state that I attended on Mrs. Emma Dwight , wife of Edwin Dwight on the 2 day of Sept. , 1903; that there was born to her on said date a male child; that said child was living March 4, 1905, and is said to have been named Hunter Dwight

                              her
                          Belle x Vinson

Witnesses To Mark: mark
   Ed Roebuck
   Isaac Jones

     Subscribed and sworn to before me this 26 day of April , 1905

                              Thos. W. Hunter
                               Notary Public.

Applications for Enrollment of Choctaw Newborn
Act of 1905   Volume V

BIRTH AFFIDAVIT.

DEPARTMENT OF THE INTERIOR.
COMMISSION TO THE FIVE CIVILIZED TRIBES.

IN RE APPLICATION FOR ENROLLMENT, as a citizen of the Choctaw Nation, of Hunter Dwight, born on the 2nd day of September, 1903

Name of Father: Edwin Dwight   a citizen of the Choctaw Nation.
Name of Mother: Emma Dwight   a citizen of the Choctaw Nation.

Postoffice   Boswell, I.T.

AFFIDAVIT OF MOTHER.

UNITED STATES OF AMERICA, Indian Territory,
Central   DISTRICT.

I, Emma Dwight, on oath state that I am 29 years of age and a citizen by blood, of the Choctaw Nation; that I am the lawful wife of Edwin Dwight, who is a citizen, by Blood of the Choctaw Nation; that a male child was born to me on 2nd day of September, 1903; that said child has been named Hunter Dwight, and was living March 4, 1905.

Emma Dwight

Witnesses To Mark:

Subscribed and sworn to before me this 25 day of Mar., 1905

⟨Seal⟩

J.R. Armstrong
Notary Public.

AFFIDAVIT OF ATTENDING PHYSICIAN OR MID-WIFE.

UNITED STATES OF AMERICA, Indian Territory,
Central   DISTRICT.

I, Belle Vinson, a Female, on oath state that I attended on Mrs. Emma Dwight, wife of Edwin Dwight on the 2nd day of Sept., 1903; that there was born to her on said date a male child; that said child was living March 4, 1905, and is said to have been named Hunter Dwight

her
Belle x Vinson
mark

Applications for Enrollment of Choctaw Newborn
Act of 1905   Volume V

Witnesses To Mark:
   { George Hunter
    Minnie Hunter

    Subscribed and sworn to before me this 25 day of   Mar.   , 1905

<Seal>

                       J.R. Armstrong
                              Notary Public.

                                              Choctaw 3604

             Muskogee, Indian Territory, March 30, 1905.

Edwin Dwight,
    Boswell, Indian Territory.

Dear Sir:

    Receipt is hereby acknowledged of the affidavits of Emma Dwight and Belle Vinson to the birth of Hunter Dwight, son of Edwin and Emma Dwight, September 22, 1903, and the same have been filed with our records as an application for the enrollment of said child.

                         Respectfully,

                         Chairman.

                      COPY

                                              N. B. 248

             Muskogee, Indian Territory, April 7, 1905.

Edwin Dwight,
    Boswell, Indian Territory.

Dear Sir:

    There is inclosed you herewith for execution application for the enrollment of your infant child, Hunter Dwight, born September 2, 1903.

    In having these affidavits executed care should be exercised to see that all names are written in full, as they appear in the body of the affidavit, and in the event that either of the persons signing the affidavit are unable to write, signatures by mark must be attested by two witnesses. Each affidavit must be executed before a Notary Public and the notarial seal and signature of the officer must be attached to each separate affidavit.

Applications for Enrollment of Choctaw Newborn
Act of 1905   Volume V

SEV 14-7.

Respectfully,
SIGNED
T. B. Needles.
Commissioner in Charge.

COPY Choctaw N.B. 248.

Muskogee, Indian Territory, May 2, 1905.

Edwin Dwight,
  Boswell, Indian Territory.

Dear Sir:

Receipt is hereby acknowledged of the affidavits of Emma Dwight and Belle Vinson to the birth of Hunter Dwight, son of Edwin and Emma Dwight, September 2, 1903, and the same have been filed with our records in the matter of the enrollment of the above named child.

Respectfully,
SIGNED
Tams Bixby
Chairman.

Choc New Born 249
  Ethel Dawron[sic]
  (Born Jan. 19, 1905)

BIRTH AFFIDAVIT.

DEPARTMENT OF THE INTERIOR.
COMMISSION TO THE FIVE CIVILIZED TRIBES.

IN RE APPLICATION FOR ENROLLMENT, as a citizen of the   Choctaw   Nation, of Ethel Damron , born on the 19th day of January , 1905

Name of Father: W. R. Damron   a citizen of the Choctaw Nation.
Name of Mother: Amanda Damron   a citizen of the Choctaw Nation.

Postoffice   Caddo Indian Territory

11

Applications for Enrollment of Choctaw Newborn
Act of 1905   Volume V

AFFIDAVIT OF MOTHER.

UNITED STATES OF AMERICA, Indian Territory,
Central   DISTRICT.

I, Amanda Damron, on oath state that I am 24 years of age and a citizen by blood, of the Choctaw Nation; that I am the lawful wife of W. R. Damron, who is a citizen, by marriage of the Choctaw Nation; that a female child was born to me on 19th day of January, 1905; that said child has been named Ethel Damron, and was living March 4, 1905.

        Amanda Damron

Witnesses To Mark:

Subscribed and sworn to before me this 25th day of March, 1905

        J L Rappolee
         Notary Public.

AFFIDAVIT OF ATTENDING PHYSICIAN OR MID-WIFE.

UNITED STATES OF AMERICA, Indian Territory,
Central   DISTRICT.

I, W. J. Melton, a Physician, on oath state that I attended on Mrs. Amanda Damron, wife of W. R. Damron on the 19th day of January, 1905; that there was born to her on said date a female child; that said child was living March 4, 1905, and is said to have been named Ethel Damron

        W. J. Melton

Witnesses To Mark:

Subscribed and sworn to before me this 25th day of March, 1905

        J L Rappolee
         Notary Public.

Applications for Enrollment of Choctaw Newborn
Act of 1905   Volume V

Choc New Born 250
    Valley Ester[sic] Izard
    (Born May 16. 1904)

NEW-BORN AFFIDAVIT.

Number..............

...Choctaw Enrolling Commission...

IN THE MATTER OF THE APPLICATION FOR ENROLLMENT, as a citizen of the Choctaw Nation, of Valley Esther Izard

born on the 16 day of May 190 4

Name of father   John C Izard   a citizen of   Choctaw Nation final enrollment No. 10276
Name of mother   Tommie J Izard   a citizen of   United States Nation final enrollment No. _____

                         Postoffice   Ego, I.T.

AFFIDAVIT OF MOTHER.

UNITED STATES OF AMERICA
INDIAN TERRITORY
    Central   DISTRICT

    I   Tommie J Izard   , on oath state that I am 22 years of age and a citizen by Intermarriage of the Choctaw Nation, and as such have been placed upon the final roll of the _____ Nation, by the Honorable Secretary of the Interior my final enrollment number being _____; that I am the lawful wife of John C Izard , who is a citizen of the Choctaw Nation, and as such has been placed upon the final roll of said Nation by the Honorable Secretary of the Interior, his final enrollment number being 10276 and that a Female child was born to me on the 16 day of May 190 4; that said child has been named   Valley Esther , and is now living.

Witnesseth.   Tommie J Izard
   Must be two ⎤   D S Moran
   Witnesses who ⎬
   are Citizens. ⎦   Lenora M Morgan

Applications for Enrollment of Choctaw Newborn
Act of 1905 Volume V

Subscribed and sworn to before me this 18 day of Jan 190 5

J. T. Hoover
Notary Public.

My commission expires: Feb 26 - 1906

AFFIDAVIT OF ATTENDING PHYSICIAN OR MIDWIFE

UNITED STATES OF AMERICA
INDIAN TERRITORY
 Central DISTRICT

I, Thos M Morgan a Physician on oath state that I attended on Mrs. Tommie J. Izard wife of John C Izard on the 16 day of May , 190 4 , that there was born to her on said date a Female child, that said child is now living, and is said to have been named Valley Esther Izard

Thos M Morgan

Subscribed and sworn to before me this, the 18 day of January 190 5

WITNESSETH:
Must be two witnesses who are citizens
 { D S Moran
   Lenora M Morgan

J. T. Hoover Notary Public.

We hereby certify that we are well acquainted with Thos M Morgan a Physician and know him to be reputable and of good standing in the community.

D S Moran

Lenora M Morgan

BIRTH AFFIDAVIT.

DEPARTMENT OF THE INTERIOR.
COMMISSION TO THE FIVE CIVILIZED TRIBES.

IN RE APPLICATION FOR ENROLLMENT, as a citizen of the Choctaw Nation, of Valley Esther Izard , born on the 16 day of May , 1904

Name of Father: John C. Izard a citizen of the Choctaw Nation.
Name of Mother: Tommie Izard a citizen of the U. S. Nation.

Applications for Enrollment of Choctaw Newborn
Act of 1905   Volume V

Postoffice   Ego, I.T.

AFFIDAVIT OF MOTHER.

UNITED STATES OF AMERICA, Indian Territory,
Western   DISTRICT.

I, Tommie Izard, on oath state that I am 22 years of age and a citizen by marriage, of the Choctaw Nation; that I am the lawful wife of John C. Izard, who is a citizen, by blood of the Choctaw Nation; that a female child was born to me on 16th day of May, 1904; that said child has been named Valley Esther Izard, and was living March 4, 1905.

Tommie Izard

Witnesses To Mark:
  D S Moran
  Lenora M Morgan

Subscribed and sworn to before me this 17th day of March, 1905

J B Campbell
Notary Public.

AFFIDAVIT OF ATTENDING PHYSICIAN OR MID-WIFE.

UNITED STATES OF AMERICA, Indian Territory,
.... DISTRICT.

I, T.M. Morgan, a Physician, on oath state that I attended on Mrs. Tommie Izard, wife of John C Izard on the 16 day of May, 1904; that there was born to her on said date a female child; that said child was living March 4, 1905, and is said to have been named Valley Esther Izard

T. M. Morgan M.D.

Witnesses To Mark:
  D S Moran
  Lenora M Morgan

Subscribed and sworn to before me this 18th day of March, 1905

J.T. Hoover
Notary Public.

Applications for Enrollment of Choctaw Newborn
Act of 1905   Volume V

7-3635

Muskogee, Indian Territory, March 23, 1905.

John C. Izard,
    Ego, Indian Territory.

Dear Sir:

    Receipt is hereby acknowledged of the affidavits of Tommie Izard and T. M. Morgan to the birth of Vallie[sic] Esther Izard, daughter of John C. and Tommie Izard May 16, 1904, and the same have been filed with our records as an application for the enrollment of said child.

                  Respectfully,

                              Chairman.

COPY   7 NB 250

Muskogee, Indian Territory, May 11, 1905.

John C. Izard,
    Ego, Indian Territory.

Dear Sir:

    You are hereby notified that before the application for the enrollment of your minor child, Valley Esther Izard, can be finally disposed of, it will be necessary for you to furnish the Commission with either the original or a certified copy of the license and certificate of your marriage to Tommie Izard.

    Please give this matter your immediate attention.

                  Respectfully,
                  SIGNED

                          Tams Bixby
                          Chairman.

Applications for Enrollment of Choctaw Newborn
Act of 1905   Volume V

Wm O.B.

REFER IN REPLY TO THE FOLLOWING:
7-NB-250
7---3635

DEPARTMENT OF THE INTERIOR,
COMMISSIONER TO THE FIVE CIVILIZED TRIBES.

Muskogee, Indian Territory, August 26, 1905.

Tommie Izard,
    Eagletown, Indian Territory.

Dear Madam:

    Receipt is hereby acknowledged of your letter of August 17, 1905, asking if the enrollment of yourself and child, Vallie[sic] Esther Izard has been approved.

    In reply to your letter you are advised that your name has been placed upon a schedule of intermarried citizens of the Choctaw Nation, which has been forwarded to the Secretary of the Interior, and the name of your child, Valley Esther Izard, has been placed upon a schedule of citizens by blood of said nation, and you will be notified when your enrollment is approved by the Department.

                  Respectfully,

                              Tams Bixby
                              Commissioner.

<u>Choc New Born 251</u>
    Douglas D. Creecy
    (Born Dec. 4, 1903)

BIRTH AFFIDAVIT.

DEPARTMENT OF THE INTERIOR.
COMMISSION TO THE FIVE CIVILIZED TRIBES.

IN RE APPLICATION FOR ENROLLMENT, as a citizen of the   Choctaw   Nation, of Douglas D Creecy   , born on the 4   day of Dec   , 1903

Name of Father: W C Creecy   a citizen of the   U. S.   Nation.
Name of Mother: Ula L Creecy   a citizen of the   Choctaw   Nation.

                        Postoffice   Milhum[sic] Ind Te

Applications for Enrollment of Choctaw Newborn
Act of 1905 Volume V

AFFIDAVIT OF MOTHER.

UNITED STATES OF AMERICA, Indian Territory,
Southern DISTRICT.

I, Ula L Creecy , on oath state that I am 30 years of age and a citizen by Blood , of the Choctaw Nation; that I am the lawful wife of W. C. Creecy , who is a citizen, ~~by~~ U.S. of the ——— Nation; that a male child was born to me on 4 day of Dec , 1903, that said child has been named Douglas D Creecy, and is now living.

Ula L Creecy

Witnesses To Mark:
  C E Renfrow
  WB Lucken

Subscribed and sworn to before me this 8 day of Mar , 1905.

J.T. Gardner
Notary Public.

AFFIDAVIT OF ATTENDING PHYSICIAN OR MID-WIFE.

UNITED STATES OF AMERICA, Indian Territory,
Southern DISTRICT.

I, F W Skillern , a Physician , on oath state that I attended on Mrs. Ula L Creecy , wife of W C Creecy on the 4 day of Dec , 1903; that there was born to her on said date a .... child; that said child is now living and is said to have been named ....

F W Skillern

Witnesses To Mark:

Subscribed and sworn to before me this 8 day of Mar , 1905.

J.T. Gardner
Notary Public.

Applications for Enrollment of Choctaw Newborn
Act of 1905 Volume V

BIRTH AFFIDAVIT.

DEPARTMENT OF THE INTERIOR.
COMMISSION TO THE FIVE CIVILIZED TRIBES.

IN RE APPLICATION FOR ENROLLMENT, as a citizen of the Choctaw Nation, of Douglas D Creecy, born on the 4th day of December, 1903

Name of Father: W C Creecy   a citizen of the U. S. Nation.
Name of Mother: Ula L Creecy   a citizen of the Choctaw Nation.

Postoffice   Milburn, Ind Ter

AFFIDAVIT OF MOTHER.

UNITED STATES OF AMERICA, Indian Territory,}
Southern   DISTRICT.

I, Ula L Creecy, on oath state that I am 30 years of age and a citizen by Blood, of the Choctaw Nation; that I am the lawful wife of W C Creecy, who is a citizen, by ——— of the United States Nation; that a Male child was born to me on 4th day of December, 1903; that said child has been named Douglas D Creecy, and was living March 4, 1905.

                         Ula L Creecy

Witnesses To Mark:
{ C E Renfrow
{ C.B. Thompson

Subscribed and sworn to before me this 24 day of May, 1905

                         J T Gardner
                         Notary Public.

AFFIDAVIT OF ATTENDING PHYSICIAN OR MID-WIFE.

UNITED STATES OF AMERICA, Indian Territory,}
Southern   DISTRICT.

I, F W Skillern MD, a Physician, on oath state that I attended on Mrs. Ula L Creecy, wife of W.C. Creecy on the 4th day of December, 1903; that there was born to her on said date a male child; that said child was living March 4, 1905, and is said to have been named Douglas D Creecy

                         F W Skillern M.D.

Applications for Enrollment of Choctaw Newborn
Act of 1905 Volume V

Witnesses To Mark:

{

    Subscribed and sworn to before me this 24 day of May , 1905

                                J T Gardner
                                     Notary Public.

7-3636

Muskogee, Indian Territory, March 13, 1905.

Ula L. Creecy,
    Milburn, Indian Territory.

Dear Madam:

    Receipt is hereby acknowledged of your affidavit and the affidavit of F. W. Skillern to the birth of Douglas D. Creecy, infant son of Ula L. and W. C. Creecy, December 4, 1903, and the same have been filed as an application for the enrollment of said child.

                        Respectfully,

                                           Chairman.

---

7 N.B. 251.

Muskogee, Indian Territory May 29, 1905.

W. C. Creecy,
    Milburn, Indian Territory.

Dear Sir:

    Receipt is hereby acknowledged of the affidavits of Ula L. Creecy and F. W. Skillern to the birth of Douglas D. Creecy, son of W. C. and Ula L. Creecy, December 4, 1903, and the same have been filed with our records in the matter of the enrollment of said child.

                        Respectfully,

                                           Chairman.

Applications for Enrollment of Choctaw Newborn
Act of 1905 Volume V

Choc New Born 252
    Clem Riddle
    (Born Jan. 17, 1903)

BIRTH AFFIDAVIT.

Department of the Interior,
COMMISSION TO THE FIVE CIVILIZED TRIBES.

IN RE APPLICATION FOR ENROLLMENT, as a citizen of the Choctaw Nation, of Clem Riddle, born on the 17 day of Jan, 190 3

Name of Father: J. T. Riddle   a citizen of the U. S. Nation.
Name of Mother: Mary A Riddle   a citizen of the Coctaw[sic] Nation.

Post-Office: Bokchito I.T.

AFFIDAVIT OF MOTHER.

UNITED STATES OF AMERICA,
   INDIAN TERRITORY,
  Central   District.

I, Mary A Riddle, on oath state that I am 27 years of age and a citizen by Birth, of the Choctaw Nation; that I am the lawful wife of J T Riddle, who is a citizen, by Birth of the U. S. ~~Nation~~; that a ~~Female~~ Male child was born to me on 17 day of Jan, 1903, that said child has been named Clem Riddle, and is now living.

                                     Mary A Riddle

WITNESSES TO MARK:

Subscribed and sworn to before me this 25 day of August, 190 3

                                     R F Moon
                                        Notary Public.

Applications for Enrollment of Choctaw Newborn
Act of 1905   Volume V

AFFIDAVIT OF ATTENDING PHYSICIAN OR MID-WIFE.

UNITED STATES OF AMERICA,
    INDIAN TERRITORY,
    Central   District.

I, A C Gardner, a Midwife, on oath state that I attended on Mrs. Mary A Riddle, wife of J T Riddle on the 17 day of Jan, 190 3; that there was born to her on said date a Male child; that said child is now living and is said to have been named Clem Riddle

                              her
                          A C x Gardner
WITNESSES TO MARK: mark
    { R F Moon
      J C Dabbor

Subscribed and sworn to before me this 25 *day of* August, 190 3

                    R F Moon
                         Notary Public.

AFFIDAVIT OF ATTENDING PHYSICIAN OR MIDWIFE

State of Missouri
~~UNITED STATES OF AMERICA~~
City of St Louis   } SS.
~~INDIAN TERRITORY~~
~~Central~~   ~~DISTRICT~~

I, J J Breaker a Practicing Physician on oath state that I attended on Mrs. Mary A Riddle wife of J.T. Riddle on the 17 day of Jan, 190 3, that there was born to her on said date a Male child, that said child is now living, and is said to have been named Clem Riddle

                        J J Breaker   M.D.

Subscribed and sworn to before me this, the 25th *day of* January   190 5
My time expires April 10-1908
                        Sarah J Guyre
                             Notary Public.

WITNESSETH:
   Must be two witnesses { James Boland
   who are citizens and
   know the child.   Rosa Moore

Applications for Enrollment of Choctaw Newborn
Act of 1905   Volume V

We hereby certify that we are well acquainted with   J J Breaker   a   Practicing Physician   and know   him   to be reputable and of good standing in the community.

> James Boland
> John A.M. *(Illegible)*

NEW-BORN AFFIDAVIT.

Number..............

Choctaw Enrolling Commission.

IN THE MATTER OF THE APPLICATION FOR ENROLLMENT, as a citizen of the Choctaw   Nation, of   Clem Riddle

born on the   17   day of   Jan   190 3

Name of father   J T Riddle   a citizen of   U. S.
Nation final enrollment No ....
Name of mother   Mary A Riddle   a citizen of   Choctaw Nation
Nation final enrollment No 10755

Postoffice   Bokchito I.T.

AFFIDAVIT OF MOTHER.

UNITED STATES OF AMERICA,
INDIAN TERRITORY,
Central   DISTRICT

I   Mary A Riddle   , on oath state that I am .... years of age and a citizen by   Blood   of the   Choctaw   Nation, and as such have been placed upon the final roll of the   Choctaw   Nation, by the Honorable Secretary of the Interior my final enrollment number being   10755   ; that I am the lawful wife of   J T Riddle   , who is a citizen of the   U.S.   Nation, and as such has been placed upon the final roll of said Nation by the Honorable Secretary of the Interior, his final enrollment number being .... and that a   male   child was born to me on the   17   day of   Jan   190 3; that said child has been named   Clem Riddle   , and is now living.

WITNESSETH: Mary A Riddle

Must be two Witnesses who are Citizens.   Rosa Moore
                                          A.C. Gardner

Applications for Enrollment of Choctaw Newborn
Act of 1905   Volume V

Subscribed and sworn to before me this   20   day of   Jan   190 5

R.F. Moore
Notary Public.

My commission expires   Feb 19 - 05

BIRTH AFFIDAVIT.

DEPARTMENT OF THE INTERIOR.
COMMISSION TO THE FIVE CIVILIZED TRIBES.

IN RE APPLICATION FOR ENROLLMENT, as a citizen of the   Choctaw   Nation, of   Clem Riddle   , born on the   17th day of   January   , 1903

Name of Father: J T Riddle   a citizen of the United States Nation.
Name of Mother: Mary A. Riddle   a citizen of the   Choctaw   Nation.

Postoffice   Bokchito I.T.

AFFIDAVIT OF MOTHER.

UNITED STATES OF AMERICA, Indian Territory,
Central Judicial   DISTRICT.

I,   Mary A. Riddle   , on oath state that I am   28   years of age and a citizen by   blood   , of the   Choctaw   Nation; that I am the lawful wife of   J. T. Riddle   , who is a citizen, by ——— of the   United States   Nation; that a   male   child was born to me on   17th day of   January   , 1903; that said child has been named   Clem   , and was living March 4, 1905.

Mary A Riddle

Witnesses To Mark:

Subscribed and sworn to before me this 12   day of   April   , 1905

J M Moore
Notary Public.

24

Applications for Enrollment of Choctaw Newborn
Act of 1905   Volume V

AFFIDAVIT OF ATTENDING PHYSICIAN OR MID-WIFE.

UNITED STATES OF AMERICA, Indian Territory,
Central Judicial   DISTRICT.

I, J. J. Breaker, a Physician, on oath state that I attended on Mrs. Mary A. Riddle, wife of J. T. Riddle on the 17th day of January, 1903; that there was born to her on said date a male child; that said child was living March 4, 1905, and is said to have been named Clem Riddle

J. J. Breaker M.D.

Witnesses To Mark:

Subscribed and sworn to before me this 12 day of April, 1905

J M Moore
Notary Public.

N. B. 252

COPY

Muskogee, Indian Territory, April 8, 1905.

J. T. Riddle,
    Bokchito, Indian Territory.

Dear Sir:

There is inclosed you herewith for execution application for the enrollment of your infant child, Clem Riddle, born January 17, 1903.

The affidavits heretofore filed with the Commission show the child was living on August 25, 1903. It is necessary, for the child to be enrolled, that he was living on March 4, 1905. You will please insert the mother's age in space left blank for that purpose.

In having these affidavits executed care should be exercised to see that all names are written in full, as they appear in the body of the affidavit, and in the event that either of the persons signing the affidavit are unable to write, signatures by mark must be attested by two witnesses. Each affidavit must be executed before a Notary Public and the notarial seal and signature of the officer must be attached to each separate affidavit.

Respectfully,
SIGNED
T. B. Needles.
Commissioner in Charge.

LM 8-10

Applications for Enrollment of Choctaw Newborn
Act of 1905 Volume V

Choctaw N.B. 252.

Muskogee, Indian Territory, April 16, 1905.

J. T. Riddle,
    Bokchito, Indian Territory.

Dear Sir:

    Receipt is hereby acknowledged of the affidavits of Mary A. Riddle and J. J. Breaker to the birth of Clem Riddle, son of J. T. and Mary A. Riddle, January 17, 1903, and the same have been filed with our records in the matter of the enrollment of said child.

                    Respectfully,

                              Chairman.

Applications for Enrollment of Choctaw Newborn
Act of 1905   Volume V

Choc New Born 253
    Rosa Angelina Chateau
    (Born Jan. 30, 1905)

N B 253
No. 2194

Certificate of Record of Marriages.

United States of America,
The Indian Territory, } sct.
Central *District.*

I, E. J. Fannin Clerk of the United States Court in the Indian Territory and District aforesaid; do hereby CERTIFY, that the License for and Certificate of the Marriage of

Mr. Martin Chateau and
M Meda York was

filed in my office in said Territory and District the 18 day of July A.D., 190 4, and duly recorded in Book 2 of Marriage Record, Page 479

WITNESS my hand and Seal of said Court, at Atoka this 18 day of July A.D. 190 4

E.J. Fannin
        Clerk.

By J.D. Catlin Deputy.

P. O. *(Illegible)* I.T.

DEPARTMENT OF THE INTERIOR,
COMMISSION TO THE FIVE CIVILIZED TRIBES.
FILED

MAR 29 1905

Tams Bixby CHAIRMAN.

Applications for Enrollment of Choctaw Newborn
Act of 1905   Volume V

No. 2194

MARRIAGE LICENSE

United States of America,   The Indian Territory,
                                            Central DISTRICT, SS.

To any Person Authorized by Law to Solemnize Marriage, Greeting:

You are hereby commanded to Solemnize the Rite and publish the Banns of Matrimony between Mr.   Martin Chateau   of   Caney   in the Indian Territory, aged   24   years, and M iss Media[sic] York   of .... in the Indian Territory., aged   18   years, according to law, and do you officially sign and return this License to the parties therein named.

WITNESS my hand and official seal, this   25   day of   June   A. D. 190 4

E. J. Fannin
Clerk of the United States Court.

J.D. Catlin   Deputy

Certificate of Marriage.

United States of America,
The Indian Territory,   } ss.
Central   District.   I,   Wm Fronterhouse

a   Minister   , do hereby certify, that on the   26   day of June   A. D. 190 4   , I did, duly and according to law, as commanded in the foregoing License, solemnize the Rite and publish the Banns of Matrimony between the parties therein named.

Witness my hand, this   26   day of   June   A. D. 190 4

My credentials are recorded in the office of the Clerk of   Wm Fronterhouse
the United States Court in the Indian Territory,
Central District, Book   B   , Page   12   a   minister of the gospel

Note—This License and Certificate of Marriage must be returned to the Office of the Clerk of the United States Court of the Indian Territory, from whence it was issued, within sixty days from the date thereof, or the party to whom the License was issued will be liable in the amount of the One Hundred Dollars ($100.00)

Applications for Enrollment of Choctaw Newborn
Act of 1905   Volume V

BIRTH AFFIDAVIT.

DEPARTMENT OF THE INTERIOR.
COMMISSION TO THE FIVE CIVILIZED TRIBES.

IN RE APPLICATION FOR ENROLLMENT, as a citizen of the Choctaw Nation, of Rosa Angelina Chateau, born on the 30th day of January, 1905

Name of Father: Martin Chateau   a citizen of the Choctaw Nation.
Name of Mother: Media Magdalene Chateau   a citizen of the Non Citz ~~Nation~~.

Postoffice   Caney I.T.

AFFIDAVIT OF MOTHER.

UNITED STATES OF AMERICA, Indian Territory,
Central   DISTRICT.

I, Medie Magdalene Chateau, on oath state that I am 18 years of age and a ~~citizen by~~ Non Citizen, ~~of the Nation~~; that I am the lawful wife of Martin Chateau, who is a citizen, by blood of the Choctaw Nation; that a female child was born to me on 30th day of January, 1905, ~~1~~; that said child has been named Rosa Angelina Chateau, and was living March 4, 1905.

Medie Magdalene Chateau

Witnesses To Mark:
{ MF Martin

Subscribed and sworn to before me this 20th day of March, 1905

W.H. Angell
Notary Public.

AFFIDAVIT OF ATTENDING PHYSICIAN OR MID-WIFE.

UNITED STATES OF AMERICA, Indian Territory,
Central   DISTRICT.

I, Rosa York, a mid-wife, on oath state that I attended on Mrs. Medie Magdalene Chateau, wife of Martin Chateau on the 30th day of January, 1905; that there was born to her on said date a female child; that said child was living March 4, 1905, and is said to have been named Rosa Angelina Chateau

her
Rosa x York
mark

Applications for Enrollment of Choctaw Newborn
Act of 1905   Volume V

Witnesses To Mark:
  { MF Martin
    WH Angell

    Subscribed and sworn to before me this 20th day of March, 1905.

                      W.H. Angell
                         Notary Public.

                                            7-3827

                Muskogee, Indian Territory, March 30, 1905.

Martin Chateau,
    Atoka, Indian Territory.

Dear Sir:

    Receipt is hereby acknowledged of the marriage license and certificate between Martin Chateau and Miss Media York of June 25, 1904, which you offer in support of the application for the enrollment of your infant child Rosa Angelina Chateau, and the same have been filed with the record in this matter.

                Respectfully,

                                  Chairman.

                                            7-3827

                Muskogee, Indian Territory, April 4, 1905.

Martin Chateau,
    Atoka, Indian Territory.

Dear Sir:

    Receipt is hereby acknowledged of your letter of March 26, 1905, asking that your marriage certificate be returned, and requesting to be advised if you can enroll your wife as you do not remember whether or not you were married under Choctaw law.

    In reply to your letter you are advised that the marriage certificate referred to by you was forwarded in the matter of the application for the enrollment of your child Rose Angelina Chateau, and it is therefore impracticable to return the same at this time.

Applications for Enrollment of Choctaw Newborn
Act of 1905 Volume V

Relative to the enrollment of your wife as an intermarried citizen you are informed that under the provisions of the act of Congress approved July 1, 1902, no person who intermarried with a citizen of the Choctaw or Chickasaw Nation subsequent to September 25, 1902, the date of the ratification of said act, is entitled to enrollment as an intermarried citizen of either of said Nations.

Respectfully,

Chairman.

Choc New Born 254
Lida Bessie Wilson
(Born June 3, 1903)

NEW BORN AFFIDAVIT

No ....

CHOCTAW ENROLLING COMMISSION

IN THE MATTER OF THE APPLICATION FOR ENROLLMENT as a citizen of the Choctaw Nation, of Lida Wilson born on the 23 day of June 190 3

Name of father Abel Wilson a citizen of Choctaw Nation, final enrollment No. 10805
Name of mother Mary Wilson a citizen of Choctaw Nation, final enrollment No. 10806

Caney I.T. Postoffice.

AFFIDAVIT OF MOTHER

UNITED STATES OF AMERICA }
INDIAN TERRITORY }
DISTRICT Central }

I Mary Wilson , on oath state that I am 27 years of age and a citizen by blood of the Choctaw Nation, and as such

Applications for Enrollment of Choctaw Newborn
Act of 1905   Volume V

have been placed upon the final roll of the   Choctaw   Nation, by the Honorable Secretary of the Interior my final enrollment number being   10806 ; that I am the lawful wife of   Abel Wilson , who is a citizen of the   Choctaw   Nation, and as such has been placed upon the final roll of said Nation by the Honorable Secretary of the Interior, his final enrollment number being   10805   and that a   Female   child was born to me on the   23   day of   June   190 3; that said child has been named   Lida Wilson , and is now living.

WITNESSETH: Mary Wilson
Must be two witnesses ⎧ Louisa Shirky
who are citizens   ⎩ Austin Pickens

Subscribed and sworn to before me this, the   22   day of   February   190 5

A.E. Folsom
Notary Public.

My Commission Expires:
Jan 9-1909

Affidavit of Attending Physician or Midwife

UNITED STATES OF AMERICA, ⎫
    INDIAN TERRITORY,   ⎬
Central   DISTRICT   ⎭

I,   Abel Wilson   The Father attend[sic] at Birth on oath state that I attended on Mrs. Mary Wilson   wife of   my wife on the   23   day of   June , 190 3, that there was born to her on said date a   Female   child, that said child is now living, and is said to have been named   Lida Wilson

The Father
Abel Wilson   M.D.

Subscribed and sworn to before me this the   22   day of   February   1905

A.E. Folson
Notary Public.

WITNESSETH:
Must be two witnesses ⎧ Louisa Shirky
who are citizens and   ⎬
know the child.   ⎩ Austin Pickens

We hereby certify that we are well acquainted with   Abel Wilson   The Father of child   and know   him   to be reputable and of good standing in the community.

Must be two citizen ⎧ Louisa Shirky
witnesses.   ⎩ Austin Pickens

Applications for Enrollment of Choctaw Newborn
Act of 1905   Volume V

BIRTH AFFIDAVIT.

DEPARTMENT OF THE INTERIOR.
COMMISSION TO THE FIVE CIVILIZED TRIBES.

IN RE APPLICATION FOR ENROLLMENT, as a citizen of the Choctaw Nation, of Bessie Wilson, born on the 23 day of June, 1903

Name of Father: Abel Wilson   a citizen of the Choctaw Nation.
Name of Mother: Mary Wilson   a citizen of the Choctaw Nation.

Postoffice   Caddo I.T.

AFFIDAVIT OF MOTHER.

UNITED STATES OF AMERICA, Indian Territory, }
    Central   DISTRICT. }

    I, Mary Wilson, on oath state that I am 30 years of age and a citizen by blood, of the Choctaw Nation; that I am the lawful wife of Abel Wilson, who is a citizen, by blood of the Choctaw Nation; that a female child was born to me on 23rd day of June, 1903; that said child has been named Bessie Wilson, and was living March 4, 1905.

                                Mary Wilson

Witnesses To Mark:
   { Eliza Lewis
   { AND Phillips

    Subscribed and sworn to before me this 21 day of March, 1905

                                A. Denton Phillips
                                    Notary Public.

AFFIDAVIT OF ATTENDING PHYSICIAN OR MID-WIFE.

UNITED STATES OF AMERICA, Indian Territory, }
    Central   DISTRICT. }

    I, Sarah Wilson, a midwife, on oath state that I attended on Mrs. Mary Wilson, wife of Abel Wilson on the 23rd day of June, 1903; that there was born to her on said date a female child; that said child was living March 4, 1905, and is said to have been named Bessie Wilson

                                Sarah Wilson Midwife

Applications for Enrollment of Choctaw Newborn
Act of 1905 Volume V

Witnesses To Mark:
 { Eliza Lewis
 { Cornelius *(Illegible)*

    Subscribed and sworn to before me this 21 day of March, 1905

                  A. Denton Phillips
                    Notary Public.

BIRTH AFFIDAVIT.

DEPARTMENT OF THE INTERIOR.
COMMISSION TO THE FIVE CIVILIZED TRIBES.

    IN RE APPLICATION FOR ENROLLMENT, as a citizen of the Choctaw Nation, of Lida Bessie Wilson, born on the 23 day of June, 1903

Name of Father: Abel Wilson   a citizen of the Choctaw Nation.
Name of Mother: Mary Wilson   a citizen of the Choctaw Nation.

             Postoffice   Caddo I.T.

AFFIDAVIT OF MOTHER.

UNITED STATES OF AMERICA, Indian Territory, }
    Central   **DISTRICT.** }

    I, Mary Wilson, on oath state that I am 30 years of age and a citizen by Blood, of the Choctaw Nation; that I am the lawful wife of Abel Wilson, who is a citizen, by Blood of the Choctaw Nation; that a Female child was born to me on 23" day of June, 1903; that said child has been named Lida Bessie Wilson, and was living March 4, 1905.

                    Mary Wilson

Witnesses To Mark:
 { Eliza Lewis
 { AND Phillips

    Subscribed and sworn to before me this 29th day of May, 1905

                  A. Denton Phillips
                    Notary Public.

Applications for Enrollment of Choctaw Newborn
Act of 1905 Volume V

AFFIDAVIT OF ATTENDING PHYSICIAN OR MID-WIFE.

UNITED STATES OF AMERICA, Indian Territory,
Central DISTRICT.

I, N C Coleman , a attendant , on oath state that I attended on Mrs. Mary Wilson , wife of Abel Wilson on the 23" day of June , 1903; that there was born to her on said date a Female child; that said child was living March 4, 1905, and is said to have been named Lida Bessie Wilson

N C Coleman

Witnesses To Mark:

Subscribed and sworn to before me this 29 day of May , 1905

A. Denton Phillips
Notary Public.

7-NB-254.

Muskogee, Indian Territory, May 20, 1905.

Able Wilson,
Caddo, Indian Territory.

Dear Sir:

There is enclosed you herewith for execution application for the enrollment of your infant child.

In the affidavits of February 22, 1905, heretofore filed with the Commission, the name of the applicant is given as Lida Wilson, while in those of March 21, 1905, her name is given as Bessie Wilson. In the enclosed application the name of the applicant is left blank and you will please insert the correct name before executing.

In having these affidavits executed care should be exercised to see that all names are written in full, as they appear in the body of the affidavit, and in the event that either of the persons signing the affidavit are unable to write, signatures by mark must be attested by two witnesses. Each affidavit must be executed before a Notary Public and the notarial seal and signature of the officer must be attached to each separate affidavit.

Respectfully,

Chairman.

Applications for Enrollment of Choctaw Newborn
Act of 1905 Volume V

COMMISSIONERS:
TAMS BIXBY,
THOMAS B. NEEDLES,
C.R. BRECKINBRIDGE.

WM. O. BEALL
Secretary

DEPARTMENT OF THE INTERIOR,
COMMISSIONER TO THE FIVE CIVILIZED TRIBES.

Wm O.B.

REFER IN REPLY TO THE FOLLOWING:

7-3831

ADDRESS ONLY THE
COMMISSION TO THE FIVE CIVILIZED TRIBES.

Muskogee, Indian Territory, March 24, 1905.

Abel Wilson,
  Caddo, Indian Territory.

Dear Sir:

Receipt is hereby acknowledged of the affidavits of Mary Wilson and Sarah Wilson to the birth of Bessie Wilson, daughter of Abel and Mary Wilson, June 23, 1903, and the same have been filed with the records as an application for the enrollment of said child.

  Respectfully,
  Tams Bixby
  Chairman.

---

7 N.B. 254.

Muskogee, Indian Territory, June 2, 1905.

Abel Wilson,
  Caddo, Indian Territory.

Dear Sir:

Receipt is hereby acknowledged of the affidavits of Mary Wilson and N. C. Coleman to the birth of Lida Bessie Wilson, daughter of Abel and Mary Wilson, June 23, 1903, and the same have been filed with our records in the matter of the enrollment of said child.

  Respectfully,

  (Blank)

Applications for Enrollment of Choctaw Newborn
Act of 1905   Volume V

Muskogee, Indian Territory, July 25, 1905.

Chief Clerk,
    Choctaw Land Office,
        Atoka, Indian Territory.

Dear Sir:

    Refer to suplicate[sic] Choctaw New Born Roll Card No. 254, in the possession of your office and change the name of the applicant thereon to read, "Lida Bessie Wilson."

        Respectfully,

                Commissioner.

Muskogee, Indian Territory, July 25, 1905.

Chief Clerk,
    Chickasaw Land Office,
        Ardmore, Indian Territory.

Dear Sir:

    Refer to duplicate Choctaw New Born Roll Card No. 254, in the possession of your office and change the name of the applicant thereon to read, "Lida Bessie Wilson,"

        Respectfully,

                Commissioner.

Applications for Enrollment of Choctaw Newborn
Act of 1905   Volume V

Choc New Born 255
　　　Perry Anderson
　　　(Born May 7, 1904)

AFFIDAVIT OF ATTENDING PHYSICIAN OR MIDWIFE

UNITED STATES OF AMERICA
INDIAN TERRITORY
Central　　DISTRICT

　　　I,　P. L. Cane　　a　　Physician on oath state that I attended on Mrs. Elsie Anderson　wife of　Frank Anderson on the　7th　day of　May　, 190 4, that there was born to her on said date a　male child, that said child is now living, and is said to have been named　Perry Anderson

　　　　　　　　　　　　　　　　　　　P. L. Cain　　　　M.D.
　　Subscribed and sworn to before me this, the　20th　day of　January　　190 5

　　　　　　　　　　　　　　　　　J. M. Redsor
　　　　　　　　　　　　　　　　　　　　Notary Public.

WITNESSETH:
Must be two witnesses who are citizens and know the child.
　　Robinson Anderson
　　J. J. Gardner

　　　We hereby certify that we are well acquainted with　P. L. Cane a　Physician　and know　him　to be reputable and of good standing in the community.
　　　　　　　　　　　　　　　Robinson Anderson
　　　　　　　　　　　　　　　J. J. Gardner

NEW-BORN AFFIDAVIT.

　　　　　Number..............

Choctaw Enrolling Commission.

　　IN THE MATTER OF THE APPLICATION FOR ENROLLMENT, as a citizen of the Choctaw　Nation, of　Perry Anderson

born on the　7th　day of　May　190 4

Name of father　Frank Anderson　　　　a citizen of　Choctaw
Nation final enrollment No　10587
Name of mother　Elsie Anderson　　　　a citizen of　Choctaw
Nation final enrollment No　10811

Applications for Enrollment of Choctaw Newborn
Act of 1905 Volume V

Postoffice Blue, I.T.

AFFIDAVIT OF MOTHER.

UNITED STATES OF AMERICA,
INDIAN TERRITORY,
Central DISTRICT

I Elsie Anderson, on oath state that I am 24 years of age and a citizen by blood of the Choctaw Nation, and as such have been placed upon the final roll of the Choctaw Nation, by the Honorable Secretary of the Interior my final enrollment number being 10811; that I am the lawful wife of Frank Anderson, who is a citizen of the Choctaw Nation, and as such has been placed upon the final roll of said Nation by the Honorable Secretary of the Interior, his final enrollment number being 10587 and that a male child was born to me on the 7th day of May 1904; that said child has been named Elsie Anderson, and is now living.

WITNESSETH: Elsie Anderson

Must be two Witnesses who are Citizens.
Robinson D. Anderson
J. J. Gardner

Subscribed and sworn to before me this 16 day of Jan 1905

W. A. Shoney
Notary Public.

My commission expires Jan. 11, 1909

BIRTH AFFIDAVIT.

DEPARTMENT OF THE INTERIOR.
COMMISSION TO THE FIVE CIVILIZED TRIBES.

IN RE APPLICATION FOR ENROLLMENT, as a citizen of the Choctaw Nation, of Perry Anderson, born on the 7th day of May, 1904

Name of Father: Frank Anderson   a citizen of the Choctaw Nation.
Name of Mother: Elsie Anderson   a citizen of the Choctaw Nation.

Postoffice Blue, I.T.

Applications for Enrollment of Choctaw Newborn
Act of 1905   Volume V

AFFIDAVIT OF MOTHER.

UNITED STATES OF AMERICA, Indian Territory, }
Central   DISTRICT.

I, Elsie Anderson, on oath state that I am 24 years of age and a citizen by blood, of the Choctaw Nation; that I am the lawful wife of Frank Anderson, who is a citizen, by blood of the Choctaw Nation; that a male child was born to me on 7th day of May, 1904; that said child has been named Perry Anderson, and was living March 4, 1905.

                              Elsie Anderson

Witnesses To Mark:
{

Subscribed and sworn to before me this 23rd day of March, 1905

                              W.H. Angell
                                  Notary Public.

AFFIDAVIT OF ATTENDING PHYSICIAN OR MID-WIFE.

UNITED STATES OF AMERICA, Indian Territory, }
Central   DISTRICT.

I, P. L. Cain, a Physician, on oath state that I attended on Mrs. Elsie Anderson, wife of Frank Anderson on the 7th day of May, 1904; that there was born to her on said date a male child; that said child was living March 4, 1905, and is said to have been named Perry Anderson

                              P. L. Cain

Witnesses To Mark:
{

Subscribed and sworn to before me this 21st day of March, 1905

                              J.M. Reasor
                                  Notary Public.

Applications for Enrollment of Choctaw Newborn
Act of 1905   Volume V

Choc New Born 256
    Opal Baxter
    (Born March 1, 1904)

Affidavit of Attending Physician or Midwife

UNITED STATES OF AMERICA,
    INDIAN TERRITORY,
  Central   DISTRICT

I, W. R. Bowman a physician on oath state that I attended on Mrs. Alta Baxter wife of Walter W. Baxter on the 1st. day of March, 190 4, that there was born to her on said date a female child, that said child is now living, and is said to have been named Willie O. Baxter

    W.R. Bowman   M. D.

Subscribed and sworn to before me this the 17th. day of January 1905

(Name Illegible)
Notary Public.

WITNESSETH:
Must be two witnesses who are citizens and know the child.
    F. Manning
    J. F. Boydstun

We hereby certify that we are well acquainted with W. R. Bowman a physician and know him to be reputable and of good standing in the community.

Must be two citizen witnesses.
    F Manning
    J. F. Boydston

Applications for Enrollment of Choctaw Newborn
Act of 1905   Volume V

NEW-BORN AFFIDAVIT.

Number..............

Choctaw Enrolling Commission.

IN THE MATTER OF THE APPLICATION FOR ENROLLMENT, as a citizen of the Choctaw Nation, of   Willie O. Baxter

born on the 1st day of   March   1904

Name of father   Walter W Baxter   a citizen of   Choctaw
Nation final enrollment No   15467
Name of mother   Alta Baxter   a citizen of   Choctaw
Nation final enrollment No   Choctaw D. 741.

Postoffice   Caddo, Ind. Ter.

AFFIDAVIT OF MOTHER.

UNITED STATES OF AMERICA,
INDIAN TERRITORY,
Central   DISTRICT

I   Alta Baxter   , on oath state that I am   22   years of age and a citizen by   intermarriage   of the   Choctaw   Nation, and as such have been placed upon the final roll of the   Choctaw   Nation, by the Honorable Secretary of the Interior my final enrollment number being   Choc. D. 741 ; that I am the lawful wife of   Walter W. Baxter   , who is a citizen of the   Choctaw   Nation, and as such has been placed upon the final roll of said Nation by the Honorable Secretary of the Interior, his final enrollment number being   15467   and that a   female   child was born to me on the   1st   day of   March   1904; that said child has been named   Willie O. Baxter   , and is now living.

WITNESSETH: Alta Baxter

Must be two ⎫ F Manning
Witnesses who ⎬
are Citizens. ⎭ J.F. Boydstun

Subscribed and sworn to before me this   17th   day of   January   1905

(Name Illegible)
                                          Notary Public.

My commission expires   Sept. 21st - 1905.

Applications for Enrollment of Choctaw Newborn
Act of 1905   Volume V

BIRTH AFFIDAVIT.

DEPARTMENT OF THE INTERIOR.
COMMISSION TO THE FIVE CIVILIZED TRIBES.

IN RE APPLICATION FOR ENROLLMENT, as a citizen of the   Choctaw   Nation, of   Opal Baxter   , born on the   1st.   day of   March , 1904

Name of Father: Walter W. Baxter   a citizen of the   Choctaw   Nation.
Name of Mother: Alta Baxter   a citizen of the   Choctaw   Nation.

Postoffice   Caddo, Ind. Ter.

AFFIDAVIT OF MOTHER.

UNITED STATES OF AMERICA, Indian Territory, }
  Central   DISTRICT.

I,   Alta Baxter   , on oath state that I am   22   years of age and a citizen by intermarriage   , of the   Choctaw   Nation; that I am the lawful wife of   Walter W. Baxter   , who is a citizen, by   blood   of the   Choctaw   Nation; that a   female   child was born to me on   1st.   day of   March   , 1904; that said child has been named   Opal Baxter   , and was living March 4, 1905.

Alta Baxter

Witnesses To Mark:
  {

Subscribed and sworn to before me this   18th.   day of   March   , 1905

(Name Illegible)
Notary Public.

AFFIDAVIT OF ATTENDING PHYSICIAN OR MID-WIFE.

UNITED STATES OF AMERICA, Indian Territory, }
  Central   DISTRICT.

I,   Mrs. Siner Overstreet   , a   midwife   , on oath state that I attended on Mrs.   Alta Baxter   , wife of   Walter W. Baxter   on the   1st.   day of   March   , 1904; that there was born to her on said date a   female   child; that said child was living March 4, 1905, and is said to have been named   Opal Baxter

Siner Overstreet

Witnesses To Mark:
  {

Applications for Enrollment of Choctaw Newborn
Act of 1905   Volume V

Subscribed and sworn to before me this 18th. day of   March   , 1905

                                 (Name Illegible)
                                   Notary Public.

                                      7-3672

                   Muskogee, Indian Territory, March 22, 1905.

Walter W. Baxter,
      Caddo, Indian Territory.

Dear Sir:

      Receipt is hereby acknowledged of the affidavits of Alta Baxter and Siner Overstreet to the birth of Opal Baxter, daughter of Walter W. and Alta Baxter, March 1, 1904, and the same have been filed with our records as an application for the enrollment of said child.

                         Respectfully,

                                            Chairman.

<u>Choc New Born 257</u>
        Ruth Lawrence
        (Born Dec. 5, 1904)

BIRTH AFFIDAVIT.
                         DEPARTMENT OF THE INTERIOR.
COMMISSION TO THE FIVE CIVILIZED TRIBES.

      IN RE APPLICATION FOR ENROLLMENT, as a citizen of the   Choctaw   Nation, of Ruth Lawrence   , born on the Fifth   day of December , 1904

Name of Father: Frank T. Lawrence   a citizen of the   Choctaw   Nation.
Name of Mother: Ida V. Lawrence   a citizen of the   Choctaw   Nation.

                         Postoffice   Caddo, Ind. Ter.

Applications for Enrollment of Choctaw Newborn
Act of 1905 Volume V

AFFIDAVIT OF MOTHER.

UNITED STATES OF AMERICA, Indian Territory,
Central DISTRICT.

I, Ida V. Lawrence, on oath state that I am 23 years of age and a citizen by Intermarriage, of the Choctaw Nation; that I am the lawful wife of Frank T. Lawrence, who is a citizen, by blood of the Choctaw Nation; that a Female child was born to me on Fifth day of December, 1904; that said child has been named Ruth Lawrence, and was living March 4, 1905.

                            Ida V. Lawrence

Witnesses To Mark:

Subscribed and sworn to before me this 27th day of March, 1905

                            D.H. Linebaugh
                                Notary Public.

AFFIDAVIT OF ATTENDING PHYSICIAN OR MID-WIFE.

UNITED STATES OF AMERICA, Indian Territory,
Central DISTRICT.

I, W. J. Melton, a Physician, on oath state that I attended on Mrs. Ida V. Lawrence, wife of Frank T. Lawrence on the fifth day of December, 1904; that there was born to her on said date a Female child; that said child was living March 4, 1905, and is said to have been named Ruth Lawrence

                            W. J. Melton

Witnesses To Mark:

Subscribed and sworn to before me this 25th day of March, 1905

                            J.L. Rappolee
                               Notary Public.

Applications for Enrollment of Choctaw Newborn
Act of 1905   Volume V

Choc New Born 258
    Lloyd O. Manning
    (Born June 29, 1903)

NEW BORN AFFIDAVIT

No ....

CHOCTAW ENROLLING COMMISSION

IN THE MATTER OF THE APPLICATION FOR ENROLLMENT as a citizen of the Choctaw Nation, of   Lloyd O. Manning   born on the 29th day of June   190 3

Name of father   Forbis Manning   a citizen of   Choctaw   Nation, final enrollment No.   10533
Name of mother   Laura Manning   a citizen of   Choctaw   Nation, final enrollment No.   346

Caddo I.T.   Postoffice.

AFFIDAVIT OF MOTHER

UNITED STATES OF AMERICA
    INDIAN TERRITORY
DISTRICT   Central

I   Laura Manning   , on oath state that I am   31   years of age and a citizen by   Intermarriage   of the   Choctaw   Nation, and as such have been placed upon the final roll of the   Choctaw   Nation, by the Honorable Secretary of the Interior my final enrollment number being   346 ; that I am the lawful wife of   Forbis Manning   , who is a citizen of the   Choctaw   Nation, and as such has been placed upon the final roll of said Nation by the Honorable Secretary of the Interior, his final enrollment number being   10532   and that a   Male   child was born to me on the   29th day of   June   190 3; that said child has been named   Lloyd O. Manning   , and is now living.

WITNESSETH: Laura Manning
  Must be two witnesses ⎰ Amelia Harris
  who are citizens   ⎱ S.J. Homer

Applications for Enrollment of Choctaw Newborn
Act of 1905   Volume V

Subscribed and sworn to before me this, the 8th day of February 1905

A.E. Folsom
Notary Public.

My Commission Expires:
Jan 9 - 1909

Affidavit of Attending Physician or Midwife

UNITED STATES OF AMERICA,
INDIAN TERRITORY,
Central DISTRICT

I, Le Roy Long a Practicing Physician on oath state that I attended on Mrs. Laura Manning wife of Forbis Manning on the 29th day of June, 1903, that there was born to her on said date a male child, that said child is now living, and is said to have been named Lloyd O Manning

LeRoy Long   M. D.

Subscribed and sworn to before me this the 13th day of Feby 1905

(Name Illegible)
Notary Public.

Com Ex 3/6/07

WITNESSETH:

Must be two witnesses who are citizens and know the child.
- Amelia Harris
- S.J. Homer

We hereby certify that we are well acquainted with Le Roy Long a Physician and know him to be reputable and of good standing in the community.

Must be two citizen witnesses.
- Amelia Harris
- S.J. Homer

Applications for Enrollment of Choctaw Newborn
Act of 1905   Volume V

BIRTH AFFIDAVIT.

DEPARTMENT OF THE INTERIOR.
COMMISSION TO THE FIVE CIVILIZED TRIBES.

IN RE APPLICATION FOR ENROLLMENT, as a citizen of the Choctaw Nation, of LLoyd[sic] O. Manning, born on the 29th day of June, 1903

Name of Father: Forbis Manning   a citizen of the   Choctaw   Nation.
Name of Mother: Laura Manning   a citizen of the   Choctaw   Nation.

Postoffice   Caddo, I.T.

AFFIDAVIT OF MOTHER.

UNITED STATES OF AMERICA, Indian Territory,
   Central   **DISTRICT.**

I, Laura Manning, on oath state that I am 31 years of age and a citizen by Intermarriage, of the Choctaw Nation; that I am the lawful wife of Forbis Manning, who is a citizen, by Blood of the Choctaw Nation; that a male child was born to me on 29th day of June, 1903; that said child has been named LLoyd O. Manning, and was living March 4, 1905.

Laura Manning

Witnesses To Mark:
{

Subscribed and sworn to before me this 21st day of March, 1905

C.H. *(Illegible)*
Notary Public.

AFFIDAVIT OF ATTENDING PHYSICIAN OR MID-WIFE.

UNITED STATES OF AMERICA, Indian Territory,
   Central   **DISTRICT.**

I, LeRoy Long, a Physician, on oath state that I attended on Mrs. Laura Manning, wife of Forbis Manning on the 29th day of June, 1903; that there was born to her on said date a male child; that said child was living March 4, 1905, and is said to have been named LLoyd O. Manning

LeRoy Long

Witnesses To Mark:
{

Applications for Enrollment of Choctaw Newborn
Act of 1905   Volume V

Subscribed and sworn to before me this 24   day of   March   , 1905

Com Ex 3/6/07

(Name Illegible)
Notary Public.

Choctaw 3721

Muskogee, Indian Territory, March 30, 1905.

F. Manning,
    Caddo, Indian Territory.

Dear Sir:

    Receipt is hereby acknowledged of your letter of March 25, inclosing affidavits of Laura Manning and LeRoy Long to the birth of Lloyd O. Manning, son of Forbis and Laura Manning, June 29, 1903, and the same have been filed with our records as an application for the enrollment of said child.

        Respectfully,

                Chairman.

7-3721

Muskogee, Indian Territory, May 7, 1906.

Forbis Manning,
    Caddo, Indian Territory.

Dear Sir:

    Receipt is hereby acknowledged of the affidavits of Laura Manning and W. R. Bowman to the birth of Vera Manning, child of Forbis and Laura Manning, October 4, 1905, and the same have been filed as an application for the enrollment of said child.

        Respectfully,

                Acting Commissioner.

Applications for Enrollment of Choctaw Newborn
Act of 1905 Volume V

Choc New Born 259
    Francis Leader
    (Born Nov. 25, 1902)

BIRTH AFFIDAVIT.

DEPARTMENT OF THE INTERIOR,
COMMISSION TO THE FIVE CIVILIZED TRIBES.

IN RE Application for Enrollment, as a citizen of the Choctaw Nation, of Francis Leader, born on the 25 day of Nov., 1902
Name of Father: ~~Joel~~ Silas Leader   a citizen of the Choctaw Nation.
Name of Mother: Agnes Johnson   a citizen of the Choctaw Nation.

              Post-Office: Peck, Ind. Ter.

AFFIDAVIT OF MOTHER.

UNITED STATES OF AMERICA, }
   INDIAN TERRITORY.
   Cent.   District.

    Agnes Johnson
  I, ~~Francis Leader~~, on oath state that I am 25 years of age and a citizen by blood, of the Choctaw Nation; xxxxxxxxxxxxxxxxxxxxxxxxxxxxxx, xxxxxxxxxxxxxxxxxxxxxxxx .... of the .... xxxion; that a female child was born to me on 25th day of November, 1902, that said child has been named Francis Leader, and is now living.

                      Agnes Johnson

WITNESSES TO MARK:

  Subscribed and sworn to before me this   29th   *day of* July, 1904

                    (Name Illegible)
                        NOTARY PUBLIC.

Applications for Enrollment of Choctaw Newborn
Act of 1905   Volume V

AFFIDAVIT OF ATTENDING PHYSICIAN OR MID-WIFE.

UNITED STATES OF AMERICA,
    INDIAN TERRITORY.
  Central   District.

        Icey Leader
    I, ~~Sisily Hotubby~~ , a   mid-wife   , on oath state that I attended on xxx.   Agnes Johnson   , xxxxxx ....on the   25th   day of November   , 1904[sic]; that there was born to her on said date a   female   child; that said child is now living and is said to have been named   Francis Leader

                                            her
                                   Icey x Leader
WITNESSES TO MARK: mark
    { N.S. Farmer
      Culberson Lewis

Subscribed and sworn to before me this   3rd   *day of*   August   , 1904

                                    N.S. Farmer
                                       NOTARY PUBLIC.

DEPARTMENT OF THE INTERIOR,
COMMISSIONER TO THE FIVE CIVILIZED TRIBES.

Durant, Indian Territory, January 18, 1907.
_____ooOoo_____

    In the matter of the application for the enrollment, as a citizen of the Choctaw Nation, of Francis Leader, on New Born Card Number 260.

    Testimony taken at Lewis, Indian Territory, December 15, 1906.

    <u>CULBERSON LEWIS</u>, being duly sworn, by Lacey P. Bobo, Notary Public in and for the Central District of Indian Territory, testified as follows:

                Jacob Homer, Official Interpreter.

<u>BY THE COMMISSIONER</u>:

Q Are you duly enrolled as a member of one of the five civilized tribes, if so which one?
A Choctaw.
Q How does your name appear upon the approved Choctaw roll?
A Culberson Lewis.
Q How old are you? A 24.
Q Did you know a little Choctaw girl named Francis Leader?

Applications for Enrollment of Choctaw Newborn
Act of 1905 Volume V

A Yes.
Q Who was the father of this child? A Silas Leader.
Q Who was the mother? A Agnes Johnson.
Q Was this child born in lawful wedlock? A No, sir.
Q Do you know when the child was born? A No.
Q Do you know when the child died? A Yes.
Q You may state when? A September 17, 1904.
Q Have you a record of this child's death? A Yes.
Q Is same a private or official record? A Private.
Q How old was this child at the time of her death judging from her size?
A Maybe about two years old, maybe about a year and a half.
Q What was its sex? A Girl.
Q Were you present at the death of this child?
A Yes.
Q Did you assist in the burial?
A Yes, I was the step-father of the child.
Q Did the child's mother survive it?
A Yes, the mother lived about two months after the child died?[sic]
Q When did the child's mother's death occur?
A November 24, 1904.
Q How many years has this child and her mother been dead?
A A little over two years.

Witness Excused.

Testimony taken at Caney, Indian Territory, December 17, 1906.

JOSLIH[sic] LEWIS, being duly sworn, by Lacey P. Bobo, Notary Public in and for the Central District of Indian Territory, testified as follows:

Jacob Homer, Official Interpreter.

BY THE COMMISSIONER:

Q What is your name? A Joslin Lewis.
Q What is your age? A 26.
Q Are you a citizen by blood of the Choctaw Nation? A Yes.
Q What is your post office? A Caney, I. T.
Q Were you acquainted with Silas Leader, a Choctaw who resided at or near Caney, I. T?
A Yes.
Q Were you likewise acquainted with Agnes Johnson? A Yes.
Q Did Agnes Johnson have a minor child, if so what was its name?
A Francis.
Q Who was the father of this child? A Silas Leader.
Q When was the child born? A I do not know.

Applications for Enrollment of Choctaw Newborn
Act of 1905   Volume V

Q When did it die? A In the fall of 1904.
Q How old was it at the time of its death?
A About two years old.
Q You state as a matter of fact and upon oath that this child was not living March 4, 1905, and died in the fall previous?
A Yes.

Witness Excused.

W. P. Covington, being duly sworn, states that the above and foregoing is a full, true and correct transcript of his stenographic notes taken in said case on said date.

Subscribed and sworn to before me, this 19 day of Jany 1907.

Lacey P. Bobo
Notary Public.

7-3726

Muskogee, Indian Territory, August 6, 1904.

Agnes Johnson,
    Peck, Indian Territory.

Dear Madam :-

    Receipt is hereby acknowledged of your affidavit and that of Icey Leader, relative to the birth of your infant daughter, Francis Leader, November 25, 1902, which it is presumed have been forwarded to this office as an application for enrollment of said child as a citizen by blood of the Choctaw Nation.

    The Act of Congress approved July 1, 1902, which was ratified by the citizens of the Choctaw and Chickasaw Nations, September 25, 1902, among other things provides that no child born to a citizen of the Choctaw or Chickasaw Nation subsequent to the date of said ratification shall be entitled to enrollment. citizen or freedman of the Choctaw or Chickasaw Nations subsequent to the date of said ratification shall be entitled to be enrolled, or to participate in the distribution of the tribal property of the Choctaw and Chickasaws.

Respectfully,

Commissioner in Charge.

Applications for Enrollment of Choctaw Newborn
Act of 1905 Volume V

N. B. 260[sic]

COPY

Muskogee, Indian Territory, April 8, 1905.

Silas Leader,
    Peck, Indian Territory.

Dear Sir:

    There is inclosed you herewith for execution application for the enrollment of your infant child, Francis Leader, born November 25, 1902.

    The affidavits heretofore filed with the Commission show the child was living on August 3, 1904. It is necessary, for the child to be enrolled, that he was living on March 4, 1905. You will please insert the mother's age in space provided for that purpose.

    In having these affidavits executed care should be exercised to see that all names are written in full, as they appear in the body of the affidavit, and in the event that either of the persons signing the affidavit are unable to write, signatures by mark must be attested by two witnesses. Each affidavit must be executed before a Notary Public and the notarial seal and signature of the officer must be attached to each separate affidavit.

                        Respectfully,
                          SIGNED
                        T. B. Needles.

LM 8-12.   Commissioner in Charge.

7-NB-260[sic].

Muskogee, Indian Territory, May 20, 1905.

Agnes Johnson,
    Peck, Indian Territory.

Dear Madam:

    There is enclosed you herewith for execution application for the enrollment of your infant child, Francis Leader, born November 25, 1902.

    Your attention is called to the Commissions[sic] letter of the 8th ultimo, which contained application similar to the one above mentioned. Before this matter can be finally determined it will be necessary for you to file the enclosed application, properly executed, in this office. The affidavits heretofore filed with the Commission show the child was living on August 3, 1904. It is necessary, for the child to be enrolled, that she was living on March 4, 1905.

Applications for Enrollment of Choctaw Newborn
Act of 1905   Volume V

In having these affidavits executed care should be exercised to see that all names are written in full, as they appear in the body of the affidavit, and in the event that either of the persons signing the affidavit are unable to write, signatures by mark must be attested by two witnesses. Each affidavit must be executed before a Notary Public and the notarial seal and signature of the officer must be attached to each separate affidavit.

Respectfully,

VR 20-13.   Chairman.

7-NB-260[sic]

Muskogee, Indian Territory, July 29, 1905.

Agnes Johnson,
    Peck, Indian Territory.

Dear Madam:

Your attention is called to a communication addressed to you by the Commission to the Five Civilized Tribes under date of May 24, 1905, with which was inclosed for execution application for the enrollment of your infant child, Francis Leader, born November 25, 1902.

In said letter you were advised that the affidavits heretofore filed in this case, show the child was living August 3, 1904, and that it was necessary for the child to be enrolled that he[sic] was living March 4, 1905. No reply to this letter has been received.

The matter should receive your immediate attention as no further action can be taken relative to his[sic] enrollment until this evidence is supplied.

Respectfully,

Commissioner.

7-NB-260[sic]

Muskogee, Indian Territory, January 25, 1907.

Agnes Johnson,
    Peck, Indian Territory.

Dear Madam:

You are hereby advised that on January 25, 1907, it appearing from the records of this office that your minor child, Francis Leader died prior to March 4, 1905, the

Applications for Enrollment of Choctaw Newborn
Act of 1905   Volume V

Commissioner dismissed the application for his enrollment as a new born citizen of the Choctaw Nation.

                        Respectfully,

                                              Commissioner.

Choc New Born 260
    Claud Hassel Harkins
    (Born April 26, 1903)
    Mable Harkins
    (Born March 2, 1905)

BIRTH AFFIDAVIT.

DEPARTMENT OF THE INTERIOR,
COMMISSION TO THE FIVE CIVILIZED TRIBES.

IN RE Application for Enrollment, as a citizen of the Choctaw Nation, of Claud Hassel Harkins , born on the 26 day of April , 1903

Name of Father: George W. Harkins   a citizen of the Choctaw Nation.
Name of Mother: Hattie Harkins   a citizen of the Choctaw Nation.

                Post-Office: Owl, I.T.

AFFIDAVIT OF MOTHER.

UNITED STATES OF AMERICA, }
    INDIAN TERRITORY.
  Cent.   District.

    I, Hattie Harkins , on oath state that I am 38 years of age and a citizen by Marriage , of the Choctaw Nation; that I am the lawful wife of George W. Harkins , who is a citizen, by Blood of the Choctaw Nation; that a male child was born to me on 26 day of April , 1903 , that said child has been named Claud Hassel Harkins , and is now living.

                                    Hattie Harkins

WITNESSES TO MARK:

Applications for Enrollment of Choctaw Newborn
Act of 1905 Volume V

Subscribed and sworn to before me this 18 *day of* Jan , 1904

R.T. Breedlane
NOTARY PUBLIC.

AFFIDAVIT OF ATTENDING PHYSICIAN OR MID-WIFE.

UNITED STATES OF AMERICA,
   INDIAN TERRITORY.
  Cent   District.

I, Dr. J.H. Arnold , a Physician , on oath state that I attended on Mrs. Hattie Harkins , wife of G.W. Harkins on the 26 day of April , 1903; that there was born to her on said date a male child; that said child is now living and is said to have been named Claud Hassel Harkins

Dr. J.H. Arnold

WITNESSES TO MARK:

Subscribed and sworn to before me this 18 *day of* Jan , 1904

R.T. Breedlane
NOTARY PUBLIC.

BIRTH AFFIDAVIT.

DEPARTMENT OF THE INTERIOR.
COMMISSION TO THE FIVE CIVILIZED TRIBES.

IN RE APPLICATION FOR ENROLLMENT, as a citizen of the Choctaw Nation, of Claud H. Harkins , born on the 26 day of April , 1903

Name of Father: George W. Harkins   a citizen of the Choctaw Nation.
Name of Mother: Hattie Harkins   a citizen of the Choctaw Nation.

Postoffice   Tupelo I.T.

AFFIDAVIT OF MOTHER.

UNITED STATES OF AMERICA, Indian Territory,
  Central   **DISTRICT.**

I, Hattie Harkins , on oath state that I am 38 years of age and a citizen by Intermarriage , of the Choctaw Nation; that I am the lawful wife of

Applications for Enrollment of Choctaw Newborn
Act of 1905   Volume V

George W. Harkins, who is a citizen, by Blood of the Choctaw Nation; that a male child was born to me on 26 day of April, 1903; that said child has been named Claud H Harkins, and was living March 4, 1905.

           Hattie Harkins

Witnesses To Mark:
{

  Subscribed and sworn to before me this 7 day of April, 1905

           John H. Cross
           Notary Public.

AFFIDAVIT OF ATTENDING PHYSICIAN OR MID-WIFE.

UNITED STATES OF AMERICA, Indian Territory, }
 Central   DISTRICT.

  I, J. H. Arnold, a Physician, on oath state that I attended on Mrs. Hattie Harkins, wife of George W. Harkins on the 26 day of April, 1903; that there was born to her on said date a male child; that said child was living March 4, 1905, and is said to have been named Claud H. Harkins

           Dr. J.H. Arnold

Witnesses To Mark:
{

  Subscribed and sworn to before me this 7 day of April, 1905

           John H. Cross
           Notary Public.

BIRTH AFFIDAVIT.

      DEPARTMENT OF THE INTERIOR.
    COMMISSION TO THE FIVE CIVILIZED TRIBES.

  IN RE APPLICATION FOR ENROLLMENT, as a citizen of the Choctaw Nation, of Mable Harkins, born on the 2 day of March, 1905

Name of Father: George W. Harkins a citizen of the Choctaw Nation.
Name of Mother: Hattie Harkins   a citizen of the Choctaw Nation.

      Postoffice Tupelo I.T.

Applications for Enrollment of Choctaw Newborn
Act of 1905 Volume V

AFFIDAVIT OF MOTHER.

UNITED STATES OF AMERICA, Indian Territory, }
    Central   DISTRICT.

    I, Hattie Harkins , on oath state that I am 38 years of age and a citizen by Intermarriage , of the Choctaw Nation; that I am the lawful wife of George W. Harkins , who is a citizen, by Blood of the Choctaw Nation; that a Female child was born to me on 2 day of March , 1905; that said child has been named Mable Harkins , and was living March 4, 1905.

                                                Hattie Harkins

Witnesses To Mark:
{

    Subscribed and sworn to before me this 7 day of April , 1905

                                                John H. Cross
                                               Notary Public.

AFFIDAVIT OF ATTENDING PHYSICIAN OR MID-WIFE.

UNITED STATES OF AMERICA, Indian Territory, }
    Central   DISTRICT.

    I, J. H. Arnold , a Physician , on oath state that I attended on Mrs. Hattie Harkins , wife of George W. Harkins on the 2 day of March , 1905; that there was born to her on said date a Female child; that said child was living March 4, 1905, and is said to have been named Mable Harkins

                                                Dr. J.H. Arnold

Witnesses To Mark:
{

    Subscribed and sworn to before me this 7 day of April , 1905

                                               John H. Cross
                                             Notary Public.

Applications for Enrollment of Choctaw Newborn
Act of 1905   Volume V

7-3679

Muskogee, Indian Territory, February 4, 1904.

George W. Harkins,
    Owl, Indian Territory.

Dear Sir:

    Receipt is hereby acknowledged of the affidavits of Hattie Harkins and J. H. Arnold, relative to the birth of your infant son, Claud Hassel Harkins, April 26, 1903, which it is presumed have been forwarded to this office as an application for enrollment as a citizen by blood of the Choctaw Nation.

    You are informed that under the provisions of the act of Congress, approved July 1, 1902, (32 Stats., 641), the Commission is now without authority to receive or consider the original application for enrollment of any person whomsoever, as a citizen of the Choctaw or Chickasaw Nation.

    Respectfully,

Commissioner in Charge.

N. B. 258[sic]

Muskogee, Indian Territory, April 8, 1905.

George W. Harkins,
    Owl, Indian Territory.

Dear Sir:

    There is inclosed you herewith for execution application for the enrollment of your infant child, Claud Hassel Harkins, born April 26, 1903.

    The affidavits heretofore filed with the Commission show the child was living on January 18, 1904. It is necessary, for the child to be enrolled, that he was living on March 4, 1905. You will please insert mother's age in space left blank for that purpose.

    In having these affidavits executed care should be exercised to see that all names are written in full, as they appear in the body of the affidavit, and in the event that either of the persons signing the affidavit are unable to write, signatures by mark must be attested by two witnesses. Each affidavit must be executed before a Notary Public and the notarial seal and signature of the officer must be attached to each separate affidavit.

    Respectfully,

Commissioner in Charge.

LM 8-11

Applications for Enrollment of Choctaw Newborn
Act of 1905   Volume V

Choctaw 3679.

Muskogee, Indian Territory, April 12, 1905.

George W. Harkins,
    Tupelo, Indian Territory.

Dear Sir:

    Receipt is hereby acknowledged of the affidavits of Hattie Harkins and R. J. H. Arnold to the birth of Claud H. Harkins and Mable Harkins, Children[sic] of George W. and Hattie Harkins, April 26, 1903, and March 2, 1905, respectively, and the same have been filed with our records as an application for the enrollment of said children.

    Respectfully,

    Commissioner in Charge.

Choc New Born 261
    Ella Frazier
    (Born Feb. 1, 1903)

BIRTH AFFIDAVIT.

DEPARTMENT OF THE INTERIOR,
COMMISSION TO THE FIVE CIVILIZED TRIBES.

IN RE Application for Enrollment, as a citizen of the Choctaw Nation, of Ella Frazier, born on the 1st day of February, 1903

Name of Father: John Frazier   a citizen of the Choctaw Nation.
Name of Mother: Mary Frazier   a citizen of the Choctaw Nation.

    Post-Office: Boswell I.T.

Applications for Enrollment of Choctaw Newborn
Act of 1905   Volume V

AFFIDAVIT OF MOTHER.

UNITED STATES OF AMERICA, }
    INDIAN TERRITORY.
Central   District.

I, Mary Frazier, on oath state that I am Thirty three years of age and a citizen by blood, of the Choctaw Nation; that I am the lawful wife of John Frazier, who is a citizen, by blood of the Choctaw Nation; that a female child was born to me on 1st day of February, 1903, that said child has been named Ella Frazier, and is now living.

                                   Mary Frazier

WITNESSES TO MARK:

{

Subscribed and sworn to before me this 28th *day of* Nov , 1903

                                   J R Armstrong
                                     NOTARY PUBLIC.

        3/11/1907

AFFIDAVIT OF ATTENDING PHYSICIAN OR MID-WIFE.

UNITED STATES OF AMERICA, }
    INDIAN TERRITORY.
Central   District.

I, Ellen Walhubbie, a Midwife, on oath state that I attended on Mrs. Mary Frazier, wife of John Frazier on the 1st day of February, 1903; that there was born to her on said date a female child; that said child is now living and is said to have been named Ella Frazier

                                 her
                        Ellen x Wachubbie[sic]
WITNESSES TO MARK: mark
{ John Frazier
  J.A. Scott

Subscribed and sworn to before me this 28th *day of* Nov , 1903

                              J R Armstrong
                                NOTARY PUBLIC.
                        Com Ex Mar 11, 1907

Applications for Enrollment of Choctaw Newborn
Act of 1905   Volume V

BIRTH AFFIDAVIT.

DEPARTMENT OF THE INTERIOR.
COMMISSION TO THE FIVE CIVILIZED TRIBES.

IN RE APPLICATION FOR ENROLLMENT, as a citizen of the Choctaw Nation, of Ella Frazier, born on the 1st day of Feb. 1903, 1......

Name of Father: John Frazier   a citizen of the Choctaw Nation.
Name of Mother: Mary Frazier   a citizen of the Choctaw Nation.

Postoffice   Boswell, I. T.

AFFIDAVIT OF MOTHER.

UNITED STATES OF AMERICA, Indian Territory,
Central   DISTRICT.

I, Mary Frazier, on oath state that I am about 36 years of age and a citizen by blood, of the Choctaw Nation; that I am the lawful wife of John Frazier, who is a citizen, by blood of the Choctaw Nation; that a female child was born to me on 1st day of Feb. 1903, 1......; that said child has been named Ella Frazier, and was living March 4, 1905.

Mary Frazier

Witnesses To Mark:

Subscribed and sworn to before me this 25th day of Mra[sic] 1905, 190....

(seal)   JR Armstrong
                      Notary Public.
Commission Expires Mar 11, 1907

AFFIDAVIT OF ATTENDING PHYSICIAN OR MID-WIFE.

UNITED STATES OF AMERICA, Indian Territory,
Central   DISTRICT.

I, Ellen Waichubbie[sic], a midwife, on oath state that I attended on Mrs. Mary Frazier, wife of John Frazier on the 1st day of Feb. 1903, 1......; that there was born to her on said date a female child; that said child was living March 4, 1905, and is said to have been named Ella Frazier

                         her
              Ellen x Waichubbie
                        mark

Applications for Enrollment of Choctaw Newborn
Act of 1905 Volume V

Witnesses To Mark:
{ *(Name Illegible)*
{ TH Bayles

Subscribed and sworn to before me this 25th day of Mra[sic] 1905 , 190....

(seal)   JR Armstrong
                              Notary Public.

BIRTH AFFIDAVIT.

DEPARTMENT OF THE INTERIOR.
COMMISSION TO THE FIVE CIVILIZED TRIBES.

IN RE APPLICATION FOR ENROLLMENT, as a citizen of the Choctaw Nation, of Ella Frazier , born on the 1" day of Feby. , 1903

Name of Father: John Frazier   a citizen of the Choctaw Nation.
Name of Mother: Mary Frazier   a citizen of the Choctaw Nation.

Postoffice   Boswell, I. T.

AFFIDAVIT OF MOTHER.

UNITED STATES OF AMERICA, Indian Territory, }
.... DISTRICT. }

I, Mary Frazier , on oath state that I am about 36 years of age and a citizen by blood , of the Choctaw Nation; that I am the lawful wife of John Frazier , who is a citizen, by blood of the Choctaw Nation; that a female child was born to me on 1" day of Feby. , 1903; that said child has been named Ella Frazier , and was living March 4, 1905.

                              Mary Frazier

Witnesses To Mark:
{

Subscribed and sworn to before me this 20 day of April , 1905

                              JR Armstrong
                              Notary Public.

Applications for Enrollment of Choctaw Newborn
Act of 1905   Volume V

AFFIDAVIT OF ATTENDING PHYSICIAN OR MID-WIFE.

UNITED STATES OF AMERICA, Indian Territory, }
.... DISTRICT. }

I,.. , a .... , on oath state that I attended on Mrs. Mary Frazier , wife of John Frazier on the 1" day of Feby , 1903; that there was born to her on said date a female child; that said child was living March 4, 1905, and is said to have been named Ella Frazier

her
Ellen x Warchubbie
mark

Witnesses To Mark:
{ JR Armstrong
{ *(Name Illegible)*

Subscribed and sworn to before me this 20 day of April , 1905

JR Armstrong
Notary Public.

7-3749

Muskogee, Indian Territory, March 31, 1905.

John Frazier,
    Boswell, Indian Territory.

Dear Sir:

Receipt is hereby acknowledged of the affidavits of Mary Frazier and Ellen Warchubbie to the birth of Ella Frazier daughter of John and Mary Frazier, February 1, 1903, and the same have been filed with our records as an application for the enrollment of said child.

Respectfully,

Chairman.

Applications for Enrollment of Choctaw Newborn
Act of 1905   Volume V

N. B. 261

COPY

Muskogee, Indian Territory, April 10, 1905.

John Frazier,
    Boswell, Indian Territory.

Dear Sir:

    There is inclosed you herewith for execution application for the enrollment of your infant child, Ella Frazier, born February 1, 1903.

    In having these affidavits executed care should be exercised to see that all names are written in full, as they appear in the body of the affidavit, and in the event that either of the persons signing the affidavit are unable to write, signatures by mark must be attested by two witnesses. Each affidavit must be executed before a Notary Public and the notarial seal and signature of the officer must be attached to each separate affidavit.

                      Respectfully,
                        SIGNED
                      T. B. Needles.

SEV 1-10.   Commissioner in Charge.

Choctaw N.B. 261.

Muskogee, Indian Territory, April 22, 1905.

John Frazier,
    Boswell, Indian Territory.

Dear Sir:

    Receipt is hereby acknowledged of the affidavits of Mary Frazier and Ellen Waichubbee to the birth of Ella Frazier, daughter of John and Mary Frazier, February 1, 1903, and the same have been filed with our records in the matter of the enrollment of said child.

                      Respectfully,

                                  Chairman.

Applications for Enrollment of Choctaw Newborn
Act of 1905   Volume V

Choc New Born 262
    Sam LeFlore
    (Born Dec. 4, 1903)

BIRTH AFFIDAVIT.

DEPARTMENT OF THE INTERIOR.
COMMISSION TO THE FIVE CIVILIZED TRIBES.

IN RE APPLICATION FOR ENROLLMENT, as a citizen of the Choctaw Nation, of Sam LeFlore, born on the 4 day of Dec, 1903

Name of Father: Joshua LeFlore   a citizen of the Choctaw Nation.
Name of Mother: Litie LeFlore   a citizen of the Choctaw Nation.

Postoffice

AFFIDAVIT OF MOTHER.

UNITED STATES OF AMERICA, Indian Territory,
Central Judicial   DISTRICT.

I, Litie LeFlore, on oath state that I am about 24 years of age and a citizen by blood, of the Choctaw Nation; that I am the lawful wife of Joshua LeFlore, who is a citizen, by blood of the Choctaw Nation; that a male child was born to me on 4 day of December, 1903; that said child has been named Sam, and was living March 4, 1905.

                her
          Litie x LeFlore
Witnesses To Mark: mark
  V Branaugh
  L.D. Horton

Subscribed and sworn to before me this 25 day of Mch, 1905

          L.D. Horton
              Notary Public.

Applications for Enrollment of Choctaw Newborn
Act of 1905   Volume V

AFFIDAVIT OF ATTENDING PHYSICIAN OR MID-WIFE.

UNITED STATES OF AMERICA, Indian Territory, }
Central Judicial   DISTRICT.

I, Besie[sic] Wilson, a midwife, on oath state that I attended on Mrs. Litie LeFlore, wife of Joshua LeFlore on the 4 day of December, 1903; that there was born to her on said date a .... child; that said child was living March 4, 1905, and is said to have been named Sam

             her
         Besie x Wilson
Witnesses To Mark: mark
 { V Branaugh
   L.D. Horton

  Subscribed and sworn to before me this 25 day of Mch, 1905

        L.D. Horton
         Notary Public.

          N. B. 262
     COPY
  Muskogee, Indian Territory, April 10, 1905.

Joshua LeFlore,
 Boswell, Indian Territory.

Dear Sir:

  Referring to the affidavits heretofore forwarded, relative to the birth of Sam LeFlore it is stated in the affidavit of the mother, Lita[sic] LeFlore, that she is a citizen by blood of the Choctaw Nation.

  If this is correct you are requested to state when, where and under what name she was listed for enrollment, the names of her parents and other members of her family for whom application was made at the same time, and if she has selected an allotment, give her roll number as the same appears upon her allotment certificate.

      Respectfully,
      SIGNED

      T. B. Needles.
      Commissioner in Charge.

Applications for Enrollment of Choctaw Newborn
Act of 1905   Volume V

Choc New Born 263
    Maggie Hoparkentubbi
    (Born Nov. 15, 1902)

NEW BORN
Choctaw Nation, Choctaw Roll
Act of Congress approved March 3rd, 1905, (Public No. 212).
Card No. 263

Residence Choctaw Nation   *Post Office* Bennington I.T.
Roll No. N.B. 1284   *Name 1.* Hoparkentubbi, Maggie
Age March 4, 1905 2   *Sex* F   *Blood* Full
Name of Father David Hoparkentubbi Deceased   *Father's Roll No.* 10592
Name of Mother Isabelle Jones   *Mothers Roll No.* 14810
Born November 15, 1902

For Father's enrollment see Choctaw Roll Card No. 3752
For Mother's enrollment see Choctaw Roll Card No. 3752

Remarks Application for enrollment of No 1 received March 4, 1905. David Hoparkentubbi Roll No. 10592 father No 1 died May 14, 1902; Enrollment cancelled by Department July 8, 1904. Isabelle Jones mother of No 1 is identified as Isabelle Hoparkentubbi; No. 2 on Choctaw Card 3752.

DUPLICATE.

Enrollment of No. 1284 *Approved*   *Date* Apr. 15, 1905
By Secretary of Interior Aug 22, 1905

    Approved July 28, 1905
        Tams Bixby
        ~~Chairman~~. Commissioner.

Copy
BIRTH AFFIDAVIT.
DEPARTMENT OF THE INTERIOR.
COMMISSION TO THE FIVE CIVILIZED TRIBES.

    IN RE APPLICATION FOR ENROLLMENT, as a citizen of the Choctaw Nation, of Maggie Hoparkentubbi , born on the 15 day of Novem[sic] , 1902

Name of Father: David Hoparkentubbi   a citizen of the Choctaw Nation.
Name of Mother: Isabelle "   a citizen of the " Nation.

    Postoffice Bennington I.T.

Applications for Enrollment of Choctaw Newborn
Act of 1905 Volume V

AFFIDAVIT OF MOTHER.

UNITED STATES OF AMERICA, Indian Territory,
Central DISTRICT.

I, Isabelle Hoparkentubbi , on oath state that I am 23 years of age and a citizen by blood , of the Choctaw Nation; that I am the lawful wife of David Hoparkentubbi , who is a citizen, by blood of the Choctaw Nation; that a Female child was born to me on 15 day of November , 1902; that said child has been named Maggie Hoparkentubbi , and ~~was living March 4, 1905~~. is now living

                                          her
                  Signed   Isabelle x Hoparkentubbi
                                       mark

Witnesses To Mark:
   { Jas M Johnson
    R.L. Smith
(Seal)

      Subscribed and sworn to before me this 6th day of January , 1903

                                (Signed) CC McClard
                                                 Notary Public.

AFFIDAVIT OF ATTENDING PHYSICIAN OR MID-WIFE.

UNITED STATES OF AMERICA, Indian Territory,
Central DISTRICT.

I, Sisley Homer , a midwife , on oath state that I attended on Mrs. Isabelle Hoparkentubbi , wife of David Hoparkentubbi on the 15 day of November , 1902; that there was born to her on said date a Female child; that said child was living March 4, 1905, and is said to have been named Maggie Hoparkentubbi

                                      her
                  (Signed) Sisley x Homer
Witnesses To Mark: mark
(Seal){ Jas M Johnson
      R.L. Smith

      Subscribed and sworn to before me this 6th day of January , 1903

                              (Signed) CC McClard
                                             Notary Public.

Applications for Enrollment of Choctaw Newborn
Act of 1905 Volume V

BIRTH AFFIDAVIT. *Copy*

DEPARTMENT OF THE INTERIOR.
COMMISSION TO THE FIVE CIVILIZED TRIBES.

IN RE APPLICATION FOR ENROLLMENT, as a citizen of the Choctaw Nation, of Maggie Hoparkentubbi , born on the 15 day of November , 1902

Name of Father: David Hoparkentubbi   a citizen of the Choctaw Nation.
Name of Mother: Isabelle   "   a citizen of the   "   Nation.

Postoffice   Bennington I.T.

AFFIDAVIT OF MOTHER.

UNITED STATES OF AMERICA, Indian Territory,
.... DISTRICT.

I, Isabelle Hoparkentubbi , on oath state that I am 25 years of age and a citizen by blood , of the Choctaw Nation; that I am the lawful wife of David Hoparkentubbi , who is a citizen, by blood of the Choctaw Nation; that a female child was born to me on 15th day of November , 1902; that said child has been named Maggie Hoparkentubbi , and ~~was living March 4, 1905~~. is now living   her

(signed) Isabelle x Hoparkentubbi
                       mark

Witnesses To Mark:
{ G.D. Duncan
{ R. M. Jones

Subscribed and sworn to before me this 9th day of June , 1905

(Seal)   J.R. Armstrong
                              Notary Public.

AFFIDAVIT OF ATTENDING PHYSICIAN OR MID-WIFE.

UNITED STATES OF AMERICA, Indian Territory,
.... DISTRICT.

I, ... , a .... on oath state that I attended on Mrs. Isabelle Hoparkentubbi , wife of David Hoparkentubbi on the 15th day of November , 1902; that there was born to her on said date a female child; that said child was living March 4, 1905, and is said to have been named Maggie Hoparkentubbi

(signed / D.A. Homer [sic]

Applications for Enrollment of Choctaw Newborn
Act of 1905   Volume V

Witnesses To Mark:

{

Subscribed and sworn to before me this 9th day of   June   , 1905

(Seal)   J.R. Armstrong
                                          Notary Public.

COPY   N. B. 263

Muskogee, Indian Territory, April 7, 1905.

David Hoparkentubbi,
  Bennington, Indian Territory.

Dear Sir:

There is inclosed you herewith for execution application for the enrollment of your infant child, Maggie Hoparkentubbi, born November 15, 1901.

The affidavits heretofore filed with the Commission show the child was living on January 6, 1903. It is necessary, for the child to be enrolled, that she was living on March 4, 1905. You will please insert the mother's age in the place left blank for that purpose.

In having these affidavits executed care should be exercised to see that all names are written in full, as they appear in the body of the affidavit, and in the event that either of the persons signing the affidavit are unable to write, signatures by mark must be attested by two witnesses. Each affidavit must be executed before a Notary Public and the notarial seal and signature of the officer must be attached to each separate affidavit.

                              Respectfully,
                              SIGNED
                              T. B. Needles.
SEV 12-7.   Commissioner in Charge.

Applications for Enrollment of Choctaw Newborn
Act of 1905   Volume V

Muskogee, Indian Territory, July 25, 1905.

Chief Clerk,
    Choctaw Land Office,
        Atoka, Indian Territory.

Dear Sir:

    Refer to duplicate Choctaw New Born Roll Card No. 263, in the possession of your office and change the name of mother of applicant thereon to read, "Isabelle Jones" instead of "Isabelle Hoparkentubbi", and note on said card the following notation:

        "Isabelle Jones, mother of No. 1, is identified as Isabelle Hoparkentubbi, number 2, on Choctaw roll card number 3752."

Respectfully,

Commissioner.

Ardmore, Indian Territory, December 9, 1905.

COPY

Commissioner to the Five Civilized Tribes.
    Muskogee, Indian Territory.

Dear Sir:-

    There is herewith transmitted the original and four carbon copies of the testimony of J. W. Hargrave and Fred V. Kinkade taken at this office on December 8, 1905, in the matter of the selection of an allotment for Maggie Hoparkentubbi, deceased, Choctaw new born Card No. 263, Choctaw new born final Roll No. 1284. It would appear from the testimony that a fraud has been attempted in the selection of the allotment in the name of said Maggie Hoparkentubbi, and the matter is referred to your office for such consideration as may be deemed necessary.

Respectfully,

Fred T. Marr,

Chief Clerk.

WRC.-3-

Applications for Enrollment of Choctaw Newborn
Act of 1905   Volume V

Muskogee, Indian Territory, December 18, 1905.

Chief Clerk,
    Choctaw Land Office,
        Atoka, Indian Territory.

Dear Sir:

    A question having arisen as to whether Maggie Hoparkentubbi, Choctaw New Born, Roll No. 1284, was living on March 3, 1905, you are directed to take no further action relative to an allotment to the said Maggie Hoparkentubbi until you are further advised by this office.

                      Respectfully,

                                Commissioner.

(The above letter given again.)

**DEPARTMENT OF THE INTERIOR,
COMMISSIONER TO THE FIVE CIVILIZED TRIBES.**

REFER IN REPLY TO THE FOLLOWING:

Muskogee, Indian Territory, December 18, 1905.

Chief Clerk,
    Choctaw Land Office,
        Atoka, Indian Territory.

Dear Sir:

    A question having arisen as to whether Maggie Hoparkentubbi, Choctaw New Born, Roll No. 1284, was living on March 3, 1905, you are directed to take no further action relative to an allotment to the said Maggie Hoparkentubbi until you are further advised by this office.

                      Respectfully,

                      Tams Bixby   Commissioner.

Applications for Enrollment of Choctaw Newborn
Act of 1905   Volume V

7-NB-263

Muskogee, Indian Territory, April 21, 1906.

Lacey P. Bobo,
    Valliant, Indian Territory.

Dear Sir[sic]:

    Receipt is hereby acknowledged of your letter of April 16, 1906, in the matter of the enrollment of Maggie Hoparkentubbi Choctaw new born roll No. 1284, with which you return copy of the affidavit of D. A. Homer which appears to have been executed by himself as Notary Public; you ask if this is in error that you be furnished a correct copy of the original; you also refer to the affidavit of Isabel[sic] Hoparkentubbi of November 27, 1905, which gives the date of the death of her daughter Maggie Hoparkentubbi as the _____ day of March 1905; you also ask to be advised if this is in error.

    There is inclosed you herewith correct affidavit of D. A. Homer to the birth of Maggie Hoparkentubbi which was executed before J. R. Armstrong, Notary Public. You are advised that the date of the death of Maggie Hoparkentubbi appears in the affidavit of Isabel Hoparkentubbi of November 27, 1905, as the "_____ day of March 1905" as indicated in your letter.

                                  Respectfully,

KB 2-20   Acting Commissioner.

7-NB-263

Muskogee, Indian Territory, April 30, 1906.

Napoleon B. McClure,
    Bennington, Indian Territory.

Dear Sir:

    Receipt is hereby acknowledged of your letter of April 26, 1906, in which you state that you find on investigation that Maggie Hoparkentubbi was born on or about July 10, 1902, an died on or about November 1, 1903, and you ask for blank for the purpose of furnishing proof of death.

    In compliance with your request there is inclosed herewith blank form for the proof of death. You are advised, however, that it appears from the records of this office that Maggie Hoparkentubbi was born November 15, 1902.

                                  Respectfully,

D. C.   Commissioner.

Applications for Enrollment of Choctaw Newborn
Act of 1905   Volume V

7-NB-263

Muskogee, Indian Territory, June 12, 1907.

Napoleon B. McClure,
    Bennington, Indian Territory.

Dear Sir:

    Receipt is hereby acknowledged of your letter of May 28, 1907, in which you ask what has been done with the case of Maggie Hopkentubby[sic] as you are anxious to file on land for her before all the valuable land is taken.

    In reply to your letter you are advised that on August 22, 1905, the Secretary of the Interior approved the enrollment of Maggie Hoparkentubbi as a new born citizen of the Choctaw Nation under the Act of Congress approved March 3, 1905, and selection of allotment May now be made in her behalf in accordance with the rules and regulations governing the selection of allotments and the designation of homesteads in the Choctaw and Chickasaw Nations.

                            Respectfully,

                                      Commissioner.

Muskogee, Oklahoma, April 18, 1908.

Subject:

Enrollment and allot-
ment of Maggie
Hoparkentubbi, deceased,
a new born Choctaw.
....

The Honorable,
    The Secretary of the Interior.

Sir:

    I have the honor to transmit herewith the record in the matter of the enrollment of Maggie Hoparkentubbi, whose name appears opposite No. 1234 upon a schedule constituting a part of the final roll of citizens by blood of the Choctaw Nation, enrolled under the Act of Congress approved March 3, 1905, as number provisions of the Act of Congress approved March 3, 1905 (33 Stats., 1048), approved by the Secretary of the Interior August 22, 1905, and the selection of an allotment in her name.

Applications for Enrollment of Choctaw Newborn
Act of 1905   Volume V

A copy of the decision of the Acting Commissioner to the Five Civilized Tribes of February 25, 1908, was, on February 26, 1908, furnished Napoleon B. McClure, Bennington, Oklahoma, the administrator of the estate of Maggie Hoparkentubbi, deceased, by registered mail, and he was notified that he would be allowed to show cause and introduce testimony before the Commissioner, at his office in Muskogee, Oklahoma, on Thursday, March 28, 1908, at two o'clock, P. M., why recommendation should not be made to the Secretary of the Interior for the cancellation of the allotment selected by him as administrator of the estate of the said Maggie Hoparkentubbi, deceased, at the Chickasaw Land Office on December 1, 1905, for the reason that the said Maggie Hoparkentubbi was not living on March 4, 1905, and not, therefore, entitled to an allotment under the provisions of the Act of Congress approved March 3, 1905 (33 Stats., 1048).

No appearance was made by said administrator, or his proper representative, before the Commissioner at the time stated in the above notice, and no action, whatever, appears to have been taken by him with reference to this case.

The records of this office show that Chickasaw Homestead Certificate No. 16634 was mailed to the administrator, Napoleon B. McClure, on June 29, 1906; that Chickasaw Allotment Certificates No's. 20663. 20664 and 20665 were mailed to him on June 30, 1906, and none of said certificates have been returned to this office.

As the result of the investigation had in this case I am of the opinion that the evidence clearly shows that Maggie Hoparkentubbi was not living on March 4, 1905, and not entitled, therefore, to an allotment under the provisions of the Act of Congress approved March 3, 1905 (33 Stats., 1048), and I have the honor ro recommend that there be placed upon the final roll of citizens enrolled under the Act of Congress approved March 3, 1905, as number above Act of Congress and the copy thereof in the possession of the Department and Indian Office opposite the name of the said Maggie Hoparkentubbi, appearing thereon at No. 1284, the following notation:

"Not living on March 4, 1905; not entitled to land or money".

I have the honor to further recommend that I be authorized to place a like notation upon the copies of said roll in the possession of this office, and to cancel and set aside the allotment selection made in the name of Maggie Hoparkentubbi, deceased, at the Chickasaw Land Office on December 1, 1905.

In view of the fact that the certificates of allotment for the land allotted to the said Maggie Hoparkentubbi, deceased, are outstanding, I have the honor to request that this office be specifically advised whether, upon the cancellation of this allotment upon the records of this office, the further allotment of any of said land shall be permitted prior to the cancellation of the certificates of allotment.

Applications for Enrollment of Choctaw Newborn
Act of 1905   Volume V

Respectfully,

WPC(VR 532)
Through the
    Commissioner of
        Indian Affairs.

Acting Commissioner.

Choc New Born 264
    Mitchell Hampton
    (Born Oct. 13, 1904)

BIRTH AFFIDAVIT.

DEPARTMENT OF THE INTERIOR.
COMMISSION TO THE FIVE CIVILIZED TRIBES.

IN RE APPLICATION FOR ENROLLMENT, as a citizen of the   Choctaw   Nation, of Mitchell Hampton   , born on the 13th day of   October   , 1904

Name of Father: Isaac Hampton   a citizen of the   Choctaw   Nation.
Name of Mother: Martha Hampton   a citizen of the   Choctaw   Nation.

Postoffice   Bennington I.T.

AFFIDAVIT OF MOTHER.

UNITED STATES OF AMERICA, Indian Territory,
   Central   DISTRICT.

    I,   Martha Hampton   , on oath state that I am   23   years of age and a citizen by Blood   , of the   Choctaw   Nation; that I am the lawful wife of   Isaac Hampton , who is a citizen, by   Blood   of the   Choctaw   Nation; that a   male   child was born to me on   13th   day of   October   , 1904, that said child has been named Mitchell Hampton   , and is now living.

                                            her
                                Martha x Hampton
Witnesses To Mark: mark
  { Robert J. Barnes
    Joshua Leflore

Applications for Enrollment of Choctaw Newborn
Act of 1905   Volume V

Subscribed and sworn to before me this 16th   day of   January   , 1905.

                                      C.C. McClard
                                             Notary Public.

AFFIDAVIT OF ATTENDING PHYSICIAN OR MID-WIFE.

UNITED STATES OF AMERICA, Indian Territory, }
    Central   DISTRICT. }

I,   Ellen Hampton   , a midwife   , on oath state that I attended on Mrs.   Martha Hampton   , wife of   Isaac Hampton   on the   13th   day of October , 1904; that there was born to her on said date a   male   child; that said child is now living and is said to have been named   Mitchell Hampton

                                      her
                            Ellen x Hampton
Witnesses To Mark: mark
  { Robert J Barnes
    Joshua Leflore

Subscribed and sworn to before me this 16th   day of   January   , 1905.

                                      C.C. McClard
                                             Notary Public.

BIRTH AFFIDAVIT.

DEPARTMENT OF THE INTERIOR.
COMMISSION TO THE FIVE CIVILIZED TRIBES.

IN RE APPLICATION FOR ENROLLMENT, as a citizen of the   Choctaw   Nation, of Mitchell Hampton   , born on the   13 day of Oct.   , 1904

Name of Father: Isaac Hampton   a citizen of the   Choctaw   Nation.
Name of Mother: Martha Hampton   a citizen of the   Choctaw   Nation.

                          Postoffice   Bennington I.T.

AFFIDAVIT OF MOTHER.

UNITED STATES OF AMERICA, Indian Territory, }
    Central   DISTRICT. }

I,   Martha Hampton   , on oath state that I am   23   years of age and a citizen by   blood   , of the   Choctaw   Nation; that I am the lawful wife of   Isaac

Applications for Enrollment of Choctaw Newborn
Act of 1905 Volume V

Hampton   , who is a citizen, by blood of the   Choctaw   Nation; that a male   child was born to me on 13" day of   October   , 1904; that said child has been named Mitchell Hampton   , and was living March 4, 1905.

                          her
                    Martha x Hampton
Witnesses To Mark: mark
{ *(Name Illegible)*
{ J.H. Baruthers

    Subscribed and sworn to before me this 26th   day of   April   , 1905

                      C.C. McClard
                      Notary Public.

AFFIDAVIT OF ATTENDING PHYSICIAN OR MID-WIFE.

UNITED STATES OF AMERICA, Indian Territory, }
   Central   DISTRICT. }

    I, Ellen Hampton   , a midwife   , on oath state that I attended on Mrs. Martha Hampton   , wife of Isaac Hampton   on the 13" day of October, 1904; that there was born to her on said date a   male   child; that said child was living March 4, 1905, and is said to have been named Mitchell Hampton

                        her
                    Ellen x Hampton
Witnesses To Mark: mark
{ J.H. Baruthers
{ Ross Frazier

    Subscribed and sworn to before me this 28th   day of   April   , 1905

                      C.C. McClard
                      Notary Public.

Applications for Enrollment of Choctaw Newborn
Act of 1905   Volume V

COPY   7-3754

Muskogee, Indian Territory, January 28, 1905.

Isaac Hampton,
    Bennington, Indian Territory.

Dear Sir:

    Receipt is hereby acknowledged of yur[sic] letter of January 23, 1905, stating that your wife Martha Hampton is the daughter of Joseph S. Durant of Bennington, Indian Territory, and was enrolled before your marriage to[sic] Martha Durant.

    In reply to your letter you are advised that the information contained therein has enabled the Commission to identify Martha Durant as having been enrolled as a citizen by blood of the Choctaw Nation, and her enrollment approved by the Secretary of the Interior.

    Referring to her affidavit and the affidavit of Ellen Hampton relative to the birth of Mitchell Hampton, infant son of Martha and Isaac Hampton, October 13, 1904, you are advised that under the provisions of the act of Congress approved July 1, 1902, no children born to citizens of the Choctaw and Chickasaw Nations subsequent to September 25, 1902, the date of the ratification of said act, are entitled to enrollment and allotment in the Choctaw and Chickasaw Nations.

                  Respectfully
                  SIGNED

                    Tams Bixby
                    Chairman.

COPY   N.B. 264

Muskogee, Indian Territory, April 7, 1905.

Isaac Hampton,
    Bennington, Indian Territory.

Dear Sir:

    There is inclosed you herewith for execution application for the enrollment of your infant child, Mitchell Hampton, born October 13, 1904.

    The affidavits heretofore filed with the Commission show the child was living on January 16, 1905. It is necessary, for the child to be enrolled, that he was living on March 4, 1905.

Applications for Enrollment of Choctaw Newborn
Act of 1905 Volume V

In having these affidavits executed care should be exercised to see that all names are written in full, as they appear in the body of the affidavit, and in the event that either of the persons signing the affidavit are unable to write, signatures by mark must be attested by two witnesses. Each affidavit must be executed before a Notary Public and the notarial seal and signature of the officer must be attached to each separate affidavit.

Respectfully,

SIGNED
T. B. Needles.
Commissioner in Charge.

SEV 11-7.

Choctaw N.B. 264

Muskogee, Indian Territory, May 2, 1905.

Isaac Hampton,
    Bennington, Indian Territory.

Dear Sir:

Receipt is hereby acknowledged of the affidavits of Martha Hampton and Ellen Hampton to the birth of Mitchell Hampton, son of Isaac and Martha Hampton, October 13, 1904, and the same have been filed with our records in the matter of the enrollment of the above named child.

Respectfully,

Chairman.

7-NB-264

Muskogee, Indian Territory, August 3, 1905.

Isaac Hampton,
    Bennington, Indian Territory.

Dear Sir:

Receipt is hereby acknowledged of your letter without date in which you ask when you can file for your child Mitchell Hampton.

In reply to your letter you are advised that on July 22, 1905, the Secretary of the Interior approved the enrollment of your child Mitchell Hampton as a citizen by blood of the Choctaw Nation, and selection of allotment may now be made in his behalf in

Applications for Enrollment of Choctaw Newborn
Act of 1905   Volume V

accordance with the rules and regulations governing the selection of allotments and the designation of homesteads in the Choctaw and Chickasaw Nations.

Respectfully,

Commissioner.

Choc New Born 265
   Robert O. Sumter, Jr.
   (Born Jan. 16, 1904)

NEW BORN AFFIDAVIT

No ....

CHOCTAW ENROLLING COMMISSION

IN THE MATTER OF THE APPLICATION FOR ENROLLMENT as a citizen of the Choctaw Nation, of   Robert Osborn Sumter Jr   born on the 16th day of   January   190 4

   Name of father   Robert O. Sumter Sr   a citizen of   Choctaw   Nation, final enrollment No.   391
   Name of mother   Lena Ramsey now Sumter   a citizen of   Choctaw   Nation, final enrollment No.   10678

Atoka, I.T.   Postoffice.

AFFIDAVIT OF MOTHER

UNITED STATES OF AMERICA }
   INDIAN TERRITORY
DISTRICT   Central

   I   Lena Ramsey now Sumter   , on oath state that I am   23   years of age and a citizen by   blood   of the   Choctaw   Nation, and as such have been placed upon the final roll of the   Choctaw   Nation, by the Honorable Secretary of the Interior my final enrollment number being   10678 ; that I am the lawful wife of   Robert O. Sumter   , who is a citizen of the   Choctaw   Nation,

83

Applications for Enrollment of Choctaw Newborn
Act of 1905   Volume V

and as such has been placed upon the final roll of said Nation by the Honorable Secretary of the Interior, his final enrollment number being   391   and that a   Male   child was born to me on the   16th   day of   January   190 4; that said child has been named   Robert Osborn Sumter, Jr   , and is now living.

Lena T Ramsey now Sumter

WITNESSETH:
Must be two witnesses who are citizens { Noah Perkins
John A Perkins

Subscribed and sworn to before me this, the   21st   day of   February   190 5

AE Folsom
Notary Public.

My Commission Expires:
Jan 9-1909

AFFIDAVIT OF ATTENDING PHYSICIAN OR MIDWIFE

UNITED STATES OF AMERICA
INDIAN TERRITORY
Central   DISTRICT

I,   Thomas Long   a   Practicing Physician on oath state that I attended on Mrs.   Lena Ramsey now Sumter   wife of   Robert O. Sumter on the   16"   day of   January , 190 4, that there was born to her on said date a   male   child, that said child is now living, and is said to have been named   Robert Osborn Sumter, Jr

T.J. Long   M.D.

WITNESSETH:
Must be two witnesses who are citizens and know the child. { Noah Perkins
John A Perkins

Subscribed and sworn to before me this, the   21"   day of   February   190 5

A E Folsom   Notary Public.

We hereby certify that we are well acquainted with   Thomas Long   a   Practicing Physician   and know   him   to be reputable and of good standing in the community.

{ Noah Perkins
John A Perkins

Applications for Enrollment of Choctaw Newborn
Act of 1905 Volume V

BIRTH AFFIDAVIT.

DEPARTMENT OF THE INTERIOR.
COMMISSION TO THE FIVE CIVILIZED TRIBES.

IN RE APPLICATION FOR ENROLLMENT, as a citizen of the Choctaw Nation, of Robert O. Sumter, Jr., born on the 16th day of Jany, 1904

Name of Father: Robert O Sumter   a citizen of the Choc Nation.
Name of Mother: Lena Sumter (nee Ramsey)   a citizen of the " Nation.

Postoffice   Atoka, I.T.

AFFIDAVIT OF MOTHER.

UNITED STATES OF AMERICA, Indian Territory,
Central DISTRICT.

I, Lena Sumter (nee Lena Ramsey), on oath state that I am 23 years of age and a citizen by blood, of the Choctaw Nation; that I am the lawful wife of Robert O. Sumter, who is a citizen, by Intermarriage of the Choctaw Nation; that a male child was born to me on 16th day of January, 1904; that said child has been named Robert O Sumter, Jr., and was living March 4, 1905.

                               Lena Sumter

Witnesses To Mark:

Subscribed and sworn to before me this 15" day of March, 1905

                               W.H. Angell
                                   Notary Public.

AFFIDAVIT OF ATTENDING PHYSICIAN OR MID-WIFE.

UNITED STATES OF AMERICA, Indian Territory,
Central DISTRICT.

I, T. J. Long, a Physician, on oath state that I attended on Mrs. Lena Sumter, wife of Robert O. Sumter on the 16th day of January, 1904; that there was born to her on said date a male child; that said child was living March 4, 1905, and is said to have been named Robert O Sumter, Jr.

                               T. J. Long M.D.

Witnesses To Mark:

Applications for Enrollment of Choctaw Newborn
Act of 1905 Volume V

Subscribed and sworn to before me this 15" day of   March   , 1905

        W.H. Angell
         Notary Public.

7-3782

Muskogee, Indian Territory, March 20, 1905.

Robert O. Sumter,
  Atoka, Indian Territory.

Dear Sir:

  Receipt is hereby acknowledged of the affidavits of Lena Sumter formerly Ramsey and T. J. Long, M. D., to the birth of Robert O. Sumter Jr., son of Robert O. and Lena Sumter, January 16, 1904, and the same have been filed with our records as an application for the enrollment of said child.

        Respectfully,

           Chairman.

Substitution

7-NB-265.

Muskogee, Indian Territory, May 17, 1905.

W. H. Angell,
  Choctaw Land Office,
    Atoka, Indian Territory.

Dear Sir:

  There is enclosed herewith affidavit of Lena Sumter, mother, and T. J. Long, attending physician to the birth of Robert O. Sumter, Jr., an applicant for enrollment as a citizen by blood of the Choctaw Nation, from which you omitted your seal.

  Please affix your seal to these affidavits and return them to this office.

        Respectfully,

V. 16-7.   Chairman.

Applications for Enrollment of Choctaw Newborn
Act of 1905 Volume V

Choc New Born 266
    Anus Earl Folsom
    (Born Sep. 7, 1903)

BIRTH AFFIDAVIT.

DEPARTMENT OF THE INTERIOR,
COMMISSION TO THE FIVE CIVILIZED TRIBES.

In Re Application for Enrollment, as a citizen of the Choctaw Nation, of Anus Earl Folsom, born on the 7 day of September, 1903

Name of Father: Jacb[sic] Folsom   a citizen of the Choctaw Nation.

Name of Mother: Mary Folsom   a citizen of the Intermarried Choctaw Nation.

Post-office   Caney, Ind Ter.

AFFIDAVIT OF MOTHER.

UNITED STATES OF AMERICA,
   INDIAN TERRITORY,
   Central District.

I, Mary Folsom, on oath state that I am 44 years of age and a citizen by Intermarriage, of the Choctaw Nation; that I am the lawful wife of Jacob Folsom, who is a citizen, by blood of the Choctaw Nation; that a male child was born to me on 7 day of September, 1903, that said child has been named Anus Earl Folsom, and is now living.

                         Mary Fulsom[sic]

WITNESSES TO MARK:
   J.N . Banister
   A Denton Phillips

Subscribed and sworn to before me this 24 day of June 1904, 190....

                         A Denton Phillips
                              NOTARY PUBLIC.

Applications for Enrollment of Choctaw Newborn
Act of 1905   Volume V

AFFIDAVIT OF ATTENDING PHYSICIAN OR MID-WIFE.

UNITED STATES OF AMERICA,
INDIAN TERRITORY,
Central   District.

I, J. H. Armstrong, a M. D., on oath state that I attended on Mrs. Mary Folsom, wife of Jacob Folsom on the 7 day of September 1903, 1......; that there was born to her on said date a Male child; that said child is now living and is said to have been named Anus Earl Folsom

J.H. Armstrong M.D.

WITNESSES TO MARK:

Subscribed and sworn to before me this 24 day of June 1904 , 190...

A Denton Phillips
NOTARY PUBLIC.

NEW BORN AFFIDAVIT

No ....

CHOCTAW ENROLLING COMMISSION

IN THE MATTER OF THE APPLICATION FOR ENROLLMENT as a citizen of the Choctaw Nation, of   Amos[sic] Earl Folsom   born on the 7th day of September   190 4

Name of father Jacob Folsom   a citizen of   Choctaw   Nation, final enrollment No. 10737
Name of mother Mary Folsom   a citizen of   Choctaw   Nation, final enrollment No. 158

Caney I.T.   Postoffice.

Applications for Enrollment of Choctaw Newborn
Act of 1905 Volume V

AFFIDAVIT OF MOTHER

UNITED STATES OF AMERICA
    INDIAN TERRITORY
DISTRICT   Central

I   Mary Folsom   , on oath state that I am   45   years of age and a citizen by   Marriage   of the   Choctaw   Nation, and as such have been placed upon the final roll of the   Choctaw   Nation, by the Honorable Secretary of the Interior my final enrollment number being   158 ; that I am the lawful wife of   Jacob Folsom   , who is a citizen of the   Choctaw   Nation, and as such has been placed upon the final roll of said Nation by the Honorable Secretary of the Interior, his final enrollment number being   10737   and that a   Male   child was born to me on the 7th day of   September   190 4; that said child has been named   Amos Earl Folsom   , and is now living.

WITNESSETH: Mary Fulsom[sic]

Must be two witnesses who are citizens { Edward E. Pitchlynn
    W. T. Smith

Subscribed and sworn to before me this, the 10th day of   Mch   190 5

A E Folsom
Notary Public.

My Commission Expires:
Jan 9 - 1909

AFFIDAVIT OF ATTENDING PHYSICIAN OR MIDWIFE

UNITED STATES OF AMERICA
INDIAN TERRITORY
Central   DISTRICT

I,   Armstrong   a   Practicing Physician on oath state that I attended on Mrs.   Mary Folsom   wife of   Jacob Folsom on the 7th day of   September   , 190 4, that there was born to her on said date a   male child, that said child is now living, and is said to have been named   Amos[sic] Earl Folsom

                  J.H. Armstrong   M.D.

WITNESSETH:
Must be two witnesses who are citizens and know the child. { Edward E. Pitchlynn
    W T Smith

Subscribed and sworn to before me this, the 10th day of   March   190 5

                  A E Folsom   Notary Public.

Applications for Enrollment of Choctaw Newborn
Act of 1905 Volume V

We hereby certify that we are well acquainted with Dr Armstrong a Practicing Physician and know him to be reputable and of good standing in the community.

{ Edward E Pitchlynn
  W T Smith

Ex
Jan 9 - 1909

BIRTH AFFIDAVIT.

DEPARTMENT OF THE INTERIOR,
COMMISSION TO THE FIVE CIVILIZED TRIBES.

In Re Application for Enrollment, as a citizen of the Choctaw Nation, of Amos[sic] Earl Folsom , born on the 7 day of September , 1903

Name of Father: Jacob Folsom   a citizen of the Choctaw Nation.
Name of Mother: Mary Folsom   a citizen of the Choctaw Nation.

Post-office Caney, Ind Ter.

AFFIDAVIT OF MOTHER.

UNITED STATES OF AMERICA,
   INDIAN TERRITORY,
  Central District.

I, Mary Folsom , on oath state that I am 45 years of age and a citizen by Intermarriage , of the Choctaw Nation; that I am the lawful wife of Jacob Folsom , who is a citizen, by blood of the Choctaw Nation; that a male child was born to me on 7 day of September , 1903 , that said child has been named Amos Earl Folsom , and is now living.

Mary Fulsom[sic]

WITNESSES TO MARK:
{ John Luvig
  Isreal Jones

Subscribed and sworn to before me this 16 day of March , 190 5

A Denton Phillips
NOTARY PUBLIC.

Applications for Enrollment of Choctaw Newborn
Act of 1905 Volume V

AFFIDAVIT OF ATTENDING PHYSICIAN OR MID-WIFE.

UNITED STATES OF AMERICA,
   INDIAN TERRITORY,
  Central   District.

I, J. H. Armstrong, a Physician, on oath state that I attended on Mrs. Mary Folsom, wife of Jacob Folsom on the 7 day of September, 1903; that there was born to her on said date a Male child; that said child is now living and is said to have been named Amos Earl Folsom

                             J.H. Armstrong M.D.

WITNESSES TO MARK:

Subscribed and sworn to before me this 16 day of March, 190 5

                             A Denton Phillips
                                NOTARY PUBLIC.

BIRTH AFFIDAVIT.   7-NB 266

DEPARTMENT OF THE INTERIOR.
COMMISSION TO THE FIVE CIVILIZED TRIBES.

IN RE APPLICATION FOR ENROLLMENT, as a citizen of the Choctaw Nation, of Anus Earl Fulsom[sic], born on the 7th day of Sep., 1903

Name of Father: Jacob Folsom   a citizen of the Choctaw Nation.
Name of Mother: Mary Folsom   a citizen of the Choctaw Nation.

                     Postoffice   Caney I.T.

AFFIDAVIT OF MOTHER.

UNITED STATES OF AMERICA, Indian Territory,
  Central   **DISTRICT.**

I, Mary Folsom, on oath state that I am 45 years of age and a citizen by Marriage, of the Choctaw Nation; that I am the lawful wife of Jacob Folsom, who is a citizen, by blood of the Choctaw Nation; that a male child was born to me on 7th day of Sep, 1903; that said child has been named Anus Earl Folsom, and was living March 4, 1905.

                              Mary Folsom

Applications for Enrollment of Choctaw Newborn
Act of 1905 Volume V

Witnesses To Mark:

{

Subscribed and sworn to before me this 7th day of August , 1905

C. J. Ralston
Notary Public.

My Commission expires Oct. 14 1907

AFFIDAVIT OF ATTENDING PHYSICIAN OR MID-WIFE.

UNITED STATES OF AMERICA, Indian Territory, }
Central   DISTRICT.

I, J H Armstrong , a Physician , on oath state that I attended on Mrs. Mary Folsom , wife of Jacob Folsom on the 7th day of Sep. , 1903; that there was born to her on said date a male child; that said child was living March 4, 1905, and is said to have been named Anus Earl Folsom

J H Armstrong

Witnesses To Mark:

{

Subscribed and sworn to before me this 7th day of August , 1905

C J Ralston
Notary Public.

My Commission expires Oct. 14 1907

7-3805

Muskogee, Indian Territory, March 21, 1905.

Jacob Fulsom[sic],
    Caney, Indian Territory.

Dear Sir:

Receipt is hereby acknowledged of the affidavits of Mary Fulsom and J. H. Armstrong to the birth of Amos Earl Fulsom son of Jacob and Mary Fulsom, September 7, 1903, and the same have been filed with our records as an application for the enrollment of said child.

Respectfully,

Chairman.

Applications for Enrollment of Choctaw Newborn
Act of 1905   Volume V

7-NB-266

Muskogee, Indian Territory, July 29, 1905.

Jacob Folsom,
    Caney, Indian Territory.

Dear Sir:

    There is inclosed you herewith for execution application for the enrollment of your infant child.

    In the affidavit of June 24, 1904, the name of the child is given as Anus Earl Folsom, the date of his birth September 7, 1903; in the affidavit of March 10, 1905, the name is given as Amos Earl Folsom, and the date of birth, September 7, 1904, and in the affidavits of March 16, 1905, the name of child is given as Amos Earl Folsom and the date of birth, September 7, 1903.

    In the inclosed affidavits the name of child and date of birth is left blank. Please insert the correct name and date and when the affidavits are properly executed return to this office immediately, as no further action can be taken relative to the enrollment of your said child until the evidence requested is supplied.

        Respectfully,

                  Commissioner

LM 6/29

7-NB-266

Muskogee, Indian Territory, August 10, 1905.

Jacob Folsom,
    Caney, Indian Territory.

Dear Sir:

    Receipt is hereby acknowledged of the affidavits of Mary Folsom and J. H. Armstrong to the birth of Anus Earl Folsom son of Jacob and Mary Folsom, September 7, 1903, and the same have been filed with the records of this office in the matter of the enrollment of said child.

        Respectfully,

                  Acting Commissioner.

Applications for Enrollment of Choctaw Newborn
Act of 1905 Volume V

Choc New Born 267
      Henry Clay Cochnauer
      (Born Feb. 16, 1903)
      Nicholas Alexander Cochnauer
      (Born Dec. 10, 1904)

BIRTH AFFIDAVIT.

DEPARTMENT OF THE INTERIOR,
COMMISSION TO THE FIVE CIVILIZED TRIBES.

In Re Application for Enrollment, as a citizen of the Choctaw Nation, of Henry Clay Cochnaeur[sic] , born on the 16th day of February , 1903

Name of Father: N. H. Cochnaeur   a citizen of the Choctaw Nation.
Name of Mother: Bettie Cochnaeur   a citizen of the Choctaw Nation.

          Post-office   Boswell Ind. Ter.

AFFIDAVIT OF MOTHER.

UNITED STATES OF AMERICA,
   INDIAN TERRITORY,
   Central   District.

    I, Bettie Cochnaeur , on oath state that I am 27 years of age and a citizen by blood , of the Choctaw Nation; that I am the lawful wife of N. H. Cochnaeur , who is a citizen, by blood of the Choctaw Nation; that a male child was born to me on 16th day of Feb. , 1903 , that said child has been named Henry Clay Cochnaeur , and is now living.

                            her
                       Bettie x Cochnaeur
WITNESSES TO MARK: mark
   John Frazier
   E.T. Dwight

    Subscribed and sworn to before me this 12th day of September , 1903

                    J.R. Armstrong
                         NOTARY PUBLIC.
          Commission Ex 3/11/1908

Applications for Enrollment of Choctaw Newborn
Act of 1905 Volume V

AFFIDAVIT OF ATTENDING PHYSICIAN OR MID-WIFE.

UNITED STATES OF AMERICA,
INDIAN TERRITORY,
Central   District.

I, Martha A. Morress[sic], a Midwife, on oath state that I attended on Mrs. Bettie Cochnaeur, wife of N. H. Cochnaeur on the 16th day of February, 1903 ; that there was born to her on said date a male child; that said child is now living and is said to have been named Henry Clay Cochnauer

Martha A Morress

WITNESSES TO MARK:

Subscribed and sworn to before me this 12th day of September , 1903

J.R. Armstrong
NOTARY PUBLIC.
Commission Ex 3/11/1908

BIRTH AFFIDAVIT.

DEPARTMENT OF THE INTERIOR.
COMMISSION TO THE FIVE CIVILIZED TRIBES.

IN RE APPLICATION FOR ENROLLMENT, as a citizen of the Choctaw Nation, of Henry Clay Cochnauer, born on the 16 day of February , 1903

Name of Father: Nicholas Cochnauer   a citizen of the Choctaw Nation.
Name of Mother: Bettie Cochnauer   a citizen of the Choctaw Nation.

Postoffice   Boswell, Ind. Ter.

AFFIDAVIT OF MOTHER.

UNITED STATES OF AMERICA, Indian Territory,
Central   DISTRICT.

I, Bettie Cochnauer, on oath state that I am 32 years of age and a citizen by Blood, of the Choctaw Nation; that I am the lawful wife of Nicholas Cochnauer, who is a citizen, by Blood of the Choctaw Nation; that a Male child was born to me on 16" day of February , 1903; that said child has been named Henry Clay Cochnauer, and was living March 4, 1905.

Applications for Enrollment of Choctaw Newborn
Act of 1905   Volume V

                              her
                          Bettie x Cochnauer

Witnesses To Mark: mark
{ Sophie Leflore
{ J.L. Trout

Subscribed and sworn to before me this 22nd day of April, 1905.

                        S.H. Downing
                          Notary Public.

AFFIDAVIT OF ATTENDING PHYSICIAN OR MID-WIFE.

UNITED STATES OF AMERICA, Indian Territory, }
   Central   DISTRICT. }

   I, Martha Manus, a Midwife, on oath state that I attended on Mrs. Bettie Cochnauer, wife of Nicholas Cochnauer on the 16" day of February, 1903; that there was born to her on said date a Male child; that said child was living March 4, 1905, and is said to have been named Henry Clay Cochnauer

                            her
                        Martha x Manus

Witnesses To Mark: mark
{ D.A. Bridges
{ J. C. Parker

Subscribed and sworn to before me this 17" day of April, 1905.

                        S. H. Downing
                          Notary Public.

BIRTH AFFIDAVIT.

DEPARTMENT OF THE INTERIOR.
COMMISSION TO THE FIVE CIVILIZED TRIBES.

IN RE APPLICATION FOR ENROLLMENT, as a citizen of the Choctaw Nation, of Henry Clay Cochnauer, born on the 16 day of February, 1903

Name of Father: Nicholas Cochnauer   a citizen of the Choctaw Nation.
Name of Mother: Betty Cochnauer   a citizen of the Choctaw Nation.

                        Postoffice   Boswell I.T.

Applications for Enrollment of Choctaw Newborn
Act of 1905   Volume V

AFFIDAVIT OF MOTHER.

UNITED STATES OF AMERICA, Indian Territory, }
Central   DISTRICT.

I, Betty Cochnauer, on oath state that I am 32 years of age and a citizen by blood, of the Choctaw Nation; that I am the lawful wife of Nicholas Cochnauer, who is a citizen, by blood of the Choctaw Nation; that a Male child was born to me on 16" day of February, 1903; that said child has been named Henry Clay Cochnauer, and was living March 4, 1905.

        her
      Betty x Cochnauer
Witnesses To Mark: mark
 { S.C. Boswell
  J. J. Nale

Subscribed and sworn to before me this 5" day of April, 1905

      S.H. Downing
        Notary Public.

AFFIDAVIT OF ATTENDING PHYSICIAN OR MID-WIFE.

UNITED STATES OF AMERICA, Indian Territory, }
Central   DISTRICT.

I, Martha Manus, a Midwife, on oath state that I attended on Mrs. Betty Cochnauer, wife of Nicholas Cochnauer on the 16" day of February, 1903; that there was born to her on said date a Male child; that said child was living March 4, 1905, and is said to have been named Henry Clay Cochnauer

        her
      Martha x Manus
Witnesses To Mark: mark
 { S.C. Boswell
  J. J. Nale

Subscribed and sworn to before me this 5" day of April, 1905

      S.H. Downing
        Notary Public.

Applications for Enrollment of Choctaw Newborn
Act of 1905 Volume V

BIRTH AFFIDAVIT.

DEPARTMENT OF THE INTERIOR.
COMMISSION TO THE FIVE CIVILIZED TRIBES.

IN RE APPLICATION FOR ENROLLMENT, as a citizen of the Choctaw Nation, of Nicholas Alexander Cochnauer, born on the 10 day of December, 1904

Name of Father: Nicholas Cochnauer   a citizen of the Choctaw Nation.
Name of Mother: Betty Cochnauer   a citizen of the Choctaw Nation.

Postoffice Boswell I.T.

AFFIDAVIT OF MOTHER.

UNITED STATES OF AMERICA, Indian Territory, } Central DISTRICT.

I, Betty Cochnauer, on oath state that I am 32 years of age and a citizen by blood, of the Choctaw Nation; that I am the lawful wife of Nicholas Cochnauer, who is a citizen, by blood of the Choctaw Nation; that a Male child was born to me on 10" day of December, 1904; that said child has been named Nicholas Alexander Cochnauer, and was living March 4, 1905.

                 her
         Betty x Cochnauer
Witnesses To Mark: mark
{ S.C. Boswell
  J. J. Nale

Subscribed and sworn to before me this 5" day of April, 1905

         S.H. Downing
            Notary Public.

AFFIDAVIT OF ATTENDING PHYSICIAN OR MID-WIFE.

UNITED STATES OF AMERICA, Indian Territory, } Central DISTRICT.

I, Martha Manus, a Midwife, on oath state that I attended on Mrs. Betty Cochnauer, wife of Nicholas Cochnauer on the 10" day of December, 1904; that there was born to her on said date a Male child; that said child was living March 4, 1905, and is said to have been named Nicholas Alexander Cochnauer

Applications for Enrollment of Choctaw Newborn
Act of 1905   Volume V

                                              her
                                  Martha x Manus

Witnesses To Mark: mark
  { S.C. Boswell
    J. J. Nale

        Subscribed and sworn to before me this 5" day of   April   , 1905

                                      S.H. Downing
                                               Notary Public.

                                                        7-3840

                        Muskogee, Indian Territory, September 18, 1903.

N. H. Cochnauer,
       Boswell, Indian Territory.

Dear Sir:

       Receipt is hereby acknowledged of the affidavits of Bettie Cochnauer and Martha A. Morris relative to the birth of Henry Clay Cochnauer, infant son of N. H. and Bettie Cochnauer, born February 16, 1903, which it is presumed have been forwarded to this office as an application for enrollment as a citizen by blood of the Choctaw Nation of the above named child.

        You are informed that under the provisions of the Act of Congress, approved July 1, 1902 (32 Stats., 641), which was ratified by the citizens of the Choctaw and Chickasaw Nations September 25, 1902, this Commission is now without authority to receive or consider the original application of any person whomsoever for enrollment as a citizen of the Choctaw or Chickasaw Nation.

                              Respectfully,

                                                    Chairman.

Applications for Enrollment of Choctaw Newborn
Act of 1905 Volume V

N. B. 267

COPY

Muskogee, Indian Territory, April 7, 1905.

Nicholas Cochnauer,
    Boswell, Indian Territory.

Dear Sir:

    There is inclosed you herewith for execution application for the enrollment of your infant child, Henry Clay Cochnauer, born February 16, 1903.

    The affidavits heretofore filed with the Commission show the child was living on September 12, 1903. It is necessary, for the child to be enrolled, that he was living on March 4, 1905. You will please insert the age of the mother in space left blank for that purpose.

    In having these affidavits executed care should be exercised to see that all names are written in full, as they appear in the body of the affidavit, and in the event that either of the persons signing the affidavit are unable to write, signatures by mark must be attested by two witnesses. Each affidavit must be executed before a Notary Public and the notarial seal and signature of the officer must be attached to each separate affidavit.

                                Respectfully,
                                SIGNED
                                T. B. Needles.
LM 7-19.   Commissioner in Charge.

7-3840

Muskogee, Indian Territory, April 10, 1905.

Nicholas Cochnauer,
    Boswell, Indian Territory..

Dear Sir:

    Receipt is hereby acknowledged of the affidavits of Betty Cochnauer and Martha Manus to the birth of Henry Clay Cochnauer and Nicholas Alexander Cochnauer, children of Nicholas and Betty Cochnauer, February 16, 1903, and December 10, 1904, and the same have been filed with our records as application for the enrollment of said children.

                                Respectfully,

                                Commissioner in Charge.

Applications for Enrollment of Choctaw Newborn
Act of 1905   Volume V

7 NB 267

Muskogee, Indian Territory, April 26, 1905.

Nicholas Cochnauer,
    Boswell, Indian Territory.

Dear Sir:

    Receipt is hereby acknowledged of the affidavits of Bettie Cochnauer and Martha Manus to the birth of Henry Clay Cochnauer, son of Nicholas and Bettie Cochnauer, February 16, 1903, and the same have been filed with our records in the matter of the enrollment of the above named child.

                Respectfully,

                            Chairman.

Choc New Born 268
    Cleo Zion
    (Born Aug. 15, 1903)

BIRTH AFFIDAVIT.

DEPARTMENT OF THE INTERIOR,
COMMISSION TO THE FIVE CIVILIZED TRIBES.

    In Re Application for Enrollment, as a citizen of the Choctaw Nation, of Cleo Zion , born on the 15 day of August , 1903

Name of Father: Henry W. Zion   a citizen of the White Nation.
Name of Mother: Ora Zion   a citizen of the Choctaw Nation.

                Post-office   Caney Ind Ter

Applications for Enrollment of Choctaw Newborn
Act of 1905 Volume V

AFFIDAVIT OF MOTHER.

UNITED STATES OF AMERICA, }
   INDIAN TERRITORY,
   Central   District.

    I, Ora Zion, on oath state that I am 19 years of age and a citizen by blood, of the Choctaw Nation; that I am the lawful wife of Henry W. Zion, who is a citizen, by White man of the ~~United~~ Nation; that a Female child was born to me on 15 day of August, 1903, that said child has been named Cleo Zion, and is now living.

                                Ora Zion

WITNESSES TO MARK:
   { AD Phillips
   { *(Name Illegible)*

    Subscribed and sworn to before me this 7 day of April, 1904

                              A Denton Phillips
                                  NOTARY PUBLIC.

AFFIDAVIT OF ATTENDING PHYSICIAN OR MID-WIFE.

UNITED STATES OF AMERICA, }
   INDIAN TERRITORY,
   .... District.

    I, J H Armstrong, a Physician, on oath state that I attended on Mrs. Ora Zion, wife of Henry W Zion on the 15 day of Aug, 1903; that there was born to her on said date a Female child; that said child is now living and is said to have been named Cleo Zion

                                J H Armstrong

WITNESSES TO MARK:
   {

    Subscribed and sworn to before me this 7 day of April, 1904

                              A Denton Phillips
                                 NOTARY PUBLIC.

Applications for Enrollment of Choctaw Newborn
Act of 1905   Volume V

NEW-BORN AFFIDAVIT.

Number...............

...Choctaw Enrolling Commission...

IN THE MATTER OF THE APPLICATION FOR ENROLLMENT, as a citizen of the Choctaw Nation, of Cleo Zion born on the 15th day of August 1903

Name of father   H.W. Zion   a citizen of   ———
Nation final enrollment No. ——
Name of mother   Ora Matoy, now Zion   a citizen of   Choctaw
Nation final enrollment No. 10886

Postoffice   Caney I.T.

AFFIDAVIT OF MOTHER.

UNITED STATES OF AMERICA
INDIAN TERRITORY
   Central   DISTRICT

I   Ora Matoy, now Zion   , on oath state that I am 20 years of age and a citizen by blood of the Choctaw Nation, and as such have been placed upon the final roll of the Choctaw Nation, by the Honorable Secretary of the Interior my final enrollment number being 10886; that I am the lawful wife of H.W. Zion , who is a citizen of the Choctaw Nation, and as such has been placed upon the final roll of said Nation by the Honorable Secretary of the Interior, his final enrollment number being ——— and that a Female child was born to me on the 15th day of August 1903; that said child has been named Cleo Zion , and is now living.

Witnesseth.   Ora Matoy now Zion

Must be two ⎫ John N Folsom
Witnesses who ⎬
are Citizens. ⎭ N J Talbert

Subscribed and sworn to before me this 15 day of February 1905

A.E. Folsom
Notary Public.

My commission expires:

Applications for Enrollment of Choctaw Newborn
Act of 1905   Volume V

Affidavit of Attending Physician or Midwife

UNITED STATES OF AMERICA,
    INDIAN TERRITORY,
Central   DISTRICT

I, J.H. Armstrong a Practicing Physician on oath state that I attended on Mrs. Ora Matoy now Zion wife of A[sic].W. Zion on the 15th day of August, 190 3, that there was born to her on said date a Female child, that said child is now living, and is said to have been named Cleo Zion

J H Armstrong   M. D.

Subscribed and sworn to before me this the 15th day of February 1905

A.E. Folsom
Notary Public.

WITNESSETH:
Must be two witnesses who are citizens and know the child.
    John N Folsom
    N J Talbert

We hereby certify that we are well acquainted with Dr Armstrong a Practicing Physician and know him to be reputable and of good standing in the community.

Jan 9-1909

Must be two citizen witnesses.
    John N. Folsom
    N.J. Talbert

BIRTH AFFIDAVIT.

DEPARTMENT OF THE INTERIOR.
COMMISSION TO THE FIVE CIVILIZED TRIBES.

IN RE APPLICATION FOR ENROLLMENT, as a citizen of the Choctaw Nation, of Cleo Zion, born on the 15" day of August, 1903

Name of Father: Henry W. Zion   a citizen of the U. S. Nation.
Name of Mother: Ora Zion (Matoy)   a citizen of the Choctaw Nation.

Postoffice   Caney, Ind. Ter.

Applications for Enrollment of Choctaw Newborn
Act of 1905   Volume V

AFFIDAVIT OF MOTHER.

UNITED STATES OF AMERICA, Indian Territory,
Central   DISTRICT.

I, Ora Zion (Matoy), on oath state that I am 20 years of age and a citizen by Blood, of the Choctaw Nation; that I am the lawful wife of Henry W. Zion, who is a citizen, by ——— of the United States Nation; that a Female child was born to me on 15" day of August, 1903; that said child has been named Cleo Zion, and was living March 4, 1905.

Ora Zion (Matoy)

Witnesses To Mark:
{ H. A. Moody

Subscribed and sworn to before me this 19 day of April, 1905

A Denton Phillips
Notary Public.

AFFIDAVIT OF ATTENDING PHYSICIAN OR MID-WIFE.

UNITED STATES OF AMERICA, Indian Territory,
Central   DISTRICT.

I, J H Armstrong, a M. D., on oath state that I attended on Mrs. Ora Zion (Matoy), wife of Henry W. Zion on the 15" day of August, 1903; that there was born to her on said date a Female child; that said child was living March 4, 1905, and is said to have been named Cleo Zion

J H Armstrong M.D.

Witnesses To Mark:
{

Subscribed and sworn to before me this 19 day of April, 1905

A Denton Phillips
Notary Public.

Applications for Enrollment of Choctaw Newborn
Act of 1905 Volume V

N. B. 268

COPY

Muskogee, Indian Territory, April 7, 1905.

Henry W. Zion,
    Caney, Indian Territory.

Dear Sir:

There is inclosed you herewith for execution application for the enrollment of your infant child, Cleo Zion, born August 15, 1903.

The affidavits heretofore filed with the Commission show the child was living on April 27, 1904. It is necessary, for the child to be enrolled, that she was living on March 4, 1905. You will please insert the age of the mother in space left blank for that purpose.

In having these affidavits executed care should be exercised to see that all names are written in full, as they appear in the body of the affidavit, and in the event that either of the persons signing the affidavit are unable to write, signatures by mark must be attested by two witnesses. Each affidavit must be executed before a Notary Public and the notarial seal and signature of the officer must be attached to each separate affidavit.

Respectfully,
SIGNED
T. B. Needles.
Commissioner in Charge.

LM 7-17.

Choctaw N.B. 268

Muskogee, Indian Territory, April 22, 1905.

Henry W. Zion,
    Caney, Indian Territory.

Dear Sir:

Receipt is hereby acknowledged of the affidavits of Ora Zion (Matoy) and J. H. Armstrong to the birth of Cleo Zion, daughter of Henry W. and Ora Zion, Agust 15, 1903, and the same have been filed with our records in the matter of the enrollment of said child.

Respectfully,

Chairman.

Applications for Enrollment of Choctaw Newborn
Act of 1905   Volume V

(The letter below does not belong with the current applicant.)

7--3860.

COPY

Muskogee, Indian Territory, May 9, 1905.

W. E. Zion,
    Matoy, Indian Territory.

Dear Sir:

    Receipt is hereby acknowledged of the affidavits of Susan Zion and Dr. W. T. Lindsey to the birth of Floyd Zion and Ray Zion, children of W. E. and Susan Zion, May 31, 1903 and January 15, 1905, respectively, and the same have been filed with our records as an application for the enrollment of said children.

                  Respectfully,

                                    Commissioner in Charge.

Choc New Born 269
    Clorie Smith
    (Born Nov. 9, 1904)

NEW-BORN AFFIDAVIT.

            Number..............

...Choctaw Enrolling Commission...

    IN THE MATTER OF THE APPLICATION FOR ENROLLMENT, as a citizen of the Choctaw Nation, of Clora Smith

born on the 9 day of November 190 4

Name of father   Rice Smith   a citizen of   Choctaw
Nation final enrollment No. ──
Name of mother   Sarah E Smith (nee Mathews)   a citizen of   Choctaw
Nation final enrollment No. 10719

                                Postoffice   Midway I.T.

Applications for Enrollment of Choctaw Newborn
Act of 1905 Volume V

AFFIDAVIT OF MOTHER.

UNITED STATES OF AMERICA
INDIAN TERRITORY
Central   DISTRICT

I   Sarah E Smith   , on oath state that I am   16   years of age and a citizen by   blood   of the   Choctaw Nation, and as such have been placed upon the final roll of the Choctaw Nation, by the Honorable Secretary of the Interior my final enrollment number being   10919; that I am the lawful wife of   Rice Smith   , who is a citizen of the   Choctaw Nation, and as such has been placed upon the final roll of said Nation by the Honorable Secretary of the Interior, his final enrollment number being   white   and that a   female   child was born to me on the   9   day of   November   190 4; that said child has been named   Clora Smith   , and is now living.

Witnesseth.   Mrs Sarah Smith

Must be two Witnesses who are Citizens.
 Wallace G Plummer
 Henrietta Brown

Subscribed and sworn to before me this   18   day of   Jan   190 5

                                   J W Jones
                                          Notary Public.

My commission expires: Oct. 18th 1907

AFFIDAVIT OF ATTENDING PHYSICIAN OR MIDWIFE

UNITED STATES OF AMERICA
INDIAN TERRITORY
Central   DISTRICT

I,   R D Cody   a   Practicing Physician   on oath state that I attended on Mrs.   Sarah E Smith   wife of   Rice Smith   on the   9   day of   November   , 190 4, that there was born to her on said date a   Female   child, that said child is now living, and is said to have been named   Clora Smith

                       RD Cody   M.D.

Subscribed and sworn to before me this, the   25   day of   Jan   190 5

                            John H Cross
                                  Notary Public.

WITNESSETH:
Must be two witnesses who are citizens and know the child.
 T.W. Jones
 Ben Wolf

Applications for Enrollment of Choctaw Newborn
Act of 1905   Volume V

We hereby certify that we are well acquainted with R.D. Cody a Physician and know him to be reputable and of good standing in the community.

> T.W. Jones
>
> Ben Wolf

BIRTH AFFIDAVIT.

DEPARTMENT OF THE INTERIOR.
COMMISSION TO THE FIVE CIVILIZED TRIBES.

IN RE APPLICATION FOR ENROLLMENT, as a citizen of the Choctaw Nation, of Clorie Smith, born on the 9th day of November, 1904

Name of Father: R. C. Smith   a citizen of the United States ~~Nation~~.
(nee Sarah E Mathews)
Name of Mother: Sarah E Smith   a citizen of the Choctaw Nation.

Postoffice   Wesley India Territory

AFFIDAVIT OF MOTHER.

UNITED STATES OF AMERICA, Indian Territory,
Central   DISTRICT.

I, Sarah E Smith (nee Sarah E Mathews), on oath state that I am 17 years of age and a citizen by blood, of the Choctaw Nation; that I am the lawful wife of R. C. Smith, who is a citizen, ~~by~~ .... of the Choctaw Nation; that a female child was born to me on 9th day of November, 1904; that said child has been named Clorie Smith, and was living March 4, 1905.

Mrs Sarah E Smith

Witnesses To Mark:

Subscribed and sworn to before me this 21st day of March, 1905

D.H. Linebaugh
Notary Public.

Applications for Enrollment of Choctaw Newborn
Act of 1905 Volume V

AFFIDAVIT OF ATTENDING PHYSICIAN OR MID-WIFE.

UNITED STATES OF AMERICA, Indian Territory,
Central   DISTRICT.

I, R. D. Cody, a Physician, on oath state that I attended on Mrs. Sarah E Smith, wife of R. C. Smith on the 9th day of November, 1904; that there was born to her on said date a female child; that said child was living March 4, 1905, and is said to have been named Clorie Smith

R.D. Cody MD

Witnesses To Mark:

Subscribed and sworn to before me this 21st day of March, 1905

John H. Cross
Notary Public.

Choc New Born 270
Frances Hokubbi
(Born March 26, 1903)

BIRTH AFFIDAVIT.

DEPARTMENT OF THE INTERIOR.
COMMISSION TO THE FIVE CIVILIZED TRIBES.

IN RE APPLICATION FOR ENROLLMENT, as a citizen of the Choctaw Nation, of Frances Hokubbi, born on the 26th day of March, 1903

Name of Father: Peter Hokubbi   a citizen of the Choc Nation.
Name of Mother: Sisley   "   a citizen of the   "   Nation.

Postoffice   Atoka I T

Applications for Enrollment of Choctaw Newborn
Act of 1905 Volume V

AFFIDAVIT OF MOTHER.

UNITED STATES OF AMERICA, Indian Territory, }
    Central   DISTRICT. }

I, Sisley Hokubbi, on oath state that I am 24 years of age and a citizen by blood, of the Choctaw Nation; that I am the lawful wife of Peter Hokubbi, who is a citizen, by blood of the Choctaw Nation; that a female child was born to me on 26th day of March, 1903; that said child has been named Frances Hokubbi, and ~~was living March 4, 1905~~.
                                           died July 31, 1904
                                           Her
                                  Sisley x Hokubbi
Witnesses To Mark: mark
{ *(Illegible)* Martin
{ J.D. Ward

Subscribed and sworn to before me this 17th day of March, 1905

                                 W.H. Angell
                                     Notary Public.

Department of the Interior,
COMMISSION TO THE FIVE CIVILIZED TRIBES.

In the matter of the death of Frances Hokubbi a citizen of the Choctaw Nation, who formerly resided at or near Atoka, Ind. Ter., and died on the 31 day of ~~March~~ July, 1904

AFFIDAVIT OF RELATIVE.

UNITED STATES OF AMERICA, }
  INDIAN TERRITORY,
    Cent.   District. }

I, Peter Hokubbi, on oath state that I am 24 years of age and a citizen by blood, of the Nation; that my postoffice address is Atoka I.T., Ind. Ter.; that I am Father of Frances Hokubbi who was a citizen, by blood, of the Choctaw Nation and that said Frances Hokubbi died on the 31 day of July, 1904

                                  Peter Hokubbi

Witnesses To Mark:
{
{

Applications for Enrollment of Choctaw Newborn
Act of 1905 Volume V

Subscribed and sworn to before me this 26 *day of* May, 1905.

                              JW Jones
                                    Notary Public.

AFFIDAVIT OF ACQUAINTANCE.

UNITED STATES OF AMERICA, }
   INDIAN TERRITORY,
   Cent   District.

    I, Ramsey Roberts, on oath state that I am 34 years of age, and a citizen by blood of the Choctaw Nation; that my postoffice address is Caney, Ind. Ter.; that I was personally acquainted with Frances Hokubbi who was a citizen, by blood, of the Choctaw Nation; and that said Frances Hokubbi died on the 31 day of July, 1904

                                Ramsey Roberts

Witnesses To Mark:
{

Subscribed and sworn to before me this 26 *day of* May, 1905.

                              J.W. Jones
                                  Notary Public.

                                            7-NB-270.

                    Muskogee, Indian Territory, May 20, 1905.

Peter Hokubbi,
    Atoka, Indian Territory.

Dear Sir:

    Referring to the application for the enrollment of your infant child, Frances Hokubbi, born March 26, 1903, heretofore filed in this office, it is noted that you state that the applicant died July 31, 1904.

    If this is correct you will please execute the enclosed proof of death and return it to this office.

    In having these affidavits executed care should be exercised to see that all names are written in full, as they appear in the body of the affidavit and in the event that either of the persons signing the affidavit are unable to write, signatures by mark must be attested by two witnesses. Each affidavit must be executed before a Notary Public and the notarial seal and signature of the officer must be attached to each separate affidavit.

Applications for Enrollment of Choctaw Newborn
Act of 1905 Volume V

Respectfully,
SIGNED *Tams Bixby*
Chairman.

Excl. D/C.

7-N.B. 270.

Muskogee, Indian Territory, May 31, 1905.

Peter Hokubbi,
    Atoka, Indian Territory.

Dear Sir:

    Receipt is hereby acknowledged of your affidavit and the affidavit of Ramsey Roberts to the death of your daughter, Frances Hokubbi, which occurred July 31, 1904, and the same have been filed with our records as evidence of the death of the above named citizen. of death of the above named person.

Respectfully,
SIGNED

Tams Bixby
Chairman.

W.J.
7-NB-270

DEPARTMENT OF THE INTERIOR,
COMMISSION TO THE FIVE CIVILIZED TRIBES.

    In the matter of the application for the enrollment of Frances Hokubbi as a citizen by blood of the Choctaw Nation.

---oOo---

    It appears from the record herein that on April 17, 1905 there was filed with the Commission application for the enrollment of Frances Hokubbi as a citizen by blood of the Choctaw Nation.

    It further appears from the record in this case and the records of the Commission that the applicant was born on March 26, 1903; that she is a daughter of Peter Hokubbi and Sisley Hokubbi, recognized and enrolled citizens by blood of the Choctaw Nation whose names appear as numbers 11750 and 19024, respectively, upon the final roll of citizens by blood of the Choctaw Nation, approved by the Secretary of the Interior March 10, 1903 and February 4, 1903, respectively; and that said applicant died on July 31, 1904.

Applications for Enrollment of Choctaw Newborn
Act of 1905   Volume V

The Act of Congress approved March 3, 1905 (Public No. 212) among other things provides:

"That the Commission to the Five Civilized Tribes is authorized for sixty days after the date of the approval of this act to receive and consider applications for enrollment of children born subsequent to September twenty-fifth, nineteen hundred and two, and prior to March fourth, nineteen hundred and five, and who were living on said latter date, to citizens by blood of the Choctaw and Chickasaw tribes of Indians whose enrollment has been approved by the Secretary of the Interior prior to the date of the approval of this act; and to enroll and make allotments to such children."

It is, therefore, hereby ordered that the application for the enrollment of Frances Hokubbi as a citizen by blood of the Choctaw Nation be dismissed in accordance with the order of the Commission of March 31, 1905.

COMMISSION TO THE FIVE CIVILIZED TRIBES,

Tams Bixby
Chairman.

Muskogee, Indian Territory.
JUN 15 1905

---

7 NB 270

Muskogee, Indian Territory, June 15, 1905.

Peter Hokubbi,
   Atoka, Indian Territory. **COPY**

Dear Sir:

Inclosed herewith you will find a copy of the order of this Commission, dated June 15, 1905, dismissing the application for the enrollment of your infant child, Frances Hokubbi as a citizen by blood of the Choctaw Nation.

Respectfully,
SIGNED
Tams Bixby
Chairman.

Registered.
Incl. 7- NB-270.

Applications for Enrollment of Choctaw Newborn
Act of 1905   Volume V

7-NB-270

Muskogee, Indian Territory, June 15, 1905.

Mansfield, McMurray & Cornish, **COPY**
   Attorneys for Choctaw and Chickasaw Nations,
      South McAlester, Indian Territory.

Gentlemen:

    Inclosed herewith you will find a copy of the order of this Commission, dated June 15, 1905, dismissing the application for the enrollment of Frances Hokubbi as a citizen by blood of the Choctaw Nation.

                Respectfully,
                SIGNED

Incl. 7-NB-270   *Tams Bixby*
                             Chairman.

---

7 N.B. 270

Frances Hokubbi
One dismissed
died prior to March 4, 1905.

Applications for Enrollment of Choctaw Newborn
Act of 1905   Volume V

Choc New Born 271
    John Clinton Paddock
    (Born Nov. 19, 1904)

No. 1897

Certificate of Record of Marriages.

United States of America,
The Indian Territory, } sct.
Central   District.

I,   E. J. Fannin   Clerk of the United States Court, in the Indian Territory and District aforesaid, do hereby CERTIFY, that the License for and Certificate of the Marriage of

Mr.   John Paddock   and

M   Novie Dunlap   was

filed in my office in said Territory and District the 28 day of August A.D., 190 3 , and duly recorded in Book 2 of Marriage Record, Page 331

WITNESS my hand and Seal of said Court, at Atoka this 9" day of May A.D. 190 5

E.J. Fannin
                Clerk.
By   J.D. Collins   Deputy.

P. O.

DEPARTMENT OF THE INTERIOR,
COMMISSION TO THE FIVE CIVILIZED TRIBES.

FILED

May 18 1905

Tams Bixby   CHAIRMAN.

Applications for Enrollment of Choctaw Newborn
Act of 1905 Volume V

No. 1897

MARRIAGE LICENSE

United States of America,   The Indian Territory,
                                                                  Central DISTRICT, SS.

To any Person Authorized by Law to Solemnize Marriage, Greeting:

You are hereby commanded to Solemnize the Rite and publish the Banns of Matrimony between Mr.   John Paddick
of   Caddo   *in the Indian Territory, aged*   19   *years, and M* iss Novie Dunlap   *of* ....
in the Indian Territory., aged   18   *years, according to law, and do you officially sign and return this License to the parties therein named.*

                       WITNESS my hand and official seal, this   28   *day of*   August   *A. D. 190* 3

                                                            E. J. Fannin
                                        Clerk of the United States Court.

                     JD Cotton   *Deputy*

                                      Certificate of Marriage.

United States of America, ⎫
   The Indian Territory, ⎬ *ss.*
     Central   District. ⎭   *I,*   James D Catlin

a   Minister   *, do hereby certify, that on the*   28   *day of* August   *A. D. 190* 3 *, I did, duly and according to law, as commanded in the foregoing License, solemnize the Rite and publish the Banns of Matrimony between the parties therein named.*

                 Witness my hand, this   28   *day of*   August   *A. D. 190* 3

My credentials are recorded in the office of the Clerk of ⎫   James D Catlin
the United States Court in the Indian Territory,   ⎬
Central District, Book   B   *, Page*   112   ⎭   *a*   Minister

     Note—This License and Certificate of Marriage must be returned to the Office of the Clerk of the United States Court of the Indian Territory, from whence it was issued, within sixty days from the date thereof, or the party to whom the License was issued will be liable in the amount of the One Hundred Dollars ($100.00)

Applications for Enrollment of Choctaw Newborn
Act of 1905 Volume V

BIRTH AFFIDAVIT.

DEPARTMENT OF THE INTERIOR.
COMMISSION TO THE FIVE CIVILIZED TRIBES.

IN RE APPLICATION FOR ENROLLMENT, as a citizen of the Choctaw Nation, of John Clinton Paddock, born on the 19th day of November, 1904

Name of Father: John S. Paddock   a citizen of the Choctaw Nation.

                                                  Intermarried

Name of Mother: Novie Paddock   a citizen of the Choctaw Nation.

                            Postoffice   Lindsey Ind. Ter.

AFFIDAVIT OF MOTHER.

UNITED STATES OF AMERICA, Indian Territory,
Southern DISTRICT.

I, Novie Paddock, on oath state that I am 20 years of age and a citizen by Intermarriage, of the Choctaw Nation; that I am the lawful wife of John S. Paddock, who is a citizen, by Blood of the Choctaw Nation; that a male child was born to me on 19th day of November, 1904, that said child has been named John Clinton Paddock, and is now living.

                                    Novie Paddock

Witnesses To Mark:

Subscribed and sworn to before me this 10th day of March, 1905.
My commission expires
Dec 4th 1907,   F.E. Rice
                                      Notary Public.

AFFIDAVIT OF ATTENDING PHYSICIAN OR MID-WIFE.

State of Texas
~~UNITED STATES OF AMERICA, Indian Territory,~~
County of Hale   ~~DISTRICT.~~

I, J.J. Merrill, a Practicing Physician, on oath state that I attended on Mrs. Novie Paddock, wife of John S. Paddock on the 19th day of November, 1904; that there was born to her on said date a male child; that said child is now living and is said to have been named John Clinton Paddock

                                    J J Merrill

Applications for Enrollment of Choctaw Newborn
Act of 1905   Volume V

Witnesses To Mark:

{

    Subscribed and sworn to before me this 23^د day of   March   , 1905. My commission expires May 31st 1905

                             N M Akeson
                                  Notary Public.
                               Hale Co. Texas

                                                  7-3880

                        Muskogee, Indian Territory, March 30, 1905.

John S. Paddock,
    Lindsay, Indian Territory.

Dear Sir:

    Receipt is hereby acknowledged of the affidavits in duplicate of Marie Novie Paddock and T. J. Merrill to the birth of John Quinton[sic] Paddock, son of John S. and Marie Novie Paddock, November 19, 1904, and the same have been filed with our records as an application for the enrollment of said child.

                              Respectfully,

                                                  Chairman.

                                                  N. B. 271

COPY   Muskogee, Indian Territory, April 7, 1905.

John S. Paddock, *Care of F.E. Rice 4/28/05*
    Lindsay, Indian Territory.

Dear Sir:

    You are hereby advised that before the application for the enrollment of your infant child, John Clinton Paddock, can be finally disposed of, it will be necessary for you to furnish the Commission either the original or a certified copy of the license and certificate of marriage of yourself and Novie Paddock.

    Please give this matter your prompt attention.

                              Respectfully,
                         SIGNED *T. B. Needles*.
                                Commissioner in Charge.

Applications for Enrollment of Choctaw Newborn
Act of 1905 Volume V

7-388

Muskogee, Indian Territory, May 16, 1905.

Mrs. Novie Paddock,
    Pauls Valley, Indian Territory.

Dear Madam:

    Receipt is hereby acknowledged of your letter of May 8, stating that you will forward evidence of your marriage as soon as possible.

    In reply to your letter you are advised that this matter should receive immediate attention in order that proper disposition may be made of the application for the enrollment of your child, John Clinton Paddock.

                  Respectfully,

                                      Chairman.

Choctaw N B 271

Muskogee, Indian Territory, May 19, 1905.

John S. Paddock,
    Care F. E. Rice,
        Lindsay, Indian Territory.

Dear Sir:

    Receipt is hereby acknowledged of marriage license and certificate between John Paddick[sic] and Novie Dunlap which you offer in support of the application for the enrollment of your child, John Clinton Paddock, and the same have been filed with the record in this case.

                  Respectfully,

                                      Chairman.

Applications for Enrollment of Choctaw Newborn
Act of 1905   Volume V

7 N.B. 271.

Muskogee, Indian Territory, June 1, 1905.

Novie Paddock,
    Pauls Valley, Indian Territory.

Dear Madam:

Receipt is hereby acknowledged of your letter of May 22, stating that you forwarded your marriage certificate to this office and asking if the same has been received.

In reply to your letter you are advised that the evidence of marriage between yourself and your husband was filed in this office May 18, 1905, and it will not be necessary for you to forward further evidence in this matter.

Respectfully,

Commissioner in Charge.

7-NB-271

Muskogee, Indian Territory, September 25, 1905.

Novie Paddock,
    Pauls Valley, Indian Territory.

Dear Madam:

Your letter of the 7th instant in reference to the enrollment of your child, John Clinton Paddock, has been referred by the Secretary of the Interior to this office for consideration and appropriate action.

I reply thereto you are advised that on July 22, 1905, the Secretary of the Interior approved the enrollment of your minor son, John Clinton Paddock, as a citizen by blood of the Choctaw Nation and his name appears upon the final roll of new-born citizens by blood of the Choctaw Nation opposite number 268. Notice of the approval by the Secretary of the Interior of the enrollment of your child was forwarded you at Lindsay, Indian Territory, early in August of the present year.

The child is now entitled to an allotment and selection thereof should be made without delay at the land office for the nation in which the prospective allotment is located. It appears from the records of this office that you are a non-citizen white woman and it would therefore be required that the allotment be selected by the father of the child, John S. Paddock.

Applications for Enrollment of Choctaw Newborn
Act of 1905   Volume V

Respectfully,

Commissioner.

Choc New Born 272
    Mary Patricia Pike
    (Born March 24, 1904)

BIRTH AFFIDAVIT.

DEPARTMENT OF THE INTERIOR,
COMMISSION TO THE FIVE CIVILIZED TRIBES.

In Re Application for Enrollment, as a citizen of the Choctaw Nation, of Mary Patricia Pike, born on the 24 day of March, 1904

Name of Father: F E Pike   a citizen of the United States Nation.
Name of Mother: Ella Belle Freeney Pike   a citizen of the Choctaw Nation.

Post-office   Lindsay, Ind Ter

AFFIDAVIT OF MOTHER.

UNITED STATES OF AMERICA, }
    INDIAN TERRITORY,
    Southern Dist   District.

    I, Ella Belle Freeney Pike, on oath state that I am 21 years of age and a citizen by Blood, of the Choctaw Nation; that I am the lawful wife of F. E. Pike, who is a citizen, by .... of the United States ~~Nation~~; that a Female child was born to me on 24 day of March, 1904, that said child has been named Mary Patricia Pike, and is now living.

                         Ella Belle Freeney Pike

WITNESSES TO MARK:
    { LW Wilborne
    { *(Name Illegible)*

    Subscribed and sworn to before me this 20th day of April, 1904

                     FM Bell
                        NOTARY PUBLIC.

Applications for Enrollment of Choctaw Newborn
Act of 1905   Volume V

AFFIDAVIT OF ATTENDING PHYSICIAN OR MID-WIFE.

UNITED STATES OF AMERICA,
  INDIAN TERRITORY,
  Southern   District.

I,   S W Wilson   , a   Physician   , on oath state that I attended on Mrs. Ella Belle Freeney Pike , wife of F. E. Pike on the 24 day of March , 1904 ; that there was born to her on said date a   Female   child; that said child is now living and is said to have been named Mary Patricia Pike

S W Wilson M.D.

WITNESSES TO MARK:
  John Gallahan
  FM Bell

Subscribed and sworn to before me this 20th day of April , 1904

FM Bell

NOTARY PUBLIC.

BIRTH AFFIDAVIT.

DEPARTMENT OF THE INTERIOR.
COMMISSION TO THE FIVE CIVILIZED TRIBES.

IN RE APPLICATION FOR ENROLLMENT, as a citizen of the   Choctaw   Nation, of Mary P. Pike   , born on the 24th day of March , 1904

Name of Father: Fred E Pike   a citizen of the   Nation.
Name of Mother: Ella B. Freeney, now Pike   a citizen of the   Choctaw   Nation.

Postoffice   Lindsay Ind Ter

AFFIDAVIT OF MOTHER.

UNITED STATES OF AMERICA, Indian Territory,
  Southern   DISTRICT.

I,   Ella B Freeney now Pike   , on oath state that I am 22   years of age and a citizen by   Choctaw   blood   , of the   Choctaw   Nation; that I am the lawful wife of   Fred E. Pike   , who is a citizen, by ——— of the ——— Nation; that a female   child was born to me on 24th   day of   March   , 1904; that said child has been named   Mary P. Pike   , and was living March 4, 1905.

Applications for Enrollment of Choctaw Newborn
Act of 1905 Volume V

Ella B. Freeney Pike

Witnesses To Mark:
{

Subscribed and sworn to before me this 25 day of March , 1905

Claire L. McArthur
Notary Public.

AFFIDAVIT OF ATTENDING PHYSICIAN OR MID-WIFE.

UNITED STATES OF AMERICA, Indian Territory, }
Southern DISTRICT. }

I, S. W. Wilson , a Physician , on oath state that I attended on Mrs. Ella B. Pyke[sic] , wife of Fred E Pike on the 24th day of March , 1904; that there was born to her on said date a female child; that said child was living March 4, 1905, and is said to have been named S.W. Wilson M.D.

S. W. Wilson M.D.

Witnesses To Mark:
{

Subscribed and sworn to before me this day of , 1905

Notary Public.

7-3897

Muskogee, Indian Territory, April 28, 1904.

F. E. Pike,
    Lindsay, Indian Territory.

Dear Sir:

    Receipt is hereby acknowledged of the affidavits of Ella Belle Freeney Pike and S. W. Wilson, relative to the birth of your infant daughter, Mary Patricia Pike, March 24, 1904, which it is presumed have been forwarded as an application for enrollment of said child.

    You are informed that under the provisions of the Act of Congress, approved July 1, 1902, the Commission is now without authority to receive or consider the original

Applications for Enrollment of Choctaw Newborn
Act of 1905   Volume V

application for enrollment of any person whomsoever as a citizen of the Choctaw or Chickasaw Nation.

Respectfully,

Chairman.

(The letter below does not belong with the current applicant.)

7-3897

Muskogee, Indian Territory, April 5, 1905.

Daniel W. Oakes,
    Atlas, Indian Territory.

Dear Sir:

    Receipt is hereby acknowledged of the affidavits of Mary A. Oakes and Isabell Reynolds to the birth of Mary Margarite Oakes daughter of Daniel W. and Mary A. Oakes, November 23, 1903, and the same have been filed with our records as an application for the enrollment of said child.

Respectfully,

Commissioner in Charge.

Choc New Born 273
    Alton H. Dickey
    (Born Sep. 10, 1903)

BIRTH AFFIDAVIT.

DEPARTMENT OF THE INTERIOR.
COMMISSION TO THE FIVE CIVILIZED TRIBES.

IN RE APPLICATION FOR ENROLLMENT, as a citizen of the Choctaw Nation, of Alton H. Dickey, born on the 10th day of September, 1903

                                 non
Name of Father: Steward E. Dickey   a^citizen of the ....Nation.
                Enrolled as Mary McLellan[sic]
Name of Mother: Mary Dickey   ^   a citizen of the Choctaw Nation.

Applications for Enrollment of Choctaw Newborn
Act of 1905   Volume V

Postoffice   Nail P.O.

AFFIDAVIT OF MOTHER.

UNITED STATES OF AMERICA, Indian Territory,
Central   DISTRICT.

I, Mary Dickey, on oath state that I am 21 years of age and a citizen by Blood, of the Choctaw Nation; that I am the lawful wife of Steward E Dickey, who is a non citizen, by ~~of the~~ Nation; that a male child was born to me on 10th day of September, 1903; that said child has been named Alton H Dickey, and was living March 4, 1905.

Mary McLellan Dickey

Witnesses To Mark:
{

Subscribed and sworn to before me this 20 day of March, 1905

J G Reeder
Notary Public.
My commission expires *(blank)*

AFFIDAVIT OF ATTENDING PHYSICIAN OR MID-WIFE.

UNITED STATES OF AMERICA, Indian Territory,
Central   DISTRICT.

I, R. P. Dickey, a Physician, on oath state that I attended on Mrs. Mary Dickey, wife of Steward E. Dickey on the 10th day of September, 1903; that there was born to her on said date a male child; that said child was living March 4, 1905, and is said to have been named Alton H Dickey

R.P. Dickey

Witnesses To Mark:
{

Subscribed and sworn to before me this 20 day of March, 1905

J G Reeder
Notary Public.
My commission expires June 1904

Applications for Enrollment of Choctaw Newborn
Act of 1905   Volume V

7-3919

Muskogee, Indian Territory, March 25, 1905.

Steward E. Dickey,
    Nail, Indian Territory.

Dear Sir:

    Receipt is hereby acknowledged of the affidavit of Mary McLellan Dickey to the birth of Alton H. Dickey son of Steward E. and Mary Dickey, September 10, 1903, and the same has been filed with our records as an application for the enrollment of said child.

                      Respectfully,

                                Chairman.

Choc New Born 274
    Clara D. McClellan
    (Born Dec. 23, 1902)
    Samuel J. McLellan[sic]
    (Born Jan. 4, 1905)

Applications for Enrollment of Choctaw Newborn
Act of 1905   Volume V

7-3922 n.B. 274

DEPARTMENT OF THE INTERIOR,
COMMISSION TO THE FIVE CIVILIZED TRIBES.
FILED
MAR 23 1905

Tams Bixby   CHAIRMAN.

Certificate of Record of Marriage

UNITED STATES OF AMERICA,
INDIAN TERRITORY,   } sct.
SOUTHERN DISTRICT.

I, C. M. CAMPBELL, Clerk of the United States Court, in the Territory and District aforesaid do hereby certify, that the License for and Certificate of Marriage of

MR   Joseph M McLelan

and

M   Ada Skaggs

were filed in my office in said Territory and District the   10   day of   Jan   A.D., 190 2   and duly recorded in Book   F.   of Marriage Record, Page   201

WITNESS my hand and Seal of said Court, at Ardmore, this   day of   A.D. 190

C. M. Campbell
_____
CLERK.

Return this License to the United States Clerk at Ardmore, that it may be recorded, when it will be mailed to the proper address.

FILED
JAN 10 1902 4 PM
Ardmoreite Steam Print.

C. M. CAMPBELL Clerk.

Southern Dist. Ind. Ter.

Applications for Enrollment of Choctaw Newborn
Act of 1905   Volume V

MARRIAGE LICENSE

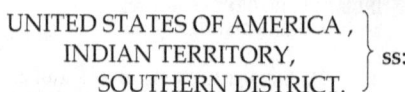

UNITED STATES OF AMERICA,
   INDIAN TERRITORY,   } ss:
      SOUTHERN DISTRICT.

To Any Person Authorized by Law to Solemnize Marriage --- Greeting:

You are hereby commanded to solemnize the Rite and publish the Banns of Matrimony between Mr. Joseph M McLelan of Franks, in the Indian Territory, aged 21 years and M Ada Skaggs of Franks in the Indian Territory aged 24 years according to law, and do you officially sign and return this License to the parties therein named.

Witness my hand and official seal, this 6 day of Jany A.D. 190 2

CM Campbell
Clerk of the United States Court

Deputy

Certificate of Marriage.

United States of America America,
   Indian Territory,   } ss.
      Southern District.

I, E A Barnett a minister of the gospel do hereby certify, that on the 7 day of January, A. D. 190 2, I did duly and according to law, as commanded in the foregoing License, solemnize the Rite and publish the Banns of Matrimony between the parties therein named.

Witness my hand, this 7 day of January, A. D. 190 2

My credentials are recorded in the office of the Clerk of the United States Court, Indian Territory, Southern District, at Ardmore, Indian Territory Book A, Page 61

NOTE:-The person officiating should fill in the spaces for book and page and sign here

E A Barnett
a minister of the gospel

NOTE (a)-The License and Certificate of Marriage must be returned to the office of the Clerk of the United States Court in the Indian Territory, at Ardmore, within sixty days from the date thereof, or the party to whom the License was issued will be liable in the amount of One Hundred Dollars ($100).

NOTE (b)-No person is authorized to perform the Marriage Ceremony in the Southern District unless the proper credentials have first been recorded in the Clerk's office.

Applications for Enrollment of Choctaw Newborn
Act of 1905 Volume V

BIRTH AFFIDAVIT.

DEPARTMENT OF THE INTERIOR.
COMMISSION TO THE FIVE CIVILIZED TRIBES.

IN RE APPLICATION FOR ENROLLMENT, as a citizen of the Choctaw Nation, of Clara D McLellan, born on the .... day of ...., 1......

Name of Father: Joseph M McLellan   a citizen of the Choctaw Nation.
Name of Mother: Ada McLellan   a citizen of the United States Nation.

Postoffice   Ashland, I.T.

AFFIDAVIT OF MOTHER.

UNITED STATES OF AMERICA, Indian Territory,
Central   DISTRICT.

I, Ada McLellan, on oath state that I am 27 years of age and a citizen by ———, of the United States Nation; that I am the lawful wife of Joseph M McLellan, who is a citizen, by blood of the Choctaw Nation; that a female child was born to me on 23rd day of December, 1902; that said child has been named Clara D. McLellan, and was living March 4, 1905.

                             Ada McLellan

Witnesses To Mark:
{

Subscribed and sworn to before me this 20th day of March, 1905.

                             W.H. Angell
                             Notary Public.

AFFIDAVIT OF ATTENDING PHYSICIAN OR MID-WIFE.

UNITED STATES OF AMERICA, Indian Territory,
Central   DISTRICT.

I, Kittie McLellan, a midwife, on oath state that I attended on Mrs. Ada McLellan, wife of Joseph M McLellan on the 23rd day of December, 1902; that there was born to her on said date a female child; that said child was living March 4, 1905, and is said to have been named Clara D McLellan

                             Kittie McLellan

Applications for Enrollment of Choctaw Newborn
Act of 1905   Volume V

Witnesses To Mark:

{

      Subscribed and sworn to before me this 20th day of   March   , 1905

                                        W.H. Angell
                                                   Notary Public.

BIRTH AFFIDAVIT.

DEPARTMENT OF THE INTERIOR.
COMMISSION TO THE FIVE CIVILIZED TRIBES.

IN RE APPLICATION FOR ENROLLMENT, as a citizen of the   Choctaw   Nation, of Samuel J McLellan   , born on the 4th day of   January   , 1905

Name of Father: Joseph M McLellan   a citizen of the   Choctaw   Nation.
Name of Mother: Ada McLellan   a citizen of the United States Nation.

                           Postoffice   Ashland, I.T.

AFFIDAVIT OF MOTHER.

UNITED STATES OF AMERICA, Indian Territory, }
    Central   DISTRICT. }

      I, Ada McLellan   , on oath state that I am   27   years of age and a citizen by ——— , of the   United States   ~~Nation~~; that I am the lawful wife of   Joseph M McLellan   , who is a citizen, by   blood   of the   Choctaw   Nation; that a male   child was born to me on   4th day of   January   , 1905; that said child has been named   Samuel J. McLellan   , and was living March 4, 1905.

                                        Ada McLellan

Witnesses To Mark:

{

      Subscribed and sworn to before me this 20th day of   March   , 1905

                                        W.H. Angell
                                               Notary Public.

Applications for Enrollment of Choctaw Newborn
Act of 1905 Volume V

AFFIDAVIT OF ATTENDING PHYSICIAN OR MID-WIFE.

UNITED STATES OF AMERICA, Indian Territory,
Central   DISTRICT.

I, Kittie McLellan, a midwife, on oath state that I attended on Mrs. Ada McLellan, wife of Joseph M McLellan on the 4th day of January, 1905; that there was born to her on said date a male child; that said child was living March 4, 1905, and is said to have been named Samuel J McLellan

Kittie McLellan

Witnesses To Mark:
{

Subscribed and sworn to before me this 20th day of March, 1905.

W.H. Angell
Notary Public.

7 NB 274

Muskogee, Indian Territory, May 22, 1905.

W. H. Angell,
   Choctaw Land Office,
      Atoka, Indian Territory.

Dear Sir:

There is enclosed herewith affidavit of Ada McLellan, mother, and Kittie McLellan, midwife to the birth of Samuel J. McLellan, born January 4, 1905, who is an applicant for enrollment as a Choctaw citizen.

Your attention is called to the fact that the affidavit of the mother was executed on March 20, 1905, while that of the midwife who apparently executed January 4, 1905, the same day on which the child was born. The date of execution given in the latter is probably an error. If so, you will please attach your own affidavit to this one showing the date on which it was executed.

Respectfully,

Chairman.

VR 22-8.

Applications for Enrollment of Choctaw Newborn
Act of 1905 Volume V

7 N B 274

Muskogee, Indian Territory, May 29, 1905.

J. M. McClelland[sic],
    Ashland, Indian Territory.

Dear Sir:

    Receipt is hereby acknowledged of your letter of May 18, relative to the enrollment of your two children, Clara D. and Samuel J. McClelland, and requesting the return of your marriage license.

    In reply to your letter you are advised that you will be informed when the enrollment of your children, Clara D. and Samuel J. McClelland, has been approved by the Secretary of the Interior.

    You are also advised that the marriage license and certificate between yourself and your wife, Ada McClelland have been filed with our records in support of the application for the enrollment of these two children, and it is impracticable at this time to comply with your request for the return thereof.

                  Respectfully,

                                      Chairman.

7-NB-274.

Muskogee, Indian Territory, September 18, 1905

Joseph M. McLellan,
    Ashland, Indian Territory.

Dear Sir:

    Receipt is hereby acknowledged of your letter of the 10th instant in which you request to be advised as to whether or not the enrollment of your minor son, Samuel J. McLellan, has been approved by the Secretary of the Interior and if not to be advised of what further evidence is necessary in said case.

    In reply to your letter you are advised that the reason your said son was not enrolled at the same time that your other child, Clara D. McLellan, was enrolled is that at that time there existed in the record in said case a discrepancy and it was necessary that the same be corrected before the rights of said Samuel J. McLellan could be finally determined. Said discrepancy has been recently corrected and you are advised that the

Applications for Enrollment of Choctaw Newborn
Act of 1905 Volume V

name of Samuel J. McLellan will be placed upon the next schedule of new born citizens to be submitted to the Secretary of the Interior for approval.

When the enrollment of said child is approved you will be duly notified.

      Respectfully,

          Acting Commissioner.

7-NB-274

      Muskogee, Indian Territory, February 20, 1906.

Joseph M. McLelland[sic],
  Ashland, Indian Territory.

Dear Sir:

  Receipt is hereby acknowledged of your letter of February 6, 1906, and replying to that portion thereof in which you ask relative to the enrollment of Samuel J. McLelland you are advised that the name of your son Samuel J. McLelland has been placed upon a schedule of new born citizens of the Choctaw Nation which has been forwarded the Secretary of the Interior and you will be notified when his enrollment is approved by the Department.

      Respectfully,

          Acting Commissioner.

Choc New Born 275
  Morley Robinson
  (Born July 22, 1903)

Applications for Enrollment of Choctaw Newborn
Act of 1905   Volume V

NEW-BORN AFFIDAVIT.

Number..........

...Choctaw Enrolling Commission...

IN THE MATTER OF THE APPLICATION FOR ENROLLMENT, as a citizen of the Choctaw Nation, of Morley Robinson

born on the 23rd[sic] day of July   190 3

Name of father   David Robinson   a citizen of   Choctaw
Nation final enrollment No. 10813
Name of mother   Allie M. Robinson   a citizen of   Choctaw
Nation final enrollment No. 351

Postoffice   Bokchito, I.T.

AFFIDAVIT OF MOTHER.

UNITED STATES OF AMERICA
INDIAN TERRITORY
Central   DISTRICT

I   Allie M Robinson   , on oath state that I am 33 years of age and a citizen by marriage of the Choctaw Nation, and as such have been placed upon the final roll of the Choctaw Nation, by the Honorable Secretary of the Interior my final enrollment number being 351 ; that I am the lawful wife of David Robinson , who is a citizen of the Choctaw Nation, and as such has been placed upon the final roll of said Nation by the Honorable Secretary of the Interior, his final enrollment number being 10813 and that a Male child was born to me on the 23[sic] day of July   190 3; that said child has been named Morley Robinson , and is now living.

Witnesseth.   Allie M Robinson

Must be two ⎫ W. M. Labor
Witnesses who⎬
are Citizens. ⎭   *(Name Illegible)*

Subscribed and sworn to before me this 23 day of February   190 5

W C Caudill
Notary Public.

My commission expires: ....

135

Applications for Enrollment of Choctaw Newborn
Act of 1905   Volume V

Affidavit of Attending Physician or Midwife

UNITED STATES OF AMERICA,
   INDIAN TERRITORY,
  Central   DISTRICT

I, N.J. Hamilton a Practicing Physician on oath state that I attended on Mrs. Allie M Robinson wife of David Robinson on the 23[sic] day of July, 190 3, that there was born to her on said date a male child, that said child is now living, and is said to have been named Morley Robinson.

                N.J. Hamilton   M. D.

Subscribed and sworn to before me this the 23 day of February 1905

                W C Caudill
                          Notary Public.

WITNESSETH:
Must be two witnesses who are citizens and know the child.
{ James Boland
  (Name Illegible)

We hereby certify that we are well acquainted with Dr. N.J. Hamilton a Physician and know him to be reputable and of good standing in the community.

            Must be two citizen { James Boland
            witnesses.   W.M. Labor

BIRTH AFFIDAVIT.

DEPARTMENT OF THE INTERIOR.
COMMISSION TO THE FIVE CIVILIZED TRIBES.

IN RE APPLICATION FOR ENROLLMENT, as a citizen of the Choctaw Nation, of Morley Robinson, born on the 23rd[sic] day of July, 1903

Name of Father: David Robinson   a citizen of the Choctaw Nation.
Name of Mother: Allie May Robinson   a citizen of the Choctaw Nation.

         Postoffice   Bokchito, I.T.

Applications for Enrollment of Choctaw Newborn
Act of 1905   Volume V

AFFIDAVIT OF MOTHER.

UNITED STATES OF AMERICA, Indian Territory,　}
　Central　　　　　　　　DISTRICT.

　　I,　Allie May Robinson　, on oath state that I am　32　years of age and a citizen by　intermarriage　, of the　Choctaw　Nation; that I am the lawful wife of David Robinson　, who is a citizen, by　Blood　of the　Choctaw　Nation; that a　male　child was born to me on　23rd　day of　July　, 1903; that said child has been named　Morley Robinson　, and was living March 4, 1905.

　　　　　　　　　　　　　　Allie May Robinson

Witnesses To Mark:

　　Subscribed and sworn to before me this 24th　day of　March　, 1905

　　　　　　　　　　　　　　WC Caudill
　　　　　　　　　　　　　　　Notary Public.

AFFIDAVIT OF ATTENDING PHYSICIAN OR MID-WIFE.

UNITED STATES OF AMERICA, Indian Territory,　}
　Central　　　　　　　　DISTRICT.

　　I,　N. J. Hamilton　, a　Physician　, on oath state that I attended on Mrs.　Allie May Robinson　, wife of　David Robinson　on the 23rd　day of July　, 1903; that there was born to her on said date a　male　child; that said child was living March 4, 1905, and is said to have been named　Morley Robinson

　　　　　　　　　　　　　　N.J. Hamilton M.D.

Witnesses To Mark:

　　Subscribed and sworn to before me this 24th　day of　March　, 1905

　　　　　　　　　　　　　　WC Caudill
　　　　　　　　　　　　　　　Notary Public.

Applications for Enrollment of Choctaw Newborn
Act of 1905   Volume V

BIRTH AFFIDAVIT.

DEPARTMENT OF THE INTERIOR.
COMMISSION TO THE FIVE CIVILIZED TRIBES.

IN RE APPLICATION FOR ENROLLMENT, as a citizen of the Choctaw Nation, of Morley Robinson, born on the 22nd day of July, 1903

Name of Father: David Robinson   a citizen of the Choctaw Nation.
Name of Mother: Allie May Robinson   a citizen of the Choctaw Nation.

Postoffice   Bokchito, Ind. Ter.

AFFIDAVIT OF MOTHER.

UNITED STATES OF AMERICA, Indian Territory,
Central   DISTRICT.

I, Allie May Robinson, on oath state that I am 32 years of age and a citizen by Intermarriage, of the Choctaw Nation; that I am the lawful wife of David Robinson, who is a citizen, by Blood of the Choctaw Nation; that a male child was born to me on 22nd day of July, 1903; that said child has been named Morley Robinson, and was living March 4, 1905.

                         Allie May Robinson

Witnesses To Mark:

Subscribed and sworn to before me this 24th day of May, 1905

                         WC Caudill
                             Notary Public.

AFFIDAVIT OF ATTENDING PHYSICIAN OR MID-WIFE.

UNITED STATES OF AMERICA, Indian Territory,
Central   DISTRICT.

I, N. J. Hamilton, a Physician, on oath state that I attended on Mrs. Allie May Robinson, wife of David Robinson on the 22nd day of July, 1903; that there was born to her on said date a male child; that said child was living March 4, 1905, and is said to have been named Morley Robinson

                         N.J. Hamilton M.D.

Witnesses To Mark:

Applications for Enrollment of Choctaw Newborn
Act of 1905   Volume V

Subscribed and sworn to before me this 24th   day of   May   , 1905

WC Caudill
Notary Public.

Choctaw 3853

Muskogee, Indian Territory, March 30, 1905.

David Robinson,
    Bokchito, Indian Territory.

Dear Sir:

    Receipt is hereby acknowledged of your letter of March 25, inclosing affidavits of Allie May Robinson and N. J. Hamilton, to the birth of Morley Robinson, son of David and Allie May Robinson, July 22, 1903, and the same have been filed with our records as an application for the enrollment of said child.

Respectfully,

Chairman.

7-NB-275.

Muskogee, Indian Territory, May 22, 1905.

David Robinson,
    Bokchito, Indian Territory.

Dear Sir:

    There is enclosed you herewith for execution application for the enrollment of your infant child, Morley Robinson.

    In the affidavits of February 22, 1905, heretofore filed in this office, the date of the applicants[sic] birth is given as July 23, 1903, while in those of March 24, 1905, it is given as July 22, 1903. In the enclosed application the date of birth is left blank, in which You will please insert the mother's age in the place left blank for that purpose. the correct date of birth, and when properly executed return it to this office.

    In having these affidavits executed care should be exercised to see that all names are written in full, as they appear in the body of the affidavit, and in the event that either of the persons signing the affidavit are unable to write, signatures by mark must be

Applications for Enrollment of Choctaw Newborn
Act of 1905   Volume V

attested by two witnesses. Each affidavit must be executed before a Notary Public and the notarial seal and signature of the officer must be attached to each separate affidavit.

                Respectfully,

                                  Chairman.

VR 22-18.

                                  7 N.B. 275.

                Muskogee, Indian Territory, May 29, 1905.

David Robinson,
    Bokchito, Indian Territory.

Dear Sir:

    Receipt is hereby acknowledged of the affidavits of Allie May Robinson and N. J. Hamilton to the birth of Morley Robinson, son of David and Allie May Robinson, July 22, 1903, and the same have been filed with our records in the matter of the enrollment of the above named child.

                Respectfully,

                                  Chairman.

Choc New Born 276
    Samuel Allen Richards
    (Born January 30, 1903)

Applications for Enrollment of Choctaw Newborn
Act of 1905   Volume V

NEW-BORN AFFIDAVIT.

Number..............

...Choctaw Enrolling Commission...

IN THE MATTER OF THE APPLICATION FOR ENROLLMENT, as a citizen of the Choctaw Nation, of   Samuel Allen Wright Richards

born on the 30th day of __January__ 190 3

Name of father   William L Richards   a citizen of   United States
Nation final enrollment No. _____
Name of mother   Clara E Richards   a citizen of   Choctaw
Nation final enrollment No. 11157

Postoffice   Bokchito, I.T.

AFFIDAVIT OF MOTHER.

UNITED STATES OF AMERICA
INDIAN TERRITORY
Central   DISTRICT

I   Clara E Richards   , on oath state that I am 35 years of age and a citizen by   blood   of the   Choctaw Nation, and as such have been placed upon the final roll of the   Choctaw Nation, by the Honorable Secretary of the Interior my final enrollment number being   11157; that I am the lawful wife of   William L. Richards   , who is a citizen of the   United States Nation, and as such has been placed upon the final roll of said Nation by the Honorable Secretary of the Interior, his final enrollment number being .... and that a   Male child was born to me on the   30th   day of   January   190 3; that said child has been named   Samuel Allen Wright Richards   , and is now living.

Witnesseth.   Clara E. Richards

Must be two ⎫ J Brooks Wright
Witnesses who⎬
are Citizens. ⎭ Elbert M Jones

Subscribed and sworn to before me this 11 day of Jan 190 5

W Richards
Notary Public.

My commission expires: Feb 5th 1905

Applications for Enrollment of Choctaw Newborn
Act of 1905 Volume V

AFFIDAVIT OF ATTENDING PHYSICIAN OR MIDWIFE

UNITED STATES OF AMERICA
INDIAN TERRITORY
Central   DISTRICT

I, M.P. Skeen a Licensed Practicing Physician on oath state that I attended on Mrs. Clara E. Richards wife of William L. Richards on the 30th day of January , 190 3 , that there was born to her on said date a male child, that said child is now living, and is said to have been named Samuel Allen Wright Richards

M. P. Skeen   M.D.

Subscribed and sworn to before me this, the 11th day of January 190 5

(Name Illegible) Notary Public.

WITNESSETH:
Must be two witnesses who are citizens
{ J Brooks Wright
  Elbert M Jones

We hereby certify that we are well acquainted with M.P. Skeen a Physician and know him to be reputable and of good standing in the community.

J Brooks Wright   Choctaw by blood _____

Elbert M Jones   Choctaw by blood _____

BIRTH AFFIDAVIT.

DEPARTMENT OF THE INTERIOR.
COMMISSION TO THE FIVE CIVILIZED TRIBES.

IN RE APPLICATION FOR ENROLLMENT, as a citizen of the Choctaw Nation, of Samuel Allen Richards , born on the 30th day of January , 1903

Name of Father: William L Richards   a citizen of the United States Nation.
Name of Mother: Clara E Richards   a citizen of the Choctaw Nation.

Postoffice   Wapanucka I.T.

Applications for Enrollment of Choctaw Newborn
Act of 1905   Volume V

AFFIDAVIT OF MOTHER.

UNITED STATES OF AMERICA, Indian Territory,
Central   DISTRICT.

I, Clara E. Richards , on oath state that I am 35 years of age and a citizen by blood , of the Choctaw Nation; that I am the lawful wife of William L Richards , who is a citizen, by .... of the United States Nation; that a male child was born to me on the 30th day of January , 1903; that said child has been named Samuel Allen Richards , and was living March 4, 1905.

Clara E. Richards

Witnesses To Mark:
{

Subscribed and sworn to before me this 21 day of March , 1905

A A Faulk
Notary Public.

AFFIDAVIT OF ATTENDING PHYSICIAN OR MID-WIFE.

UNITED STATES OF AMERICA, Indian Territory,
Central   DISTRICT.

I, M.P. Skeen , a Physician , on oath state that I attended on Mrs. Clara E Richards , wife of William L Richards on the 30th day of January , 1903; that there was born to her on said date a male child; that said child was living March 4, 1905, and is said to have been named Samuel Allen Richards

M. P. Skeen

Witnesses To Mark:
{

Subscribed and sworn to before me this 21 day of March , 1905

A A Faulk
Notary Public.

Applications for Enrollment of Choctaw Newborn
Act of 1905   Volume V

7-3984

Muskogee, Indian Territory, March 28, 1905.

W. L. Richards,
    Wapanucka, Indian Territory.

Dear Sir:

    Receipt is hereby acknowledged of your letter of March 23, 1905, enclosing affidavits of Clara E. Richards and N[sic]. P. Skeen to the birth of Samuel Allen Richards, son of William L. and Clara E. Richards, January 30, 1903, and the same have been filed with our records as an application for the enrollment of said child.

        Respectfully,

                Chairman.

7-NB-276

Muskogee, Indian Territory, August 14, 1905.

Chief Clerk,
    Choctaw Land Office,
        Atoka, Indian Territory.

Dear Sir:

    Receipt is hereby acknowledged of your letter of August 10, 1905, referring to Choctaw new born card No. 276, Samuel Allen Richards in which you state that the name of the mother of this child appears on the duplicate card in the possession of your office as Clara S. Richards, Choctaw roll by blood No. 11157 and you ask if this name should not be Clara E. Richards.

    In reply to your letter you are advised that the name of the mother of Samuel Allen Richards Choctaw new born card No. 276 appears upon the records of this office as Clara E. Richards and the duplicate card in the possession of your office shoula[sic] be corrected in conformity with this information.

        Respectfully,

                Acting Commissioner.

Applications for Enrollment of Choctaw Newborn
Act of 1905   Volume V

Choc New Born 277
    Charley Ferraute[sic]
    (Born April 10, 1903)

BIRTH AFFIDAVIT.

DEPARTMENT OF THE INTERIOR,
COMMISSION TO THE FIVE CIVILIZED TRIBES.

In Re Application for Enrollment, as a citizen of the Choctaw Nation, of Charley Ferrante , born on the 10th day of April , 1903

Name of Father: Sante Ferrante   a citizen of the Choctaw Nation.
Name of Mother: Isibinda   a citizen of the Choctaw Nation.

        Post-office   Hallaman IT

AFFIDAVIT OF MOTHER.

UNITED STATES OF AMERICA,
   INDIAN TERRITORY,
Central   District.

    I, Isi binda Ferrante , on oath state that I am 26 years of age and a citizen by Blood , of the Choctaw Nation; that I am the lawful wife of Sante Ferrante , who is a citizen, by Marriage of the Choctaw Nation; that a male child was born to me on 10th day of April , 1903 , that said child has been named Charley Ferrante , and is now living.

                          Isibinda Ferrante

WITNESSES TO MARK:
    McGee Woods
    Carolen[sic] Ferrante

    Subscribed and sworn to before me this 14th day of July , 1903

                        (Name Illegible)
                        NOTARY PUBLIC.

Applications for Enrollment of Choctaw Newborn
Act of 1905   Volume V

AFFIDAVIT OF ATTENDING PHYSICIAN OR MID-WIFE.

UNITED STATES OF AMERICA,
INDIAN TERRITORY,
Central   District.

I, S. P. Ross, a Physician, on oath state that I attended on Mrs. Isi binda Ferrante, wife of Sante Ferrante on the 10 day of April, 1903; that there was born to her on said date a male child; that said child is now living and is said to have been named Charley

S.P. Ross M.D.

WITNESSES TO MARK:

Subscribed and sworn to before me this 14th day of July, 1903.

(Name Illegible)
NOTARY PUBLIC.

BIRTH AFFIDAVIT.

DEPARTMENT OF THE INTERIOR.
COMMISSION TO THE FIVE CIVILIZED TRIBES.

IN RE APPLICATION FOR ENROLLMENT, as a citizen of the Choctaw Nation, of Charley Ferrante, born on the 10 day of April, 1903

Name of Father: Sante Ferrante   a citizen of the Choctaw Nation.
Name of Mother: Isabinda[sic] Ferrante   a citizen of the Choctaw Nation.

Postoffice   Celestine Indian Territory

AFFIDAVIT OF MOTHER.

UNITED STATES OF AMERICA, Indian Territory,
Central   DISTRICT.

I, Isabinda Ferrante, on oath state that I am 28 years of age and a citizen by blood, of the Choctaw Nation; that I am the lawful wife of Sante Ferrante, who is a citizen, by intermarriage of the Choctaw Nation; that a male child was born to me on 10 day of April, 1903; that said child has been named Charley Ferrante, and was living March 4, 1905.

Isabina[sic] Ferrante

Applications for Enrollment of Choctaw Newborn
Act of 1905 Volume V

Witnesses To Mark:
{ A J Turner
{ E.M. Jennings

    Subscribed and sworn to before me this 13th day of   April   , 1905

                              Andrew J Turner
                              Notary Public.

AFFIDAVIT OF ATTENDING PHYSICIAN OR MID-WIFE.

UNITED STATES OF AMERICA, Indian Territory,
    Central   **DISTRICT.**

    I,   S.P. Ross   , a   Physician   , on oath state that I attended on Mrs.   Isabinda Ferrante   , wife of   Sante Ferrante   on the 10 day of April , 1903; that there was born to her on said date a   male   child; that said child was living March 4, 1905, and is said to have been named Charley Ferrante

                              S.P. Ross M.D.

Witnesses To Mark:
{

    Subscribed and sworn to before me this 13 day of   April   , 1905

                              Andrew J Turner
                              Notary Public.

                                    N. B. 277
                       COPY
        Muskogee, Indian Territory, April 7, 1905.

Sante Ferrante,
    Celestine, Indian Territory.

Dear Sir:

    There is inclosed you herewith for execution application for the enrollment of your infant child, Charley Ferrante, born April 10, 1903.

    The affidavits heretofore filed with the Commission show the child was living on July 14, 1903. It is necessary, for the child to be enrolled, that he was living on March 4, 1905. You will please insert the mother's age in the place left blank for that purpose.

Applications for Enrollment of Choctaw Newborn
Act of 1905   Volume V

In having these affidavits executed care should be exercised to see that all names are written in full, as they appear in the body of the affidavit, and in the event that either of the persons signing the affidavit are unable to write, signatures by mark must be attested by two witnesses. Each affidavit must be executed before a Notary Public and the notarial seal and signature of the officer must be attached to each separate affidavit.

Respectfully,

SIGNED   *T. B. Needles.*

SEV 8-7.   Commissioner in Charge.

7 NB 277

Muskogee, Indian Territory, April 20, 1905.

Andrew J. Tiner[sic],
  Celestine, Indian Territory.

Dear Sir:

Receipt is hereby acknowledged of your letter of April 14, 1905, enclosing affidavits of Isabina Ferranta[sic] and S. P. Ross to the birth of Charley Ferrante, son of Sante Ferrante and Isabina Ferrante, April 10, 1903, and the same have been filed with our records as an application for the enrollment of said child.

Respectfully,

Chairman.

7 NB 277

Muskogee, Indian Territory, April 20, 1905.

Sante Ferrante,
  Celestine, Indian Territory.

Dear Sir:

Receipt is hereby acknowledged of your letter of April 14, 1905, asking relative to making application for the enrollment of a child born 11:30 p. m. March 4, 1905.

In reply to your letter you are advised that the act of Congress approved March 3, 1905, authorized the Commission for a period of sixty days from that date to receive applications for the enrollment of children born to enrolled citizens by blood of the

Applications for Enrollment of Choctaw Newborn
Act of 1905   Volume V

Choctaw and Chickasaw Nation prior to March 4, 1905 and living on said latter date. However, if you desire to make application for the enrollment of your child there is inclosed herewith blank which you should have executed and returned to this office as early as practicable.

                    Respectfully,

B.C.   Chairman.

---

7 NB 277

Muskogee, Indian Territory, April 24, 1905.

Andrew J. Turner,
    Celestine, Indian Territory.

Dear Sir:

    Receipt is hereby acknowledged of your letter of April 14, 1905, inclosing affidavits of Isabina Ferranta[sic] and S. P. Ross to the birth of Charley Ferrante, son of Sante Ferrante and Isabina Ferrante, April 10, 1903, and the same have been filed with our records as an application for the enrollment of said child.

                    Respectfully,

                                      Chairman.

Choc New Born 278
    Lee Freeny
    (Born Aug. 29, 1904)

BIRTH AFFIDAVIT.

IN RE-APPLICATION FOR ENROLLMENT, as a citizen of the   Choctaw   Nation, of Lee Freeny , born on the 29th day of Aug , 1904

Name of Father: Reuben Freeney   a citizen of the   Choctaw   Nation.
Name of Mother: Martha Freeny   a citizen of the   Choctaw   Nation.

                    Postoffice   Fitzhugh

Applications for Enrollment of Choctaw Newborn
Act of 1905 Volume V

AFFIDAVIT OF MOTHER.

UNITED STATES OF AMERICA, INDIAN TERRITORY, } Central District.

I, Martha Freeny, on oath state that I am 41 years of age and a citizen by Marriage, of the Choctaw Nation; that I am the lawful wife of Reuben Freeny, who is a citizen, by blood of the Choctaw Nation; that a Male child was born to me on 29th day of Aug, 1904, that said child has been named Lee Freeny, and is now living.

Martha Freeny

Witnesses To Mark:

Subscribed and sworn to before me this 20 day of Mch, 1905.

E. J. Ball
Notary Public.

AFFIDAVIT OF ATTENDING PHYSICIAN OR MID-WIFE.

UNITED STATES OF AMERICA, INDIAN TERRITORY, } Central District.

I, M. P. Skeen, a Physician, on oath state that I attended on Mrs. Martha Freeny, wife of Reuben Freeny on the 29 day of Aug, 1904; that there was born to her on said date a male child; that said child is now living and is said to have been named Lee Freeny

M. P. Skeen

Witnesses To Mark:

Subscribed and sworn to before me this 20 day of Mch, 1905.

E. J. Ball
Notary Public.

Applications for Enrollment of Choctaw Newborn
Act of 1905   Volume V

7-4000

Muskogee, Indian Territory, March 25, 1905.

Reuben Freeny,
    Fitzhugh, Indian Territory.

Dear Sir:

    Receipt is hereby acknowledged of the affidavits of Martha Freeny and M. P. Skeen to the birth of Lee Freeny, son of Reuben and Martha Freeny August 29, 1904, and the same have been filed with our records as an application for the enrollment of said child.

                      Respectfully,

                                    Chairman.

Choc New Born 279
    May Etta Emaline Krebbs
    (Born July 10, 1903)
    Amanda Krebbs
    (Born March 20, 1905)

279

NEW BORN
CHOCTAW
ENROLLMENT

May Etta Emaline Krebbs

(Born July 10, 1903)

Amanda Krebbs

(Born March 20, 1905)

Born subsequent to March 4, 1905.
  Amanda Krebbs transferred to N. B. 416 under
  Act of April 26-'06

Applications for Enrollment of Choctaw Newborn
Act of 1905   Volume V

As Citizen of the
CHOCTAW NATION
Act of Congress
Approved March 3.1905

2 decision rendered as is No. 2 June 30, 1905
  Decline to receive or consider.
  Copy of Decision forwarded, June 30, 1905
  Attorneys for Choctaw and
  Chickasaw nations[sic].
  Copy of Decision forwarded
    Applicant's Father, June 30, 1905
  Record forwarded Department, June 30, 1905
    Action approved by Secretary of interior[sic].
      Oct. 20, 1905
  Notice of departmental action forwarded
  attorneys for Choctaw and Chickasaw nations[sic].
      Oct. 31, 1905
  Notice of departmental action mailed applicant's father
      Oct. 31, 1905

279

BIRTH AFFIDAVIT.

DEPARTMENT OF THE INTERIOR,
COMMISSION TO THE FIVE CIVILIZED TRIBES.

IN RE Application for Enrollment, as a citizen of the Choctaw Nation, of May Etta Emaline Krebbs, born on the 10 day of July, 1903

Name of Father: Benjamin Krebbs   a citizen of the Choctaw Nation.
Name of Mother: Sussie B. Krebbs   a citizen of the United States Nation.

Post-Office: Allen, I.T.

Applications for Enrollment of Choctaw Newborn
Act of 1905   Volume V

AFFIDAVIT OF MOTHER.

UNITED STATES OF AMERICA,
    INDIAN TERRITORY.
  Central   District.

I, Sussie B Krebbs , on oath state that I am 20 years of age and a citizen by ...., of the United States Nation; that I am the lawful wife of Benjamin Krebbs , who is a citizen, by blood of the Choctaw Nation; that a female child was born to me on 10 day of July , 1903, that said child has been named May Etta Emaline Krebbs , and is now living.

                                      her
                                Sussie B. x Krebbs
WITNESSES TO MARK: mark
{ ? Sikes
  L.E. *(Illegible)*

Subscribed and sworn to before me this 29 *day of* July , 1903

                                W.B. Soney
My Com ex May 12, 1906   **NOTARY PUBLIC.**

AFFIDAVIT OF ATTENDING PHYSICIAN OR MID-WIFE.

UNITED STATES OF AMERICA,
    INDIAN TERRITORY.
  Central   District.

I, Waller C. Threlkeld , a Physician , on oath state that I attended on Mrs. Sussie B. Krebbs , wife of Benjamin Krebbs on the 10 day of July , 1903 ; that there was born to her on said date a female child; that said child is now living and is said to have been named May Etta Emaline Krebbs

                                Waller C. Threlkeld M.D.
WITNESSES TO MARK:
{

Subscribed and sworn to before me this 29 *day of* July , 1903

                                W.B. Soney
My Com ex May 12, 1906   **NOTARY PUBLIC.**

Applications for Enrollment of Choctaw Newborn
Act of 1905   Volume V

BIRTH AFFIDAVIT.

DEPARTMENT OF THE INTERIOR.
COMMISSION TO THE FIVE CIVILIZED TRIBES.

IN RE APPLICATION FOR ENROLLMENT, as a citizen of the Choctaw Nation, of May Etta Emaline Krebbs, born on the 10 day of July, 1903

Name of Father: Benjamin Krebbs   a citizen of the Choctaw Nation.
Name of Mother: Susie Bell Krebbs   a citizen of the United States Nation.

Postoffice ....

AFFIDAVIT OF MOTHER.

UNITED STATES OF AMERICA, Indian Territory, }
Central   DISTRICT.   }

I, Susie Bell Krebbs, on oath state that I am 22 years of age and a citizen by ...., of the United States Nation; that I am the lawful wife of Benjamin Krebbs, who is a citizen, by blood of the Choctaw Nation; that a female child was born to me on 10 day of July, 1903; that said child has been named May Etta Emaline Krebbs, and was living March 4, 1905.

                                                      her
                                      Susie Bell x Krebbs
Witnesses To Mark: mark
   { A A Caldwell
   { J.W. Reed

Subscribed and sworn to before me this 10 day of April, 1905

My commission expires   J.L. Cart
June 27 - 1908   Notary Public.

AFFIDAVIT OF ATTENDING PHYSICIAN OR MID-WIFE.

UNITED STATES OF AMERICA, Indian Territory, }
Central   DISTRICT.   }

I, W.C. Threlkeld, a physician, on oath state that I attended on Mrs. Susie Bell Krebbs, wife of Benjamin Krebbs on the 10 day of July, 1903; that there was born to her on said date a female child; that said child was living March 4, 1905, and is said to have been named May Etta Emaline Krebbs

                                        W.C. Threlkeld M.D.

Applications for Enrollment of Choctaw Newborn
Act of 1905   Volume V

Witnesses To Mark:
{

    Subscribed and sworn to before me this 10 day of April   , 1905

                                    J.L. Cart
                                                Notary Public.

BIRTH AFFIDAVIT.

DEPARTMENT OF THE INTERIOR.
COMMISSION TO THE FIVE CIVILIZED TRIBES.

    IN RE APPLICATION FOR ENROLLMENT, as a citizen of the   Choctaw   Nation, of May Etta Emaline Krebbs   , born on the 10   day of   July , 1903

Name of Father: Benjamin Krebbs   a citizen of the   Choctaw   Nation.
Name of Mother: Susie Bell Krebbs   a citizen of the United States Nation.

                          Postoffice   Allen, Indian Territory

---

                      AFFIDAVIT OF MOTHER.

UNITED STATES OF AMERICA, Indian Territory, }
    Central   **DISTRICT.** }

    I,   Susie Bell Krebbs   , on oath state that I am   22   years of age and a citizen by .... , of the   United States Nation; that I am the lawful wife of Benjamin Krebbs   , who is a citizen, by blood   of the   Choctaw Nation; that a   female   child was born to me on 10   day of   July   , 1903; that said child has been named   May Etta Emaline Krebbs   , and was living March 4, 1905.
                                    her
                              Susie Bell x Krebbs
Witnesses To Mark: mark
   { J.W. Ashford
     Bettie Cart

    Subscribed and sworn to before me this 15   day of   April   , 1905

My commission expires   J.L. Cart
   June 27 - 1908   Notary Public.

Applications for Enrollment of Choctaw Newborn
Act of 1905 Volume V

AFFIDAVIT OF ATTENDING PHYSICIAN OR MID-WIFE.

UNITED STATES OF AMERICA, Indian Territory, }
Central   DISTRICT.

I, W.C. Threlkeld , a physician , on oath state that I attended on Mrs. Susie Bell Krebbs , wife of Benjamin Krebbs on the 10 day of July , 1903; that there was born to her on said date a female child; that said child was living March 4, 1905, and is said to have been named May Etta Emaline Krebbs

W.C. Threlkeld M.D.

Witnesses To Mark:
{

Subscribed and sworn to before me this 15 day of April , 1905

My commission expires   J.L. Cart
June 27 - 1908   Notary Public.

7-4008

Muskogee, Indian Territory, August 3, 1903.

Benjamin Krebbs,
   Allen, Indian Territory.

Dear Sir:

    Receipt is hereby acknowledged of the affidavits of Sussie B. Krebbs and Walter[sic] C. Threlkeld relative to the birth of May Etta Emeline[sic] Krebbs, infant daughter of Benjamin and Sussie B. Krebbs, July 10, 1903, which it is presumed have been forwarded as an application for enrollment of the above named child as a citizen of the Choctaw Nation.

    Your attention is invited to Section 28 of the Act of Congress approved July 1, 1902 (32 Stats., 641), which was ratified by the citizens of the Choctaw and Chickasaw Nations September 25, 1902, as follows:

> "The names of all persons living on the date of the final ratification of this agreement entitled to be enrolled as provided in section 27 hereof shall be placed upon the rolls made by said Commission; and no child born thereafter to a citizen or freedman and no person intermarried thereafter to a citizen shall be entitled to enrollment or to participate in the distribution of the tribal property of the Choctaws and Chickasaws."

Applications for Enrollment of Choctaw Newborn
Act of 1905 Volume V

Under the above legislation the Commission is without authority to enroll infant children born to citizens of the Choctaw and Chickasaw Nations subsequent to the date of said ratification, September 25, 1902.

Respectfully,

Commissioner in Charge.

N. B. 279
COPY
Muskogee, Indian Territory, April 7, 1905.

Benjamin Krebbs,
    Allen, Indian Territory.

Dear Sir:

There is inclosed you herewith for execution application for the enrollment of your infant child, May Etta Emaline Krebbs, born July 10, 1903.

The affidavits heretofore filed with the Commission show the child was living on July 29, 1903. It is necessary, for the child to be enrolled, that she was living on March 4, 1905. You will please insert the mother's age in the place left blank for that purpose.

In the above mentioned affidavits, the name of your wife appears as Susie B. Krebbs while the records of the Commission show her as Susie Bell Krebbs. If these two names are of the same person, you will please fill out the inclosed application, and have it signed Susie Bell Krebbs in compliance with the records of the Commission.

In having these affidavits executed care should be exercised to see that all names are written in full, as they appear in the body of the affidavit, and in the event that either of the persons signing the affidavit are unable to write, signatures by mark must be attested by two witnesses. Each affidavit must be executed before a Notary Public and the notarial seal and signature of the officer must be attached to each separate affidavit.

Respectfully
SIGNED
T. B. Needles.
Commissioner in Charge.

SEV2-7

Applications for Enrollment of Choctaw Newborn
Act of 1905   Volume V

Choctaw 4008.

Muskogee, Indian Territory, April 18, 1905.

Benjamin Krebbs,
 Boggy Depot, Indian Territory.

Dear Sir:

Receipt is hereby acknowledged of the affidavits of Susie Bell Krebbs and W. C. Threlkeld to the birth of May Etta Emaline Krebbs, daughter of Benjamin and Susie Bell Krebbs, July 10, 1903, and the same have been filed with our records as an application for the enrollment of said child.

Receipt is also acknowledged of the affidavits of Susie Bell Krebbs and Susan Dunnigan to the birth of Amanda Krebbs, daughter of Benjamin and Susie Bell Krebbs, March 20, 1905, and you are advised that the act of Congress approved March 3, 1905, authorizes the Commission for a period of sixty days from that date to receive applicationf[sic] for the enrollment of children born to citizens by blood of the Choctaw and Chickasaw Nations, subsequent to September 25, 1902, and prior to March 4, 1905, and living on said latter date.

You will therefore see that the Commission is without authority to enroll your child, Amanda Krebbs, which was born March 30, 1905.

Respectfully,

Chairman.

Choctaw N.B. 279.

Muskogee, Indian Territory, April 21, 1905.

Benjamin Krebbs,
 Allen, Indian Territory.

Dear Sir:

Receipt is hereby acknowledged of your letter of April 15, transmitting the affidavits of Susie Bell Krebbs and W. C. Threlkeld to the birth of May Etta Emaline Krebbs, daughter of Benjamin and Susie Bell Krebbs, July 10, 1903, and the same have been filed with our records in the matter of the enrollment of the above named child. matter of the enrollment of said child.

Applications for Enrollment of Choctaw Newborn
Act of 1905   Volume V

Replying to that portion of your letter in which you state that you desire to have your wife, Susie Bell Krebbs placed upon the roll as a citizen by intermarriage of the Choctaw Nation and request a blank for this purpose, you are advised that under the provisions of the act of Congress approved July 1, 1902, the provisions of the Act of Congress approved July 1, 1902, the Commission is without authority to receive or consider applications for enrollment of intermarried citizens in the Choctaw and Chickasaw Nations, and you are further advised that the Commission has no blanks of this character for distribution.

In conclusion you request a plat of the Choctaw and Chickasaw Nations, showing all allotted lands, and in reply you are advised that the Commission has no maps of this character either for sale or distribution.

Respectfully,

Chairman.

7-NB-279

Muskogee, Indian Territory, July 24, 1905.

Benjamin Krebbs,
Allen, Indian Territory.

Dear Sir:

Receipt is hereby acknowledged of your letter of July 15, 1905, asking if Mary[sic] Etter[sic] Emeline Krebbs has been enrolled.

In reply to your letter you are advised that the name of your child May Etta Emaline Krebbs has been placed upon a schedule of citizens by blood of the Choctaw Nation which has been forwarded the Secretary of the Interior, but this office has not yet been notified of Departmental action thereon.

Respectfully,

Commissioner.

Applications for Enrollment of Choctaw Newborn
Act of 1905   Volume V

Choc New Born 280
    Elberta G. McCarter
    (Born Dec. 7, 1903)

NEW-BORN AFFIDAVIT.

Number..............

Choctaw Enrolling Commission.

IN THE MATTER OF THE APPLICATION FOR ENROLLMENT, as a citizen of the Choctaw   Nation, of   Elberta G. McCarter

born on the   7   day of   December   190 3

Name of father   Andrew L. McCarter   a citizen of   Choctaw
Nation final enrollment No   379
Name of mother   Mattie McCarter   a citizen of   Choctaw
Nation final enrollment No   11308

                    Postoffice   Owl I.T.

AFFIDAVIT OF MOTHER.

UNITED STATES OF AMERICA, ⎫
    INDIAN TERRITORY,   ⎬
  Central   DISTRICT   ⎭

    I   Mattie McCarter   , on oath state that I am   30   years of age and a citizen by   Blood   of the   Choctaw   Nation, and as such have been placed upon the final roll of the   Choctaw   Nation, by the Honorable Secretary of the Interior my final enrollment number being   11308   ; that I am the lawful wife of   Andrew L McCarter   , who is a citizen of the   Choctaw Nation, and as such has been placed upon the final roll of said Nation by the Honorable Secretary of the Interior, his final enrollment number being   379   and that a   Female child was born to me on the   7   day of   December   190 3; that said child has been named   Elberta G. McCarter   , and is now living.

WITNESSETH: Mattie McCarter
  Must be two ⎫ Richard Monds
  Witnesses who ⎬
  are Citizens. ⎭ Minerva J. Wallace

    Subscribed and sworn to before me this   19   day of   Jan   190 5

                              John H Cross

Applications for Enrollment of Choctaw Newborn
Act of 1905   Volume V

Notary Public.

My commission expires   Sept 24- 1908

AFFIDAVIT OF ATTENDING PHYSICIAN OR MIDWIFE

UNITED STATES OF AMERICA
INDIAN TERRITORY
  Central   DISTRICT

  I,   Elizabeth Goins   a   Midwife on oath state that I attended on Mrs.   Mattie McCarter   wife of   Andrew L McCarter on the   7   day of   December   , 190 3, that there was born to her on said date a Female   child, that said child is now living, and is said to have been named   Elberta G McCarter
                                                                        her   midwife
                                  Elizabeth x Goins   M.D.
                                              mark
     Subscribed and sworn to before me this, the   19 day of   Jan   190 5

                                       John H Cross
                                              Notary Public.

WITNESSETH:

Must be two witnesses who are citizens and know the child.   { Richard Monds
                                                              Minerva J Wallace

  We hereby certify that we are well acquainted with   Elizabeth Goins a   Midwife   and know   her   to be reputable and of good standing in the community.

                                   Richard Monds
                                   Minerva J Wallace

BIRTH AFFIDAVIT.

DEPARTMENT OF THE INTERIOR.
COMMISSION TO THE FIVE CIVILIZED TRIBES.

  IN RE APPLICATION FOR ENROLLMENT, as a citizen of the   Choctaw   Nation, of Elberta G. McCarter   , born on the   7   day of   Dec   , 1903

Name of Father: Andrew L McCarter   a citizen of the   Choctaw   Nation.
Name of Mother: Mattie McCarter   a citizen of the   Choctaw   Nation.

                    Postoffice   Owl I.T.

Applications for Enrollment of Choctaw Newborn
Act of 1905 Volume V

AFFIDAVIT OF MOTHER.

UNITED STATES OF AMERICA, Indian Territory, }
Central   DISTRICT.

I, Mattie McCarter, on oath state that I am 30 years of age and a citizen by Blood, of the Choctaw Nation; that I am the lawful wife of Andrew L McCarter, who is a citizen, by Intermarriage of the Choctaw Nation; that a Female child was born to me on 7 day of Dec, 1903; that said child has been named Elberta G. McCarter, and was living March 4, 1905.

Mattie McCarter

Witnesses To Mark:
{

Subscribed and sworn to before me this 27 day of March, 1905

John H Cross
Notary Public.

AFFIDAVIT OF ATTENDING PHYSICIAN OR MID-WIFE.

UNITED STATES OF AMERICA, Indian Territory, }
Central   DISTRICT.

I, Elizabeth Goins, a Midwife, on oath state that I attended on Mrs. Mattie McCarter, wife of Andrew L McCarter on the 7 day of Dec, 1903; that there was born to her on said date a Female child; that said child was living March 4, 1905, and is said to have been named Elberta G McCarter

her
Elizabeth x Goins
mark

Witnesses To Mark:
{ Sam *(Illegible)*
  M E Cross

Subscribed and sworn to before me this 27 day of March, 1905

John H Cross
Notary Public.

Applications for Enrollment of Choctaw Newborn
Act of 1905   Volume V

Choctaw N B 280
469

Muskogee, Indian Territory, May 19, 1905.

Andrew L. McCarter,
    Owl, Indian Territory.

Dear Sir:

    Receipt is hereby acknowledged of your letter of May 16, stating that some time ago you forwarded applications for the enrollment of Elberta G. McCarter and Oda Mends, but have heard nothing from them and you ask if they were received.

    In reply to your letter you are advised that the affidavits heretofore forwarded to the birth of Elberta G. McCarter and Oda Mends have been filed with our records as applications for the enrollment of said children.

                    Respectfully,

                              Chairman.

Choc New Born 281
    Leona Wallace
    (Born Feb. 22, 1904)

NEW-BORN AFFIDAVIT.

                Number............

Choctaw Enrolling Commission.

    IN THE MATTER OF THE APPLICATION FOR ENROLLMENT, as a citizen of the Choctaw   Nation, of   Leona G Wallace

born on the   22   day of   Feb   190 4

Name of father   John Wallace   a citizen of   Choctaw

Applications for Enrollment of Choctaw Newborn
Act of 1905 Volume V

Nation final enrollment No   380
Name of mother   Minerva J Wallace   a citizen of   Choctaw
Nation final enrollment No   11313
                           Postoffice   Owl I.T.

AFFIDAVIT OF MOTHER.

UNITED STATES OF AMERICA,
   INDIAN TERRITORY,
     Central   DISTRICT

     I   Minerva J Wallace   , on oath state that I am   36   years of age and a citizen by   Blood   of the   Choctaw   Nation, and as such have been placed upon the final roll of the   Choctaw   Nation, by the Honorable Secretary of the Interior my final enrollment number being   11313   ; that I am the lawful wife of   John Wallace   , who is a citizen of the   Choctaw   Nation, and as such has been placed upon the final roll of said Nation by the Honorable Secretary of the Interior, his final enrollment number being   380   and that a   Female   child was born to me on the   22   day of   Feb   190 4; that said child has been named   Leona G Wallace   , and is now living.

WITNESSETH: Minerva J Wallace
   Must be two   Richard Monds
   Witnesses who
   are Citizens.   Solomon Frazier

     Subscribed and sworn to before me this   19   day of   Jan   190 5

                           John H Cross
                                  Notary Public.

My commission expires   Sept 24 1908

AFFIDAVIT OF ATTENDING PHYSICIAN OR MIDWIFE

UNITED STATES OF AMERICA
INDIAN TERRITORY
   Central   DISTRICT

     I,   Elizabeth Goins   a   Mid wife on oath state that I attended on Mrs.   Minerva J Wallace   wife of   John Wallace on the   22   day of   Feb   , 190 4, that there was born to her on said date a   Female child, that said child is now living, and is said to have been named   Leona G Wallace
                                      her   midwife
                            Elizabeth x Goins   ~~M.D~~.
                                    mark
     Subscribed and sworn to before me this, the   19   day of   Jan   190 5

                             John H Cross
                                  Notary Public.

Applications for Enrollment of Choctaw Newborn
Act of 1905 Volume V

WITNESSETH:

Must be two witnesses who are citizens and know the child. { Richard Monds
Solomon Frazier

We hereby certify that we are well acquainted with   Elizabeth Goins a   Midwife   and know   her   to be reputable and of good standing in the community.

{ Richard Monds
Solomon Frazier

BIRTH AFFIDAVIT.

DEPARTMENT OF THE INTERIOR.
COMMISSION TO THE FIVE CIVILIZED TRIBES.

IN RE APPLICATION FOR ENROLLMENT, as a citizen of the   Choctaw   Nation, of Leona Wallace   , born on the   22   day of   Feb   , 1904

Name of Father: John Wallace   a citizen of the   Choctaw   Nation.
Name of Mother: Minerva J Wallace   a citizen of the   Choctaw   Nation.

Postoffice   Owl I.T.

AFFIDAVIT OF MOTHER.

UNITED STATES OF AMERICA, Indian Territory, }
Central   DISTRICT.

I,   Minerva J Wallace   , on oath state that I am   36   years of age and a citizen by   Blood   , of the   Choctaw   Nation; that I am the lawful wife of John Wallace   , who is a citizen, by Inter Marriage   of the   Choctaw Nation; that a   Female   child was born to me on   22 day of Feb   , 1904; that said child has been named   Leona Wallace   , and was living March 4, 1905.

Minerva J Wallace

Witnesses To Mark:
{

Subscribed and sworn to before me this   27   day of   March   , 1905

John H Cross
Notary Public.

Applications for Enrollment of Choctaw Newborn
Act of 1905 Volume V

AFFIDAVIT OF ATTENDING PHYSICIAN OR MID-WIFE.

UNITED STATES OF AMERICA, Indian Territory,
 Central   DISTRICT.

    I, Elizabeth Goins , a midwife , on oath state that I attended on Mrs. Minerva J Wallace , wife of John Wallace on the 22 day of Feb, 1904; that there was born to her on said date a Female child; that said child was living March 4, 1905, and is said to have been named Leona Wallace

                                          her
                                 Elizabeth x Goins
Witnesses To Mark: mark
   { Sam Self
     M E Cross

    Subscribed and sworn to before me this 27 day of March , 1905

                                 John H Cross
                                   Notary Public.

Choc New Born 282
      Jane Armstrong
      (Born Dec. 15, 1903)

NEW BORN AFFIDAVIT

No

CHOCTAW ENROLLING COMMISSION

    IN THE MATTER OF THE APPLICATION FOR ENROLLMENT as a citizen of the Choctaw Nation, of Jain[sic] Armstrong born on the 15th day of December 190 3

    Name of father Louis Armstrong a citizen of Choctaw Nation, final enrollment No. 23279
    Name of mother Eliza Armstrong a citizen of Choctaw Nation, final enrollment No. 11421

Applications for Enrollment of Choctaw Newborn
Act of 1905   Volume V

Atoka I.T. Postoffice.

AFFIDAVIT OF MOTHER

UNITED STATES OF AMERICA
   INDIAN TERRITORY
DISTRICT   Central

I Eliza Armstrong , on oath state that I am 27 years of age and a citizen by blood of the Choctaw Nation, and as such have been placed upon the final roll of the Choctaw Nation, by the Honorable Secretary of the Interior my final enrollment number being 11421 ; that I am the lawful wife of Louis Armstrong , who is a citizen of the Choctaw Nation, and as such has been placed upon the final roll of said Nation by the Honorable Secretary of the Interior, his final enrollment number being 12179 and that a Female child was born to me on the 15th day of December 190 3; that said child has been named Jain[sic] Armstrong , and is now living.

                                                       her
WITNESSETH: Eliza x Armstrong
  Must be two witnesses { Eastman Jacob   mark
  who are citizens   Sinnie Jacob

Subscribed and sworn to before me this, the 22nd day of February 190 5

                                      A.E. Folsom
                                                 Notary Public.

My Commission Expires:
Jan 9 - 1909

Affidavit of Attending Physician or Midwife

UNITED STATES OF AMERICA,
   INDIAN TERRITORY,
Central   DISTRICT

I, Louis Armstrong a The Father of Child on oath state that I attended on Mrs. Eliza Armstrong wife of Louis Armstrong on the 15th day of December , 190 3, that there was born to her on said date a Female child, that said child is now living, and is said to have been named Jane Armstrong

                                                             Father Child
                                       Louis Armstrong   M.D.

Subscribed and sworn to before me this the 22nd day of February 1905

                                            A E Folsom

Applications for Enrollment of Choctaw Newborn
Act of 1905 Volume V

Notary Public.

WITNESSETH:
Must be two witnesses who are citizens and know the child. { Eastman Jacob
Sinnie Jacob

We hereby certify that we are well acquainted with Louis Armstrong a The father of child and know him to be reputable and of good standing in the community.

Must be two citizen witnesses. { Eastman Jacob
Sinnie Jacob

BIRTH AFFIDAVIT.

DEPARTMENT OF THE INTERIOR.
COMMISSION TO THE FIVE CIVILIZED TRIBES.

IN RE APPLICATION FOR ENROLLMENT, as a citizen of the Choctaw Nation, of Jane Armstrong , born on the 15th day of December , 1903

Name of Father: Lewis[sic] Armstrong   a citizen of the Choctaw Nation.
Name of Mother: Eliza Armstrong   a citizen of the Choctaw Nation.

Postoffice   Atoka, I.T.

AFFIDAVIT OF MOTHER.

UNITED STATES OF AMERICA, Indian Territory, }
Central   DISTRICT.

I, Eliza Armstrong , on oath state that I am 24 years of age and a citizen by blood , of the Choctaw Nation; that I am the lawful wife of Lewis Armstrong , who is a citizen, by blood of the Choctaw Nation; that a female child was born to me on 15th day of December , 1903; that said child has been named Jane Armstrong , and was living March 4, 1905.

her
Eliza x Armstrong
mark

Witnesses To Mark:
{ Richard Shanafelt
D. Shelon

Subscribed and sworn to before me this 24th day of March , 1905

W. H. Angell

Applications for Enrollment of Choctaw Newborn
Act of 1905   Volume V

Notary Public.

Husband
AFFIDAVIT OF ~~ATTENDING PHYSICIAN OR MID-WIFE.~~

UNITED STATES OF AMERICA, Indian Territory, }
Central   DISTRICT. }

I, Lewis Armstrong   , a ———   , on oath state that I attended on Mrs. Eliza Armstrong my , wife of —————— on the 15th day of December , 1903; that there was born to her on said date a   female   child; that said child was living March 4, 1905, and is said to have been named Jane Armstrong and that there was no one present on said date except myself and said wife Eliza Armstrong

Lewis Armstrong

Witnesses To Mark:
{

Subscribed and sworn to before me this 24th day of March   , 1905

W. H. Angell
Notary Public.

BIRTH AFFIDAVIT.

DEPARTMENT OF THE INTERIOR.
COMMISSION TO THE FIVE CIVILIZED TRIBES.

IN RE APPLICATION FOR ENROLLMENT, as a citizen of the   Choctaw   Nation, of Jane Armstrong   , born on the 15th day of December , 1903

Name of Father: Lewis Armstrong   a citizen of the   Choctaw   Nation.
Name of Mother: Eliza Armstrong   a citizen of the   Choctaw   Nation.

Postoffice   Atoka, I.T.

Acquaintance
AFFIDAVIT OF ~~MOTHER~~.

UNITED STATES OF AMERICA, Indian Territory, }
Central   DISTRICT. }

I,   Morrow Armstrong   , on oath state that I am   32   years of age and a citizen by   blood   , of the   Choctaw   Nation; that I am ~~the lawful wife of~~ personally acquainted with Eliza Armstrong , who is a citizen, by blood   of the   Choctaw   Nation; that a   female   child was born to ~~me~~ her on 15th   day of

169

Applications for Enrollment of Choctaw Newborn
Act of 1905   Volume V

December   , 1903; that said child has been named   Jane Armstrong   , and was living March 4, 1905.

                                       Morrow Armstrong

Witnesses To Mark:

       Subscribed and sworn to before me this 19th day of April   , 1905

                                 W. H. Angell
                                      Notary Public.

                             Acquaintance
AFFIDAVIT OF ~~ATTENDING PHYSICIAN OR MID-WIFE.~~

UNITED STATES OF AMERICA, Indian Territory,
    Central   DISTRICT.

     I, Anna Armstrong   , a ——————— , on oath state that I ~~attended on~~ am personally acquainted with Mrs. Eliza Armstrong , wife of Lewis Armstrong and that on the 15th day of December , 1903; ~~that~~ there was born to her on said date a female   child; that said child was living March 4, 1905, and is said to have been named Jane Armstrong

                              her
                         Anna x Armstrong
Witnesses To Mark: mark
   W.J. Martin
   Arthur O. Archer

       Subscribed and sworn to before me this 19th day of April   , 1905

                                 W. H. Angell
                                      Notary Public.

Wm O. B.

| COMMISSIONERS:
TAMS BIXBY,
THOMAS B. NEEDLES,
C.R. BRECKINBRIDGE.

WM. O. BEALL
Secretary | **DEPARTMENT OF THE INTERIOR,**
COMMISSIONER TO THE FIVE CIVILIZED TRIBES. | REFER IN REPLY TO THE FOLLOWING:

N.B. 282. |

ADDRESS ONLY THE
COMMISSION TO THE FIVE CIVILIZED TRIBES.

                            Muskogee, Indian Territory, April 7, 1905.

Lewis Armstrong,
    Atoka, Indian Territory.

Dear Sir:

Applications for Enrollment of Choctaw Newborn
Act of 1905   Volume V

Referring to the application for the enrollment of your infant child, Jane Armstrong, born December 15, 1903, it appears from your affidavit on file with the Commission that there was no one except yourself in attendance upon your wife at the birth of the applicant. In this event, it will be necessary that you secure the affidavits of two persons who have actual knowledge of the fact that the child was born, when she was born, that she was living on March 4, 1905 and that Eliza Armstrong is her mother.

In having these affidavits executed care should be exercised to see that all names are written in full, as they appear in the body of the affidavit, and in the event that either of the persons signing the affidavit are unable to write, signatures by mark must be attested by two witnesses. Each affidavit must be executed before a Notary Public and the notarial seal and signature of the officer must be attached to each separate affidavit.

Respectfully,
T.B. Needles
SEV 5-7.   Commissioner in Charge.

Choc New Born 283
    Reason Jacob
    (Born Sep. 11, 1903)

NEW BORN AFFIDAVIT

No ....

CHOCTAW ENROLLING COMMISSION

IN THE MATTER OF THE APPLICATION FOR ENROLLMENT as a citizen of the Choctaw Nation, of   Reason Jacob   born on the 11th day of   September   190 3

Name of father Eastman Jacob   a citizen of   Choctaw   Nation,
final enrollment No. 11419
Name of mother Sina Jacob   a citizen of   Choctaw   Nation,
final enrollment No. 11447

Atoka I.T.   Postoffice.

Applications for Enrollment of Choctaw Newborn
Act of 1905 Volume V

AFFIDAVIT OF MOTHER

UNITED STATES OF AMERICA }
INDIAN TERRITORY }
DISTRICT   Central }

I   Sina Jacob   , on oath state that I am   34[sic]   years of age and a citizen by   blood   of the   Choctaw   Nation, and as such have been placed upon the final roll of the   Choctaw   Nation, by the Honorable Secretary of the Interior my final enrollment number being   11447   ; that I am the lawful wife of   Eastman Jacob   , who is a citizen of the   Choctaw   Nation, and as such has been placed upon the final roll of said Nation by the Honorable Secretary of the Interior, his final enrollment number being   11419   and that a   Male   child was born to me on the   11th day of   September   190 3; that said child has been named   Reason Jacob   , and is now living.

WITNESSETH: Sina Jacob

Must be two witnesses { Lewis Armstrong
who are citizens   { W.E. Dandridge

Subscribed and sworn to before me this, the   22^d day of   February   190 5

A.E. Folsom
Notary Public.

My Commission Expires:
Jan 9 - 1909

Affidavit of Attending Physician or Midwife

UNITED STATES OF AMERICA, }
INDIAN TERRITORY, }
Central   DISTRICT }

I,   Eastman Jacob   a   The Husband & father   on oath state that I attended on Mrs.   Sina Jacob   wife of   Eastman Jacob   on the   11th day of   September   , 190 3, that there was born to her on said date a   male   child, that said child is now living, and is said to have been named   Reason Jacob

Eastman Jacob   The Father   M.D.

Subscribed and sworn to before me this the   22^d day of   February   1905

A.E. Folsom
Notary Public.

Applications for Enrollment of Choctaw Newborn
Act of 1905   Volume V

WITNESSETH:

Must be two witnesses who are citizens and know the child.
{ Lewis Armstrong
  W.E. Dandridge

We hereby certify that we are well acquainted with Eastman Jacob a The Father of child and know him to be reputable and of good standing in the community.

Must be two citizen witnesses.
{ Lewis Armstrong
  W.E. Dandridge

BIRTH AFFIDAVIT.

DEPARTMENT OF THE INTERIOR.
COMMISSION TO THE FIVE CIVILIZED TRIBES.

IN RE APPLICATION FOR ENROLLMENT, as a citizen of the Choctaw Nation, of Reason Jacob , born on the 11th day of September , 1903

Name of Father: Eastman Jacob   a citizen of the Choctaw Nation.
Name of Mother: Sina Jacob   a citizen of the Choctaw Nation.

Postoffice   Atoka, I.T.

AFFIDAVIT OF MOTHER.

UNITED STATES OF AMERICA, Indian Territory,
Central   DISTRICT.

I, Sina Jacob , on oath state that I am 24 years of age and a citizen by blood , of the Choctaw Nation; that I am the lawful wife of Eastman Jacob , who is a citizen, by blood of the Choctaw Nation; that a male child was born to me on 11th day of September , 1903; that said child has been named Reason Jacob , and was living March 4, 1905.

Sina Jacob

Witnesses To Mark:

Subscribed and sworn to before me this 20th day of March , 1905

W.H. Angell
Notary Public.

Applications for Enrollment of Choctaw Newborn
Act of 1905   Volume V

Husband
AFFIDAVIT OF ~~ATTENDING PHYSICIAN OR MID-WIFE~~.

UNITED STATES OF AMERICA, Indian Territory,
Central   DISTRICT.

I, Eastman Jacob , a ——————— , on oath state that I ~~attended on~~ am the husband of Mrs. Sina Jacob , ~~wife of~~ and that on the 11th day of September , 1903; that there was born to her on said date a male child; that said child was living March 4, 1905, and is said to have been named Reason Jacob and that no one present at the time of his birth except myself and said wife

Eastman Jacob

Witnesses To Mark:

Subscribed and sworn to before me this 20th day of March , 1905

W.H. Angell
Notary Public.

BIRTH AFFIDAVIT.

DEPARTMENT OF THE INTERIOR.
COMMISSION TO THE FIVE CIVILIZED TRIBES.

IN RE APPLICATION FOR ENROLLMENT, as a citizen of the Choctaw Nation, of Reason Jacob , born on the 11th day of September , 1903

Name of Father: Eastman Jacob   a citizen of the Choctaw Nation.
Name of Mother: Sina Jacob   a citizen of the Choctaw Nation.

Postoffice   Atoka, I.T.

AFFIDAVIT OF MOTHER.

UNITED STATES OF AMERICA, Indian Territory,
Central   DISTRICT.

I, Nelson Jacob , on oath state that I am 25 years of age and a citizen by blood , of the Choctaw Nation; that I am ~~the lawful wife of~~ personally acquainted with Sina Jacob wife of Eastman Jacob , who is a citizen, by blood of

174

Applications for Enrollment of Choctaw Newborn
Act of 1905   Volume V

the   Choctaw   Nation; that a   male   child was born to ~~me~~ her on the 11th day of   September   , 1903; that said child has been named   Reason Jacob   , and was living March 4, 1905.

           Nelson Jacob

Witnesses To Mark:
{

  Subscribed and sworn to before me this   21st day of   April   , 1905

           W.H. Angell
           Notary Public.

AFFIDAVIT OF ATTENDING PHYSICIAN OR MID-WIFE.

UNITED STATES OF AMERICA, Indian Territory,
 Central   DISTRICT.

  I,   Ellis Armstrong   , a ———— , on oath state that I ~~attended on~~ am personally acquainted with Mrs.   Sina Jacob   , wife of   Eastman Jacob that on the   11th day of   September   , 1903; that there was born to her on said date a male   child; that said child was living March 4, 1905, and is said to have been named Reason Jacob

          Ellis Armstrong

Witnesses To Mark:
{

  Subscribed and sworn to before me this   21st day of   April   , 1905

           W.H. Angell
           Notary Public.

$W^m O.B.$

COMMISSIONERS:	**DEPARTMENT OF THE INTERIOR,**	REFER IN REPLY TO THE FOLLOWING:
TAMS BIXBY, THOMAS B. NEEDLES, C.R. BRECKINRIDGE.	**COMMISSIONER TO THE FIVE CIVILIZED TRIBES.**	N.B. 283
WM. O. BEALL Secretary		

ADDRESS ONLY THE
COMMISSION TO THE FIVE CIVILIZED TRIBES.

         Muskogee, Indian Territory, April 7, 1905.

Eastman Jacob,
  Atoka, Indian Territory.

Dear Sir:

Applications for Enrollment of Choctaw Newborn
Act of 1905   Volume V

    In the application for the enrollment of your infant child, Reason Jacob, born September 11, 1903, heretofore filed with the Commission, you state that there was no one except yourself in attendance upon your wife at the birth of the applicant. If this is the case, it will be necessary that you secure the affidavits of two persons who know the child was born, giving date of birth, that he was living on March 4, 1905, and that Sina Jacob was his mother.

    In having these affidavits executed, care should be exercised to see that all names are written in full, as they appear in the body of the affidavit, and in the event that either of the persons signing the affidavit are unable to write, signatures by mark must be attested by two witnesses. Each affidavit must be executed before a Notary Public and the notarial seal and signature of the officer must be attached to each separate affidavit.

                                      Respectfully,

                                                   T.B. Needles
                                                 Commissioner in Charge.

Choc New Born 284
        Octavia Belle Bolling
        (Born Aug. 12, 1903)
        Theodore Dickson Bolling
        (Born Sep. 16, 1904)

BIRTH AFFIDAVIT.

DEPARTMENT OF THE INTERIOR,
COMMISSION TO THE FIVE CIVILIZED TRIBES.

    In Re Application for Enrollment, as a citizen of the   Choctaw   Nation, of ...., born on the .... day of ...., 1........

Name of Father: Walter C. Bolling   a citizen of the Choctaw Nation.
Name of Mother: Hayzell[sic] Belle Bolling   a citizen of the Choctaw Nation.

                                Post-office   Canadian Indian Territory

AFFIDAVIT OF MOTHER.

UNITED STATES OF AMERICA, }
    INDIAN TERRITORY,

Applications for Enrollment of Choctaw Newborn
Act of 1905 Volume V

Western District.

I, Hazel Bell Bolling , on oath state that I am 19 years of age and a citizen by Intermarriage , of the Choctaw Nation; that I am the lawful wife of Walter C. Bolling , who is a citizen, by Blood of the Choctaw Nation; that a Female child was born to me on 12 day of August , 1903 , that said child has been named Octovia[sic] Belle Bolling , and is now living.

Hazel Belle[sic] Bolling

WITNESSES TO MARK:

Subscribed and sworn to before me this 21st day of Mar , 1904

J.D. Browder
NOTARY PUBLIC.

AFFIDAVIT OF ATTENDING PHYSICIAN OR MID-WIFE.

UNITED STATES OF AMERICA,
INDIAN TERRITORY,
Western District.

I, J A Adams M.D. , a Physician , on oath state that I attended on Mrs. Walter C Bolling , wife of Walter C Bolling on the 12 day of August , 1903 ; that there was born to her on said date a Female child; that said child is now living and is said to have been named Octovia Belle Bolling

J.A. Adams, M.D.

WITNESSES TO MARK:

Subscribed and sworn to before me this 21 day of Mar , 1904.

J.D. Browder
NOTARY PUBLIC.

AFFIDAVIT OF ATTENDING PHYSICIAN OR MIDWIFE

UNITED STATES OF AMERICA
INDIAN TERRITORY
Western DISTRICT

I, J A Adams a Physician

Applications for Enrollment of Choctaw Newborn
Act of 1905 Volume V

on oath state that I attended on Mrs. Hazel Bell Bolling wife of Walter C Bolling on the 12 day of Aug, 190 3, that there was born to her on said date a Female child, that said child is now living, and is said to have been named Octovia Belle Bolling

J A Adams M.D.

WITNESSETH:
Must be two witnesses who are citizens and know the child.
{ M.C. Young
  (Name Illegible) }

Subscribed and sworn to before me this, the 20th day of Feb 190 5

JD Browder Notary Public.

We hereby certify that we are well acquainted with ~~Hazel Bell Bolling~~ J A Adams a~~nd Walter C Bolling~~ Physician and know ~~them~~ him to be reputable and of good standing in the community.

{ MC Young
  (Name Illegible) }

NEW-BORN AFFIDAVIT.

Number................

...Choctaw Enrolling Commission...

IN THE MATTER OF THE APPLICATION FOR ENROLLMENT, as a citizen of the Choctaw Nation, of Octavia Belle Bolling

born on the 12th day of August 190 3

Name of father Walter C Bolling a citizen of Choctaw
Nation final enrollment No. 11467
Name of mother Hazel Belle Bolling a citizen of Choctaw
Nation final enrollment No. D775

Postoffice McAlester I.T.

AFFIDAVIT OF MOTHER.

UNITED STATES OF AMERICA
INDIAN TERRITORY
 Central DISTRICT

Applications for Enrollment of Choctaw Newborn
Act of 1905 Volume V

I Hazel Belle Bolling , on oath state that I am 20 years of age and a citizen by Marriage of the Choctaw Nation, and as such have been placed upon the final roll of the Choctaw Nation, by the Honorable Secretary of the Interior my final enrollment number being D775 ; that I am the lawful wife of Walter C Bolling , who is a citizen of the Choctaw Nation, and as such has been placed upon the final roll of said Nation by the Honorable Secretary of the Interior, his final enrollment number being 11467 and that a Female child was born to me on the 12th day of August 190 3; that said child has been named Octavia Belle Bolling , and is now living.

Witnesseth. Hazel Belle Bolling

Must be two Witnesses who are Citizens. } Gilbert Ansley

E.T. Richards

Subscribed and sworn to before me this 7th day of March 190 5

DW Hopkins
Notary Public.

My commission expires:
Dec 15th 1905

NEW-BORN AFFIDAVIT.

Number..............

...Choctaw Enrolling Commission...

IN THE MATTER OF THE APPLICATION FOR ENROLLMENT, as a citizen of the Choctaw Nation, of Theodore Dickson Bolling

born on the 16th day of September 190 4

Name of father Walter C Bolling a citizen of Choctaw Nation final enrollment No. 11467
Name of mother Hazel Belle Bolling a citizen of Choctaw Nation final enrollment No. D775

Postoffice McAlester I.T.

AFFIDAVIT OF MOTHER.

UNITED STATES OF AMERICA
INDIAN TERRITORY
 Central DISTRICT

I Hazel Belle Bolling , on oath state that I am

Applications for Enrollment of Choctaw Newborn
Act of 1905 Volume V

20 years of age and a citizen by Marriage of the Choctaw Nation, and as such have been placed upon the final roll of the Choctaw Nation, by the Honorable Secretary of the Interior my final enrollment number being D775 ; that I am the lawful wife of Walter C Bolling , who is a citizen of the Choctaw Nation, and as such has been placed upon the final roll of said Nation by the Honorable Secretary of the Interior, his final enrollment number being 11467 and that a Male child was born to me on the 16th day of September 190 4; that said child has been named Theodore Dickson Bolling , and is now living.

Witnesseth.   Hazel Belle Bolling
Must be two ⎫ Gilbert Ansley
Witnesses who ⎬
are Citizens. ⎭   E.T. Richards

Subscribed and sworn to before me this 7th day of March 190 5

DW Hopkins
Notary Public.

My commission expires:
Dec 15" 1905

AFFIDAVIT OF ATTENDING PHYSICIAN OR MIDWIFE

UNITED STATES OF AMERICA
INDIAN TERRITORY
Central   DISTRICT

I, Geo N Fleming   a   Physician on oath state that I attended on Mrs. Hazell Bell Bolling wife of Walter C Bolling on the 16th day of September , 190 4, that there was born to her on said date a Male child, that said child is now living, and is said to have been named Theodore Dickson Bolling

Geo N Fleming   M.D.

WITNESSETH:
Must be two witnesses ⎧ Gilbert Ansley
who are citizens and ⎨
know the child.   ⎩ E.T. Richards

Subscribed and sworn to before me this, the 7th day of March   190 5

D W Hopkins   Notary Public.

We hereby certify that we are well acquainted with ~~Walter C Bolling~~ Geo N Fleming a ~~Hazell Belle Bolling~~ Physician and know ~~them~~ him to be reputable and of good standing in the community.

Gilbert Ansley

180

Applications for Enrollment of Choctaw Newborn
Act of 1905 Volume V

E.T. Richards

BIRTH AFFIDAVIT.

DEPARTMENT OF THE INTERIOR.
COMMISSION TO THE FIVE CIVILIZED TRIBES.

IN RE APPLICATION FOR ENROLLMENT, as a citizen of the Choctaw Nation, of Theodore Dickson Bolling, born on the 16th day of September, 1904

Name of Father: Walter C Bolling   a citizen of the Choctaw Nation.
Name of Mother: Hazell Belle Bolling   a citizen of the Choctaw Nation.

Postoffice   McAlester Ind. Ter.

AFFIDAVIT OF MOTHER.

UNITED STATES OF AMERICA, Indian Territory, }
    Central   DISTRICT. }

I, Hazell Belle Bolling, on oath state that I am 20 years of age and a citizen by Marriage, of the Choctaw Nation; that I am the lawful wife of Walter C Bolling, who is a citizen, by Blood of the Choctaw Nation; that a Male child was born to me on 16th day of September, 1904, that said child has been named Theodore Dickson Bolling, and is now living.

                                       Hazel Belle Bolling

Witnesses To Mark:
{

Subscribed and sworn to before me this 13th day of March, 1905.

                                       DW Hopkins
                                           Notary Public.

AFFIDAVIT OF ATTENDING PHYSICIAN OR MID-WIFE.

UNITED STATES OF AMERICA, Indian Territory, }
    Central   DISTRICT. }

I, Geo N Fleming, a Physician, on oath state that I attended on Mrs. Hazel Belle Boling[sic], wife of Walter C Bolling on the 16th day of

Applications for Enrollment of Choctaw Newborn
Act of 1905 Volume V

Sept , 1904; that there was born to her on said date a Male child; that said child is now living and is said to have been named Theodore Dickson Bolling

Geo N. Fleming, M.D.

Witnesses To Mark:

{ Subscribed and sworn to before me this 13th day of March , 1905.

DW Hopkins
Notary Public.

BIRTH AFFIDAVIT.

DEPARTMENT OF THE INTERIOR.
COMMISSION TO THE FIVE CIVILIZED TRIBES.

IN RE APPLICATION FOR ENROLLMENT, as a citizen of the Choctaw Nation, of Octavia Belle Bolling , born on the 12 day of August , 1903

Name of Father: Walter C Bolling   a citizen of the Choctaw Nation.
Name of Mother: Hazel Belle Bolling   a citizen of the .... Nation.

Postoffice Canadian, I.T.

AFFIDAVIT OF MOTHER.

UNITED STATES OF AMERICA, Indian Territory, ⎫
    Central   DISTRICT. ⎭

I, Hazel Belle Bolling , on oath state that I am 20 years of age and a citizen by intermarriage , of the Choctaw Nation; that I am the lawful wife of Walter C Bolling , who is a citizen, by blood of the Choctaw Nation; that a female child was born to me on 12 day of August , 1903; that said child has been named Octavia Belle Bolling , and was living March 4, 1905.

Hazel Belle Bolling

Witnesses To Mark:

{

Subscribed and sworn to before me this 12" day of April , 1905

DW Hopkins
Notary Public.

Applications for Enrollment of Choctaw Newborn
Act of 1905 Volume V

AFFIDAVIT OF ATTENDING PHYSICIAN OR MID-WIFE.

UNITED STATES OF AMERICA, ~~Indian Territory,~~
The State of Texas
County of Rockwell   ~~DISTRICT.~~

    I, J A Adams, a Physician, on oath state that I attended on Mrs. Hazel Belle Bolling, wife of Walter C Bolling on the 12 day of August, 1903; that there was born to her on said date a female child; that said child was living March 4, 1905, and is said to have been named Octavia Belle Bolling

                                          J.A. Adams, M.D.
Witnesses To Mark:
{

    Subscribed and sworn to before me this 18th day of April, 1905

                                 Geo O Wallace Notary Public
                                 Rockwell County Tx. ~~Notary Public.~~

7-4095

Muskogee, Indian Territory, March 18, 1905.

W. C. Bolling,
    McAlester, Indian Territory.

Dear Sir:

    Receipt is hereby acknowledged of your letter of March 13, 1905, enclosing the affidavits of Hazel Belle Bolling and George N. Fleming M. D., to the birth of Theodore Dixon[sic] Bolling, infant son of Walter and Hazel Belle Bolling, September 16, 1904, and the same have been filed with our records as an application for the enrollment of said child.

                      Respectfully,

                                              Chairman.

Applications for Enrollment of Choctaw Newborn
Act of 1905 Volume V

7-4095

Muskogee, Indian Territory, March 28, 1905.

Walter C. Bolling,
    McAlester, Indian Territory.

Dear Sir:

    Receipt is hereby acknowledged of your letter of March 21, 1905, in which you state that you mailed the affidavits of your wife Hazel Belle Bolling and Dr. J. A. Adams, to the birth of your infant daughter August 12, 1903, and you ask if this application is sufficient to have your child placed upon the roll.

    In reply to your letter you are informed that the affidavits heretofore forwarded by you to the birth of your child Octavia B. Bolling August 12, 1903, have been filed with our records as an application for the enrollment of said child. In event further evidence is necessary to enable the Commission to determine her right to enrollment you will be duly notified.

                                                    Respectfully,

                                                          Chairman.

N. B. 284

Muskogee, Indian Territory, April 7, 1905.

Walter C. Bolling,
    Canadian, Indian Territory.

Dear Sir:

    There is inclosed you herewith for execution application for the enrollment of your infant child, Octavia Belle Bolling, born August 12, 1903.

    The affidavits heretofore filed with the Commission show the child was living on March 21, 1904. It is necessary, for the child to be enrolled, that she was living on March 4, 1905.

    In having these affidavits executed care should be exercised to see that all names are written in full, as they appear in the body of the affidavit, and in the event that either of the persons signing the affidavit are unable to write, signatures by mark must be attested by two witnesses. Each affidavit must be executed before a Notary Public and the notarial seal and signature of the officer must be attached to each separate affidavit.

Applications for Enrollment of Choctaw Newborn
Act of 1905   Volume V

Respectfully,

SEV 10-7.

Commissioner in Charge.

Choctaw N.B. 284.

Muskogee, Indian Territory, April 22, 1905.

Walter C. Bolling,
    McAlester, Indian Territory.

Dear Sir:

    Receipt is hereby acknowledged of your letter of April 19, transmitting the affidavits of Hazel Belle Bolling and J. A. Adams to the birth of Octavia Belle Bolling, daughter of Walter C. and Hazel Belle Bolling, August 12, 1903, and the same have been filed the our records in the matter of the enrollment of said child.

    Replying to that portion of your letter in which you ask if you can hold land pending the approval of the enrollment of your children, you are advised that no reservation of land or selection of allotment can be made for children for whom application is made under the Act of Congress approved March 3, 1905, until their enrollment is approved by the Secretary of the Interior.

Respectfully,

Chairman.

Applications for Enrollment of Choctaw Newborn
Act of 1905   Volume V

Choc New Born 285
    Sinie Carnes
    (Born Jan. 10, 1903)

Smithville, Indian Territory, April 14, 1905.

Know all men by these presents :-

That this is to certify that Mr. Ellis Carnes of Mayhew, I.T. a citizen of the Choctaw Nation and Miss Rebecca Roberts of Mayhew, I.T. a citizen of the Choctaw Nation were united by me in the Holy Bond of matrimony at Sugar Loaf Church (Nanih-Hikeya) in Jacks' Fork County, Choctaw Nation, in the presence of Jackson Graham, Indian Territory Wisey Durant and other n the 15th day of June 1901.

    This 14 day of April A.D. 1905.

                Wm H. McKinney
                Minister of the
                Gospel

United States of America,
    Indian Territory,
Central Judicial District.

    I, Ellis Carnes, after having been first duly sworn, state- I am about 34 years of age and reside in the forks of Boggy north of Boswell, I.T.

    On the 15th day of June 1901, as best I remember, I was married to Rebecca Roberts, a daughter of Laymon Roberts, a full blood Choctaw, about five miles north west of Antlers, I.T. at a place called Naneh Hekya Church by W.H. McKinney, at that time a Methodist Minister of the Gospel-His home is at or near Antlers, I.T. I did not get a certificate-Vicy Durant, Indian Territory wife of Wilson Durant living about 3 miles south of Boswell Simeon Wesley, of Antlers, Indian Territory Sarah Alison of Calloway, or Beatley, and E. D. Wesley of Antlers were present.

    My wife was enrolled as Rebecca Roberts-She died on the 8th day of August 1904- The infant I am making application to have enrolled, Sinnie Carnes was born on the 10 day of January 1903 about two miles west of the old Court grounds in the forks of Boggy- I was about two miles from home at the time -I have raised it and have it in my possession now and know that it is a daughter of myself and my said wife.

                Ellis Carnes

Applications for Enrollment of Choctaw Newborn
Act of 1905   Volume V

Subscribed and sworn to before me this the 23rd day of March 1905.

                       L.D. Horton
                               Notary Public.

(The affidavit below typed as given)

United States of America,
    Indian Territory,
Central Judicial District:

    We, J.J. Tomokins, 57 years old and Lake Oshta, about 70 years old, after being first duly sworn state--That we are residents of the Central District of the Indian Territory and resided near where Ellis Carnes lived In 1903 and continue to reside there- We are acquainted with Ellis Carnes and were acquainted with his wife Rebecca Carnes and are acquainted with the baby Siney Carnes and know of our own personal knowledge that said Siney was born about the time above mentioned and. and about the 10th day of January 1903- That we were each frequently at the house of said Ellis Carnes and that we saw said Sinie while only a few minutes old and know that it it still living.having seen said Sinie in the last two days-

                               J.J. Tompkins

Witness

    (Illegible) Phillips   Loker Oshta

    J.J. Tompkins

Subscribed and sworn to before me this the 15th day of April 1905.

                               L. D. Horton
                                  Notary Public.

BIRTH AFFIDAVIT.

DEPARTMENT OF THE INTERIOR.
COMMISSION TO THE FIVE CIVILIZED TRIBES.

    IN RE APPLICATION FOR ENROLLMENT, as a citizen of the   Choctaw   Nation, of Sinie Carnes   , born on the 10   day of January , 1903

Name of Father: Ellis Carnes   a citizen of the   Choctaw   Nation.
Name of Mother: Rebecca Carnes   a citizen of the   Choctaw   Nation.

                        Postoffice   Boswell, I.T.

Applications for Enrollment of Choctaw Newborn
Act of 1905   Volume V

Father
AFFIDAVIT OF ~~MOTHER~~.

UNITED STATES OF AMERICA, Indian Territory,
Central Judicial   DISTRICT.

I, Ellis Carnes, on oath state that I am 34 (about) years of age and a citizen by blood, of the Choctaw Nation; that I am the lawful ~~wife~~ husband of Rebecca Carnes, deceased, who ~~is~~ was a citizen, by blood of the Choctaw Nation; that a female child was born to the said Rebecca Carnes ~~me~~ on 10th day of January, 1903; that said child has been named Sinie Carnes, and was living March 4, 1905.

Ellis Carnes

Witnesses To Mark:

Subscribed and sworn to before me this 23 day of March, 1905

L.D. Horton
Notary Public.

AFFIDAVIT OF ATTENDING PHYSICIAN OR MID-WIFE.

UNITED STATES OF AMERICA, Indian Territory,
Central Judicial   DISTRICT.

I, Laymon Roberts father of Rebecca Carnes, deceased, on oath state that I attended on Mrs. Rebecca Carnes, wife of Ellis Carnes on the 10 day of January, 1903; that there was born to her on said date a female child; that said child was living March 4, 1905, and is said to have been named Sinie
I was not there the exact time Sinie was born, but in a few minutes thereafter and no other physician or midwife was present.

his
Laymon x Roberts
mark

Witnesses To Mark:
Ellis Carnes
L.D. Horton

Subscribed and sworn to before me this 24 day of March, 1905

L.D. Horton
Notary Public.

Applications for Enrollment of Choctaw Newborn
Act of 1905 Volume V

7-4100

7-4321

Muskogee, Indian Territory, March 30, 1905.

L. D. Horton,
    Attorney at Law,
        Boswell, Indian Territory.

Dear Sir:

    Receipt is hereby acknowledged of your letter of March 25, 1905, enclosing affidavits of Susan Roberts and Laymon Roberts to the birth of Vicey Roberts and Thomas Roberts, children of Laymon and Susan Roberts, October 9, 1899 and March 7, 1902, respectively; also the affidavits of Ellis Carnes and Laymon Roberts to the birth of Sinnie Carnes daughter of Ellis and Rebecca Carnes, January 10, 1903, and the same have been filed with our records as applications for the enrollment of said children.

    Receipt is also acknowledged of the affidavit of Ellis Carnes relative to his marriage to Rebecca Roberts.

    The matter of the application for the enrollment of Sam Colbert will be made the subject of another communication.

        Respectfully,

                Chairman.

(The letter below does not belong with the current applicant.)

7-4370

Muskogee, Indian Territory, April 1, 1905.

L. D. Horton,
    Boswell, Indian Territory.

Dear Sir:

    Receipt is hereby acknowledged of your letter of March 25, 1905, enclosing affidavits of Serena Colbert and Aaron Colbert to the birth of Sam Colbert son of Aaron and Serena Colbert, July 10, 1902, and the same have been filed with our records as an application for the enrollment of said child.

        Respectfully,

                Chairman.

Applications for Enrollment of Choctaw Newborn
Act of 1905 Volume V

N. B. 285

COPY

Muskogee, Indian Territory, April 8, 1905.

Ellis Carnes,
    Boswell, Indian Territory.

Dear Sir:

    Referring to the application for the enrollment of your infant child, Sinie Carnes, born January 10, 1903, as a citizen of the Choctaw Nation, it is notes that neither the affidavit of the mother of the child, nor that of the attending physician or midwife has been filed with the Commission.

    If the mother is dead or there was no physician or midwife in attendace[sic], as it appears from the above mentioned application, it will be necessary that you procure the affidavits of two persons who have actual knowledge of the fact, that the child was born, when she was born, that she was living on March 4, 1905, and that Rebecca Carnes was her mother.

    Please give this matter your prompt attention.

Respectfully,
SIGNED
T. B. Needles.
Commissioner in Charge.

~~7-3587~~

7 NB 285

Muskogee, Indian Territory, April 21, 1905.

L. D. Horton,
    Boswell, Indian Territory.

Dear Sir:

    Receipt is hereby acknowledged of your letter of April 15, 1905, enclosing affidavit of Sam Bench as to Margaret Bench, mother of Alice Bench, and the same has enabled the Commission to identify Margaret Bench as having been enrolled under the name of Margaret Belvin and the affidavits of Sam Bench, I. L. Gentry and joint affidavit of Louis Crowder and Robert Crowder heretofore forwarded have been filed with our records as an application for the enrollment of said child.

Applications for Enrollment of Choctaw Newborn
Act of 1905   Volume V

  Receipt is also acknowledged of a joint affidavit of J. J. Tompkins and H. Oshta to the birth of Sinie Carnes and the same has been filed with the record in the matter of the enrollment of this child.

  The matter of the application for the enrollment of Myrtle Lee Dowland will be made the subject of another communication.

        Respectfully,

           Chairman.

               Choctaw N.B. 285

       Muskogee, Indian Territory, May 1, 1905.

L. D. Horton,
  Boswell, Indian Territory.

Dear Sir:

  Receipt is hereby acknowledged of your letter of April 26, enclosing certificate of William H. McKinney to the marriage of Ellis Carnes and Rebecca Roberts, which is offered in support of the application for the enrollment of Siney Carnes and the same has been filed with the records in this case.

        Respectfully,

           Chairman.

Applications for Enrollment of Choctaw Newborn
Act of 1905 Volume V

Choc New Born 286
Theone Morgan
(Born Aug. 19, 1904)

NEW-BORN AFFIDAVIT.

Number..................

Choctaw Enrolling Commission.

IN THE MATTER OF THE APPLICATION FOR ENROLLMENT, as a citizen of the Choctaw Nation, of Theone Morgan

born on the 19th day of August 1904

Name of father W. K. Morgan a citizen of United United[sic]
Nation final enrollment No ....
Name of mother Stella S Morgan a citizen of Choctaw
Nation final enrollment No 11534

Postoffice Nixon, Ind. Ter.

AFFIDAVIT OF MOTHER.

UNITED STATES OF AMERICA,
INDIAN TERRITORY,
Central DISTRICT

I Stella S. Morgan , on oath state that I am 22 years of age and a citizen by blood of the Choctaw Nation, and as such have been placed upon the final roll of the Choctaw Nation, by the Honorable Secretary of the Interior my final enrollment number being 11534 ; that I am the lawful wife of W.K. Morgan , who is a citizen of the United States Nation, and as such has been placed upon the final roll of said Nation by the Honorable Secretary of the Interior, his final enrollment number being ———— and that a female child was born to me on the 19th day of August 190 4; that said child has been named Theone Morgan , and is now living.

Stella S Morgan

WITNESSETH:
Must be two
Witnesses who
are Citizens.
W.G. Plummer
J H Hampton

Subscribed and sworn to before me this 23 day of January 190 5

D.D. Brunson
Notary Public.

My commission expires Oct 22nd 1905

Applications for Enrollment of Choctaw Newborn
Act of 1905 Volume V

AFFIDAVIT OF ATTENDING PHYSICIAN OR MIDWIFE

UNITED STATES OF AMERICA
INDIAN TERRITORY
Central   DISTRICT

I, R. F. King a physician on oath state that I attended on Mrs. Stella S. Morgan wife of W K Morgan on the 19th day of August , 190 4, that there was born to her on said date a female child, that said child is now living, and is said to have been named Theone Morgan

Richard F King   M.D.

Subscribed and sworn to before me this, the 23 day of January 190 5

DD Brunson
Notary Public.

WITNESSETH:
Must be two witnesses who are citizens and know the child.
W.G. Plummer
J H Hampton

We hereby certify that we are well acquainted with R F King a physician and know him to be reputable and of good standing in the community.

W.G. Plummer
J H Hampton

BIRTH AFFIDAVIT.

DEPARTMENT OF THE INTERIOR.
COMMISSION TO THE FIVE CIVILIZED TRIBES.

IN RE APPLICATION FOR ENROLLMENT, as a citizen of the Choctaw Nation, of Theone Morgan , born on the 19th day of August , 1904

Name of Father: William Kelley Morgan   a citizen of the Not a citizen Nation.
Name of Mother: Stella Morgan   a citizen of the Choctaw Nation.

Postoffice   Nixon, Ind. Ter.

Applications for Enrollment of Choctaw Newborn
Act of 1905 Volume V

AFFIDAVIT OF MOTHER.

UNITED STATES OF AMERICA, Indian Territory,
Central DISTRICT.

I, Stella Morgan , on oath state that I am 22 years of age and a citizen by blood , of the Choctaw Nation; that I am the lawful wife of William Kelley Morgan , who is a citizen, by Not a citizen of the any tribe of nation of Indians ~~Nation~~; that a female child was born to me on 19th day of August, 1904; that said child has been named Theone Morgan , and was living March 4, 1905.

            Stella Morgan

Witnesses To Mark:

  Subscribed and sworn to before me this 21st day of March , 1905

           Geo A. Fooshee
           Notary Public.

AFFIDAVIT OF ATTENDING PHYSICIAN OR MID-WIFE.

UNITED STATES OF AMERICA, Indian Territory,
Central DISTRICT.

I, Richard F. King , a Physcian[sic] , on oath state that I attended on Mrs. Stella Morgan , wife of William Kelley Morgan on the 19th day of August , 1904; that there was born to her on said date a female child; that said child was living March 4, 1905, and is said to have been named Theone Morgan

           Richard F King M.D.

Witnesses To Mark:

  Subscribed and sworn to before me this 21st day of March , 1905

           Geo A. Fooshee
           Notary Public.

Applications for Enrollment of Choctaw Newborn
Act of 1905   Volume V

7-4113

Muskogee, Indian Territory, March 28, 1905.

William Kelly[sic] Morgan,
    Nixon, Indian Territory.

Dear Sir:

    Receipt is hereby acknowledged of the affidavits of Stella Morgan and Richard F. King to the birth of Theone Morgan, daughter of William Kelly and Stella Morgan, August 19, 1904, and the same have been filed with our records as an application for the enrollment of said child.

                              Respectfully,

                                                    Chairman.

<u>Choc New Born 287</u>
    Mike Mayers Plummer
    (Born March 8, 1903)

NEW-BORN AFFIDAVIT.

                Number..................

Choctaw Enrolling Commission.

IN THE MATTER OF THE APPLICATION FOR ENROLLMENT, as a citizen of the Choctaw   Nation, of   Mike Mayers Plummer

born on the 8th day of   March   1903

Name of father   Walter G Plummer   a citizen of by blood Choctaw
Nation final enrollment No   11533
Name of mother   Minnie Plummer   a citizen of   United States
Nation final enrollment No ....

                        Postoffice   Nixon I.T.

Applications for Enrollment of Choctaw Newborn
Act of 1905 Volume V

AFFIDAVIT OF MOTHER.

UNITED STATES OF AMERICA,
    INDIAN TERRITORY,
Central   DISTRICT

I Minnie Plummer , on oath state that I am 30 years of age and a citizen by .... of the United States Nation, and as such have been placed upon the final roll of the ———— Nation, by the Honorable Secretary of the Interior my final enrollment number being ———— ; that I am the lawful wife of Walter G Plummer , who is a citizen of the Choctaw Nation, and as such has been placed upon the final roll of said Nation by the Honorable Secretary of the Interior, his final enrollment number being 11533 and that a male child was born to me on the 8 day of March 190 3 ; that said child has been named Mike Mayers Plummer , and is now living.

WITNESSETH: Minnie Plummer

Must be two Witnesses who are Citizens.   W.C. James
                            George England

Subscribed and sworn to before me this 21 day of January 190 5

                          C H Ennis
                          Notary Public.

My commission expires Mar 3/1908

AFFIDAVIT OF ATTENDING PHYSICIAN OR MIDWIFE

UNITED STATES OF AMERICA
INDIAN TERRITORY
   Central   DISTRICT

I, H. G. Goben a physician on oath state that I attended on Mrs. Minnie Plummer wife of Walter G. Plummer on the 8 day of March , 190 3, that there was born to her on said date a Male child, that said child is now living, and is said to have been named Mike Mayers Plummer

                      H. G. Goben   M.D.

Subscribed and sworn to before me this, the 21 day of January 190 5

                        C H Ennis
                        Notary Public.

WITNESSETH:

Must be two witnesses who are citizens and know the child.   W. C. James
                            George England

Applications for Enrollment of Choctaw Newborn
Act of 1905   Volume V

We hereby certify that we are well acquainted with H. G. Goben a physician and know him to be reputable and of good standing in the community.

{ Silas James
{ W C James

BIRTH AFFIDAVIT.

DEPARTMENT OF THE INTERIOR.
COMMISSION TO THE FIVE CIVILIZED TRIBES.

IN RE APPLICATION FOR ENROLLMENT, as a citizen of the Choctaw Nation, of Mike Mayers Plummer , born on the 8th day of March , 1903

Name of Father: Walter G. Plummer a citizen of the Choctaw Nation.
Name of Mother: Minnie Plummer a citizen of the Choctaw Nation.

Postoffice   Nixon Ind. T

AFFIDAVIT OF MOTHER.

UNITED STATES OF AMERICA, Indian Territory, }
Central   DISTRICT. }

I, Minnie Plummer , on oath state that I am 30 years of age and a citizen by Intermarriage , of the Choctaw Nation; that I am the lawful wife of Walter G. Plummer , who is a citizen, by Blood of the Choctaw Nation; that a male child was born to me on 8th day of March , 1903; that said child has been named Mike Mayers Plummer , and was living March 4, 1905.

Minnie Plummer

Witnesses To Mark:
{

Subscribed and sworn to before me this 22nd day of March , 1905

W^m K Morgan
Notary Public.

Applications for Enrollment of Choctaw Newborn
Act of 1905   Volume V

AFFIDAVIT OF ATTENDING PHYSICIAN OR MID-WIFE.

UNITED STATES OF AMERICA, Indian Territory,
Central   DISTRICT.

I, Mrs L A Byrd, a Midwife, on oath state that I attended on Mrs. Minnie Plummer, wife of Walter G Plummer on the 8th day of March, 1903; that there was born to her on said date a male child; that said child was living March 4, 1905, and is said to have been named Mike Mayers Plummer

L A Byrd

Witnesses To Mark:

Subscribed and sworn to before me this 22nd day of March, 1905

W^m K Morgan
Notary Public.

7-4113

Muskogee, Indian Territory, March 28, 1905.

Fooshe & Bronson,
    Attorneys at Law.
        Coalgate, Indian Territory.

Gentlemen:

Receipt is hereby acknowledged of your letter of March 21, 1905, enclosing affidavits of Minnie Plummer and L. A. Byrd to the birth of Mike Mayers Plummer, son of Walter G. and Minnie Plummer, March 8, 1903, and the same have been filed with our records as an application for the enrollment of said child.

Respectfully,

Chairman.

Applications for Enrollment of Choctaw Newborn
Act of 1905 Volume V

Choc New Born 288
    Betsy James
    (Born May 13, 1903)

BIRTH AFFIDAVIT.

DEPARTMENT OF THE INTERIOR,
COMMISSION TO THE FIVE CIVILIZED TRIBES.

IN RE Application for Enrollment, as a citizen of the Choctaw Nation, of Betsy James, born on the 13 day of May 1903, 1..........

Name of Father: Moses James   a citizen of the Choctaw Nation.
Name of Mother: Lorena B. McClure   a citizen of the Choctaw Nation.

Post-Office: Boswell, Ind. Ter.

AFFIDAVIT OF MOTHER.

UNITED STATES OF AMERICA,
    INDIAN TERRITORY.
    Central   District.

I, Lorena B. McClure, on oath state that I am 19 years of age and a citizen by Blood, of the Choctaw Nation; that I am the lawful wife of No, who is a citizen, by Blood of the Choctaw Nation; that a Female child was born to me on 13th day of May 1903, 1........., that said child has been named Betsy James, and is now living.

                      Lorena x B McClure

WITNESSES TO MARK:
    D.C. McClure
    J H Duncan

Subscribed and sworn to before me this 13th *day of* July, 1903, 190.....

                      Thomas V McReynolds
                      NOTARY PUBLIC.
                    My Commission Expires Apr. 21. 1905

Applications for Enrollment of Choctaw Newborn
Act of 1905   Volume V

AFFIDAVIT OF ATTENDING PHYSICIAN OR MID-WIFE.

UNITED STATES OF AMERICA, }
   INDIAN TERRITORY.
  Central   District. }

I, Serane Carnes , a Midwife , on oath state that I attended on Mrs. Lorena B. McClure , wife of .... on the 13th day of May 1903 , 1......... ; that there was born to her on said date a Female child; that said child is now living and is said to have been named Betsy James

                                 Serane Carnes

WITNESSES TO MARK:
  { D.C. McClure
    J H Duncan

Subscribed and sworn to before me this 13th *day of* July, 1903 , 190.....

                             Thomas V McReynolds
                                  NOTARY PUBLIC.
                         My Commission Expires Apr. 21. 1905

BIRTH AFFIDAVIT.   7-NB-288
DEPARTMENT OF THE INTERIOR.
COMMISSION TO THE FIVE CIVILIZED TRIBES.

IN RE APPLICATION FOR ENROLLMENT, as a citizen of the Choctaw Nation, of Betsy James , born on the 13th day of May , 1903

Name of Father: Moses James   a citizen of the Choctaw Nation.
Name of Mother: Lorena B. McClure   a citizen of the Choctaw Nation.

                        Postoffice   Boswell, I.T.

AFFIDAVIT OF MOTHER.

UNITED STATES OF AMERICA, Indian Territory, }
    Central   **DISTRICT.** }

I, Lorena B. McClure , on oath state that I am 22 years of age and a citizen by Blood , of the Choctaw Nation; that I am the lawful wife of They were not Married But is , who is a citizen, by Blood of the Choctaw Nation; that a Female child was born to me on 13th day of May , 1903; that said child has been named Betsy James , and was living March 4, 1905.

Applications for Enrollment of Choctaw Newborn
Act of 1905 Volume V

                          her
                      Lorena B x McClure

Witnesses To Mark: mark
  { Douglas C McClure
    Annie B. Whitler

Subscribed and sworn to before me this 1st day of   June   , 1905

                      Perry M Clark
                           Notary Public.

AFFIDAVIT OF ATTENDING PHYSICIAN OR MID-WIFE.

UNITED STATES OF AMERICA, Indian Territory,
    Central   **DISTRICT.**

    I, Serena Colbert, a Midwife, on oath state that I attended on Mrs. Lorena B. McClure, wife of .... on the 13th day of May, 1903; that there was born to her on said date a Female child; that said child was living March 4, 1905, and is said to have been named Betsy James

                      Serena Colbert

Witnesses To Mark:
  {

Subscribed and sworn to before me this 1st day of   June   , 1905

                      Perry M Clark
                           Notary Public.

My Com Exp 3/27/09

BIRTH AFFIDAVIT.   7-NB-288
DEPARTMENT OF THE INTERIOR.
COMMISSION TO THE FIVE CIVILIZED TRIBES.

    IN RE APPLICATION FOR ENROLLMENT, as a citizen of the Choctaw Nation, of Betsy James, born on the 20 day of May, 1904

Name of Father: Moses James   a citizen of the Choctaw Nation.
Name of Mother: Lena James   a citizen of the Choctaw Nation.

                Postoffice   Boswell

Applications for Enrollment of Choctaw Newborn
Act of 1905   Volume V

AFFIDAVIT OF MOTHER.

UNITED STATES OF AMERICA, Indian Territory, }
Central Judicial   DISTRICT.

I, Lena James, on oath state that I am 23 years of age and a citizen by blood, of the Choctaw Nation; that I am the lawful wife of Moses James, who is a citizen, by blood of the Choctaw Nation; that a female child was born to me on 20 day of May, 1904; that said child has been named Betsy James, and was living March 4, 1905.

            her
           Lena x James
Witnesses To Mark: mark
 { L.D. Horton
   G D Duncan

Subscribed and sworn to before me this 1 day of May, 1905

          L. D. Horton
            Notary Public.

AFFIDAVIT OF ATTENDING PHYSICIAN OR MID-WIFE.

UNITED STATES OF AMERICA, Indian Territory, }
Central Judicial   DISTRICT.

I, Cerena Colbert, a Midwife, on oath state that I attended on Mrs. Lena James, wife of Moses James on the 20 day of May, 1904; that there was born to her on said date a female child; that said child was living March 4, 1905, and is said to have been named Betsy James

           her
         Cerena x Colbert
Witnesses To Mark: mark
 { L.D. Horton
   G D Duncan

Subscribed and sworn to before me this 1 day of May, 1905

          L. D. Horton
            Notary Public.

Applications for Enrollment of Choctaw Newborn
Act of 1905   Volume V

BIRTH AFFIDAVIT.

DEPARTMENT OF THE INTERIOR.
COMMISSION TO THE FIVE CIVILIZED TRIBES.

IN RE APPLICATION FOR ENROLLMENT, as a citizen of the   Choctaw   Nation, of Betsy James   , born on the 13   day of   May   , 1903

Name of Father: Moses James   a citizen of the   Choctaw   Nation.
Name of Mother: Lorena B. McClure   a citizen of the   Choctaw   Nation.

Postoffice   Albany, Indian Territory

AFFIDAVIT OF MOTHER.

UNITED STATES OF AMERICA, Indian Territory,
Central Judicial   DISTRICT.

I,   Lorena B. McClure   , on oath state that I am   about 24   years of age and a citizen by   blood   , of the   Choctaw   Nation; thought I was that I am the lawful wife of   Moses James   , who is a citizen, by blood   of the   Choctaw Nation; that a   female   child was born to me on   13 day of   May   , 1903; that said child has been named   Betsy James   , and was living March 4, 1905.

                          her
             Lorena B McClure x
Witnesses To Mark: mark
  Osborne Blanche
  (Name Illegible)

Subscribed and sworn to before me this 15 day of   September   , 1905

                 L. D. Horton
                    Notary Public.

(The affidavit below typed as given.)

United States of America,
    Indian Territory,
Central Judicial District.

    I, Douglas McClure, after having been first duly sworn state that I am 24 years of age and my post office address is Boswell Indian Territory. I am an enrolled citizen of the Choctaw Nation by blood and am the half brother to Leurena B. McClure who has applied to have enrolled her minor daughter Betsy. I am informed that my sister has made three affidavits for the enrollment of this daughter Betsy. In these affidavits I understand she has given the name of the baby as Betsy James. In two of these I find that

Applications for Enrollment of Choctaw Newborn
Act of 1905   Volume V

she states that Betsy was born on the 13th day of May 1903 and in the other on the 20th day of May 1904.

This Betsy McClure, or Betsy James was born at my house about the 13 day of May 1903 and I have had charge of her every since she was born and know that I am correct about her age and as to the affidavit fixing her date of birth as May 20th 1904 I cannot understand unless it was a mistake of the interpreter-She cannot understand a work of english except proper names and such as that and I account for it in that way. The woman who makes these several affidavits as midwife is Aaron Colbert's wife Cerena Colbert-She was formerly the wife of Ellis Carnes and that is the way I account for her signing one of these affidavits as Cerena Colbert and the others as Cerena Carnes-She too does not understand english and had no evil intent im making these affidavits, as I believe.

As above stated, Lourena B. McClure is my half sister- She is a full blood Choctaw and is not educated-Sometime about 1901 or 1902 as I remember, Lourena and a full blood choctaw by the name of Moses James took up together as man and wife for some months and after he (Moses James) was arrested and placed in jail this Betsy was born- This Moses James died in jail at South McAlister and Lorena perhaps thought he was her husband according to some old tribal custom of marriage-

This baby is still alive and is living with me and is a full blood choctaw and unless the marriage is legal between my sister and Moses James the baby is not legitimate and her name should be Betsy McClure.

I have been hunting for Lourena B. McClure for some days and find that she has gone up about Ardmore to look for land to allot for Betsy and have sent her word to come home as soon as she gets my message and help to straighten this matter out-

            Douglas C McClure

Subscribed and sworn to before me this the   31st   day of August 1905.

            L. D. Horton
            Notary Public.

(The affidavit below typed as given.)

Central District,
Indian Territory.

I, Osborne Blanche, after having been first duly sworn state that I am 26 years old and my post office address is Albany, I.T.

I am acquainted with Lorena B. McClure who is now present and she is living at me house. I know the McClure family and know that she is a half ~~brother~~ sister to Douglas McClure and that the baby Betsy James is now living-Having seen her to day-

I know that she is a full-blood choctaw and that she does not understand the english language and that she is not real intelligent

I further state on my oath that I did before the signing by her of the affidavit this day executed before L.D. Horton, a notary public in regard to the birth of her daughter

Applications for Enrollment of Choctaw Newborn
Act of 1905 Volume V

which she calls Betsy James, fully, fairly and honestly interprete said affidavit from the english language into the Choctaw language and that the same was fully understood by her before signing the same and that I speak and understand both the Choctaw and the english language and the said Lorena B. McClure understand the Choctaw language. And I also interpreted to her the affidavit of the birth of said Betsy this day made.

Osborne Blanche

Subscribed and sworn to before me this the   15th   day of Septembet 1905.

L.D. Horton
Notary Public.

(The affidavit below typed as given.)

Central District,
    Indian Territory.
    We, Ellis Carnes, 34 years of age and S.B. Carnes, 24 years of age, after having been first duly sworn state that we reside near Boswell and Lane Ind.Ter. respectively and are acquainted with Lorena B. McClure and have known her all her life and that she is the identical Lorena B. McClure who lived some three or four years ago with a Choctaw Indian by the name of Moses James- That Cerena Colbert was formerly the wife of affiant Ellis Carnes and is now the wife of Aaron Colbert-
    We know that Lorena has never had any other children that Betsy and that she is illiterate and ignorant and do not believe that she made applications with a view to have said child enrolled twice on the rolls of the nation?

Ellis Carnes
SB Carnes

Subscribed and sworn to before me this the 15th day of September 1905.

L.D. Horton
Notary Public.

(The affidavit below typed as given.)

UNITED STATES OF AMERICA,
    INDIAN TERRITORY,
CENTRAL JUDICIAL DISTRICT.
    I, Lorena B. mcClure after having been first duly sworn state-I am 24 years old I think, I don't know my exact age-I am the half sister to Douglas McClure- I do not know my roll number, but I am a Choctaw by blood, I think I am a full blood choctaw- I do not know the english language. I am the mother of Betsy James for whom I have made an application for enrollment- The exact date of her birth is May 13th 1903- She is still

Applications for Enrollment of Choctaw Newborn
Act of 1905 Volume V

living and is with my brother Douglas north of Boswell.Ind.Ter. I saw her to day-I have been shown and had explained to me three different applications which I have made for her enrollment- Also had explained to me the conflict in dates, names and ages given in these several affidavits- Also, I am told that Serena Colbert, the midwife has signed one of them as Serena Carnes- She was at one time the wife of Ellis Carnes and I suppose that is the only explanation for that, she is now the wife of Aaron Colbert.

Moses James mentioned in these applications is the father of Betsy, I thought we were man and wife-We lived together and he said he was my husband. About three years ago he killed a girl and they put him in jail at South McAlister and he died there-I do not know whether he was enrolled or not. He was a full blood and could talk english some.

I made all three of these applications, I did not do this to try to get my baby enrolled twice, but I get afraid I had made some of them wrong and was anxious to get her on the rolls- These mistakes in ages and dates it must have been in some way the fault of the persons who interpreted for me. G.D.Duncan interpreted the one made before L.D. Horton and I know he does not understand my language well-

I do not know who the father of Moses James was - I have not the possession of my allotment certificate, it is at my brother Douglasses house- A part of my allotment as I remember is the west half of the north west quarter of Section TWenty in Towhship five south Range 14 east- It is in the forks of the Boggies-

The reason I am so certain about Betsy being born on the 13th of May is because it was just about the middle of a month that she was born.

I prefer that my baby be enrolled in the name of Betsy James because when I lived with Moses James I though he was my husband and he said he was and if he was not I did not know it and it would be less reproach on her to be enrolled in the name of her father and not appear as illegitimate.

This is the only child I have ever had and is the only one I am applying to have enrolled.

Witness   her
                                       Lorena B McClure +
   Osborne Blanche   mark
           Ellis Carnes
SB Carnes

    Subscribed and sworn to before me this the 15th day of Sept. 1905.

                                            L.D. Horton
                                           Notary Public.

Applications for Enrollment of Choctaw Newborn
Act of 1905 Volume V

N.B. 288.

COPY

Muskogee, Indian Territory, April 8, 1905.

Moses James,
    Boswell, Indian Territory.

Dear Sir:

There is enclosed you herewith for execution application for the enrollment of your infant child, Betsy James, born May 13, 1903.

The affidavits heretofore filed with the Commission show the child was living on July 13, 1904. It is necessary, for the child to be enrolled, that she was living on March 4, 1905. You will please insert the age of the mother in the place left blank for that purpose.

In having these affidavits executed care should be exercised to see that all names are written in full, as they appear in the body of the affidavit, and in the event that either of the persons signing the affidavit are unable to write, signatures by mark must be attested by two witnesses. Each affidavit must be executed before a Notary Public and the notarial seal and signature of the officer must be attached to each separate affidavit.

                        Respectfully,
                        SIGNED
                        T. B. Needles.

LER 8-6   Commissioner in Charge.

7-NB-288.

1-6-05

Muskogee, Indian Territory, May 16, 1905.

Lorena B. McClure,
    Boswell, Indian Territory.

Dear Sir[sic]:

There is enclosed you herewith for execution application for the enrollment of your infant child, Betsy James, born May 13, 1903.

The affidavits heretofore filed with the Commission show the child was living on May 13, 1903. It is necessary, for the child to be enrolled, that she was living on March 4, 1905.

Applications for Enrollment of Choctaw Newborn
Act of 1905   Volume V

In having these affidavits executed care should be exercised to see that all names are written in full, as they appear in the body of the affidavit, and in the event that either of the persons signing the affidavit are unable to write, signatures by mark must be attested by two witnesses. Each affidavit must be executed before a Notary Public and the notarial seal and signature of the officer must be attached to each separate affidavit.

Respectfully,

Chairman.

V. 16-14.

---

7 N.B. 288.

Muskogee, Indian Territory, June 1, 1905.

L. D. Horton,
Boswell, Indian Territory.

Dear Sir:

Receipt is hereby acknowledged of your letter of May 1, transmitting the affidavits of Lena James and Cerena Colbert to the birth of Betsy James, daughter of Moses and Lena James, May 20, 1904, and the same have been filed in the matter of the enrollment of said child.

The other matter referred to in your letter was made the subject of a separate communication.

Respectfully,

Commissioner in Charge.

7-NB-288

Muskogee, Indian Territory, June 7, 1905.

Moses James,
Boswell, Indian Territory.

Dear Sir:

Receipt is hereby acknowledged of the affidavits of Lorena B. McClure and Serena Colbert to the birth of Betsy James, daughter of Moses James and Lorena B. McClure, May 13, 1903, and the same have been filed with our records as an application for the enrollment of said child.

Applications for Enrollment of Choctaw Newborn
Act of 1905   Volume V

Respectfully,

Chairman.

7-NB-288

Muskogee, Indian Territory, July 29, 1905.

L. B. Horton,
    Attorney at Law,
        Boswell, Indian Territory

Dear Sir:

    On March 1, 1905, you transmitted application for the enrollment of Betsy James, infant child, of Lena and Moses James, born May 20, 1904.

    In the affidavit of the mother, Lena James, she alleges that she is the lawful wife of Moses James, a citizen by blood of the Choctaw Nation and that her infant child Betsy James was born May 20, 1904; the affidavit of the midwife, Cerina Colbert, who attended at the birth of this child, alleges the same facts. Said application was filed in this office June 1, 1905.

    On June 7, 1905, there was filed in this office in the matter of the enrollment of Betsy James, the affidavit of Lorena B. McClure executed June 1, 1905, in which she alleges that she is not married to Moses James, that there was born to her on May 31, 1904, a female child, and that said child has been made[sic], Betsy James; the affidavit of Serena Colbert, the midwife who attended Lorena B. McClure, alleges the same facts.

    It is believed that Lorena B. McClure and Lena James are identical persons; if such is the case, you should furnish affidavits alleging such to be the fact, and also explain by affidavit the descrepancy[sic] as given to the birth of the child, and whether the mother of the child is the lawful wife of Moses James, you are also requested to furnish information by which Moses James May be identified as a citizen by blood of the Choctaw Nation; state where, and when he was enrolled, the name[sic] of his parents, and other members of his family who made application at the same time, and if he has selected an allotment, give his rolls[sic] number as it appears upon his allotment certificate.

    This matter should receive your immediate attention as no further action can be taken relative to the enrollment of said Betsy James until the evidence requested is supplied.

Respectfully,

Commissioner.

Applications for Enrollment of Choctaw Newborn
Act of 1905 Volume V

7-NB-288

Muskogee, Indian Territory, August 4, 1905.

L. D. Horton,
    Boswell, Indian Territory.

Dear Sir:

    Receipt is hereby acknowledged of your letter of July 31, 1905, in the matter of the application for the enrollment of Betsy James as infant child, in which you state that as early as practicable you will see the mother of this child and endeavor to have the affidavits to her birth properly executed.

    You will have the thanks of this office for your attention in the matter.

        Respectfully,

                Commissioner.

Choctaw N B 288

Muskogee, Indian Territory, August 9, 1905.

L. D. Horton,
    Boswell, Indian Territory.

Dear Sir:

    Receipt is hereby acknowledged of your letter of August 5 stating that Lorena B. McClure has been notified to be at your office Saturday in the matter of the enrollment of her child Betsy James, and you ask for copies of the affidavits which have heretofore been filed in order that you may get the matter straightened out if possible.

    For your information there are inclosed herewith copies of the affidavits heretofore forwarded in the matter of the application for enrollment of Betsy James as a citizen by blood of the Choctaw Nation. You will note the discrepancy in the name of the mother as given in the different affidavits and also that the date of birth is given in one set of affidavits as May 20, 1904, while the other two applications for enrollment give the date as May 13, 1903.

    You are requested to ascertain the correct date of the birth of this child and have the inclosed blank properly executed, showing the date of birth and the correct name of the mother, giving her roll number, as it appears upon her allotment certificate, if she has selected an allotment of the lands of the Choctaw and Chickasaw Nations.

Applications for Enrollment of Choctaw Newborn
Act of 1905   Volume V

Respectfully,

Acting Commissioner.

AB 1-9

7-NB-288.

Muskogee, Indian Territory, September 5, 1905.

L. D. Horton,
    Attorney at Law,
        Boswell, Indian Territory.

Dear Sir:

    Receipt is hereby acknowledged of your letter of the 31st ultimo, inclosing affidavit of Douglas C. McClure in support of the application for enrollment as a citizen by blood of the Choctaw, of Betsy James (McClure), infant child or Lorena B. McClure. You state that if other information is necessary you will be able to furnish it at once.

    In reply, you are advised that said affidavit has been filed with the record in this case.

    You are further advised that on August 9, 1905, there was forwarded to you for execution blank application for the enrollment of this child and in my letter transmitting said application you were requested to give the date of death of the child and the correct name of the mother.

    You are requested to have the affidavits executed and return to this office at the earliest possible date, as no further action can be taken relative to the enrollment of the applicant until the evidence requested in[sic] furnished.

Respectfully,

Acting Commissioner.

Applications for Enrollment of Choctaw Newborn
Act of 1905   Volume V

7-NB-288.

Muskogee, Indian Territory, September 22, 1905.

L. D. Horton,
    Attorney at Law,
        Boswell, Indian Territory.

Dear Sir:

    Receipt is hereby acknowledged of your letter of September 16, 1905, transmitting the affidavits of Lorena B. McClure, Ellis Carney and Osborne Blanche in the matter of the application for the enrollment of Betsy James as a citizen by blood of the Choctaw Nation and the same have been filed with the record in said case.

        Respectfully,

                Acting Commissioner.

7-NB-288

Muskogee, Indian Territory, December 20, 1905.

L. D. Horton,
    Attorney at Law,
        Boswell, Indian Territory.

Dear Sir:

    Receipt is hereby acknowledged of your letter of December 15, 1905, asking what action has been taken in the matter of the application for the enrollment of Betsy James, infant daughter of Moses and Lorena B. James (McClure).

    In reply to your letter you are advised that the name of Betsy James has not yet been placed upon a schedule of new born citizens of the Choctaw Nation prepared for forwarding to the Secretary of the Interior, but if further evidence is necessary to enable this office to pass upon the enrollment of this child, you will be further advised.

        Respectfully,

                Commissioner.

Applications for Enrollment of Choctaw Newborn
Act of 1905   Volume V

7-NB-288

Muskogee, Indian Territory, February 20, 1906.

L. D. Horton,
    Durant, Indian Territory.

Dear Sir:

    Receipt is hereby acknowledged of your letter of February 16, 1906, relative to the application for the enrollment of Betsy James.

    In reply to your letter you are advised that the name of Betsy James has been placed upon a schedule of new born citizens of the Choctaw Nation which has been forwarded the Secretary of the Interior and you will be notified when her enrollment is approved by the Department.

Respectfully,

Acting Commissioner.

Choc New Born 289
    Maggie Thomas
    (Born Jan. 22, 1903)
    George Thomas
    (Born Feb. 10, 1905)

BIRTH AFFIDAVIT.

DEPARTMENT OF THE INTERIOR.
COMMISSION TO THE FIVE CIVILIZED TRIBES.

IN RE APPLICATION FOR ENROLLMENT, as a citizen of the Choctaw Nation, of Maggie Thomas, born on the 22nd day of January, 1903

Name of Father: A. Thomas   a citizen of the ————Nation.
Name of Mother: Mollie M. Thomas   a citizen of the Choctaw Nation.

Postoffice   Ryan, I.T.

Applications for Enrollment of Choctaw Newborn
Act of 1905   Volume V

AFFIDAVIT OF MOTHER.

UNITED STATES OF AMERICA, Indian Territory,
.... DISTRICT.

I, Mollie M. Thomas , on oath state that I am .... years of age and a citizen by blood , of the Choctaw Nation; that I am the lawful wife of A. Thomas , who is a citizen, ~~by~~ of the .... Nation; that a female child was born to me on 22nd day of January , 1903; that said child has been named ...., and was living March 4, 1905.

Witnesses To Mark:

{ ....

....

Subscribed and sworn to before me this .... day of ...., 1905.

....
Notary Public.

AFFIDAVIT OF ATTENDING PHYSICIAN OR MID-WIFE.

UNITED STATES OF AMERICA, Indian Territory,
.... DISTRICT.

I, ..., a ...., on oath state that I attended on Mrs. Mollie M. Thomas , wife of A. Thomas on the 22nd day of January , 1903; that there was born to her on said date a .... child; that said child is now living and is said to have been named Maggie Thomas

Witnesses To Mark:

{ ....

....

Subscribed and sworn to before me this ....day of ...., 1........ .

....
Notary Public.

Applications for Enrollment of Choctaw Newborn
Act of 1905   Volume V

BIRTH AFFIDAVIT.

DEPARTMENT OF THE INTERIOR,
COMMISSION TO THE FIVE CIVILIZED TRIBES.

IN RE Application for Enrollment, as a citizen of the   Choctaw   Nation, of   Maggie Thomas , born on the   22   day of   January   , 1903

Name of Father: A Thomas   a citizen of the ——————Nation.
Name of Mother: Mollie M. Thomas   a citizen of the   Choctaw   Nation.

Post-Office: Ryan, I.T.

AFFIDAVIT OF MOTHER.

UNITED STATES OF AMERICA,
   INDIAN TERRITORY.
   Southern   District.

   I,   Mollie M. Thomas   , on oath state that I am   28   years of age and a citizen by   blood   , of the   Choctaw   Nation; that I am the lawful wife of   A. Thomas , who is a citizen, by —— of the —— Nation; that a   female   child was born to me on 22nd day of   January   , 1903 , that said child has been named   Maggie Thomas   , and is now living.

                              Mollie M Thomas

WITNESSES TO MARK:

Subscribed and sworn to before me this 31st *day of*   March   , 1903

                              E.E. Morris
                                  NOTARY PUBLIC.

AFFIDAVIT OF ATTENDING PHYSICIAN OR MID-WIFE.

UNITED STATES OF AMERICA,
   INDIAN TERRITORY.
   Southern   District.

   I,   S.K. Montgomery   , a   Physician   , on oath state that I attended on Mrs. Mollie M. Thomas   , wife of   A Thomas   on the   22   day of   January , 1903 ; that there was born to her on said date a   female   child; that said child is now living and is said to have been named   Maggie Thomas

Applications for Enrollment of Choctaw Newborn
Act of 1905 Volume V

S.K. Montgomery M.D.

WITNESSES TO MARK:

{

Subscribed and sworn to before me this 28th day of January, 1903

E.E. Morris
NOTARY PUBLIC.

BIRTH AFFIDAVIT.

DEPARTMENT OF THE INTERIOR.
COMMISSION TO THE FIVE CIVILIZED TRIBES.

IN RE APPLICATION FOR ENROLLMENT, as a citizen of the Choctaw Nation, of George Thomas, born on the 10 day of Feb, 1905

Name of Father: Anderson Thomas   a citizen of the U. S. Nation.
Name of Mother: Mollie M. Thomas   a citizen of the Choctaw Nation.

Postoffice Owl I.T.

AFFIDAVIT OF MOTHER.

UNITED STATES OF AMERICA, Indian Territory,
    Central   **DISTRICT.**

I, Mollie M. Thomas, on oath state that I am 31 years of age and a citizen by Blood, of the Choctaw Nation; that I am the lawful wife of Anderson Thomas, who is a citizen, by U. S. of the ——— Nation; that a ~~Female~~ male child was born to me on 10 day of Feb, 1905; that said child has been named George Thomas, and was living March 4, 1905.

Mollie M Thomas

Witnesses To Mark:
{ M E Cross
  J A Carmack

Subscribed and sworn to before me this 27 day of March, 1905

John H Cross
Notary Public.

Applications for Enrollment of Choctaw Newborn
Act of 1905   Volume V

AFFIDAVIT OF ATTENDING PHYSICIAN OR MID-WIFE.

UNITED STATES OF AMERICA, Indian Territory, }
Central   DISTRICT. }

I, J. A. Carmack , a Physician , on oath state that I attended on Mrs. Mollie M Thomas , wife of Anderson Thomas on the 10 day of Feb , 1905; that there was born to her on said date a male child; that said child was living March 4, 1905, and is said to have been named George Thomas

JA. Carmack M.D.

Witnesses To Mark:
{

Subscribed and sworn to before me this 27 day of March , 1905

John H Cross
Notary Public.

BIRTH AFFIDAVIT.

DEPARTMENT OF THE INTERIOR.
COMMISSION TO THE FIVE CIVILIZED TRIBES.

IN RE APPLICATION FOR ENROLLMENT, as a citizen of the Choctaw Nation, of Maggie Thomas , born on the 22 day of Jan , 1903

U. S.
Name of Father: Anderson Thomas   a citizen of the   ~~Choctaw~~ Nation.
Name of Mother: Mollie M. Thomas   a citizen of the   Choctaw Nation.

Postoffice   Owl I.T.

AFFIDAVIT OF MOTHER.

UNITED STATES OF AMERICA, Indian Territory, }
Central   DISTRICT. }

I, Mollie M. Thomas , on oath state that I am 31 years of age and a citizen by Blood , of the Choctaw Nation; that I am the lawful wife of Anderson Thomas , who is a citizen, by U. S. of the ——— Nation; that a Female child was born to me on 22 day of Jan , 1903; that said child has been named Maggie Thomas , and was living March 4, 1905.

Mollie M Thomas

Applications for Enrollment of Choctaw Newborn
Act of 1905   Volume V

Witnesses To Mark:
{ R D Cody
{ M E Cross

    Subscribed and sworn to before me this 27   day of   March   , 1905

                                   John H Cross
                                   Notary Public.

AFFIDAVIT OF ATTENDING PHYSICIAN OR MID-WIFE.

UNITED STATES OF AMERICA, Indian Territory, }
    Southern   DISTRICT. }

    I,   S.K. Montgomery   , a   Physician   , on oath state that I attended on Mrs.   Mollie M Thomas , wife of   Anderson Thomas   on the 22   day of Jan , 1903; that there was born to her on said date a   Female   child; that said child was living March 4, 1905, and is said to have been named Maggie Thomas

                               S.K. Montgomery M.D.

Witnesses To Mark:
{ S.P. Treadwell
{ *(Name Illegible)*

    Subscribed and sworn to before me this 29th   day of   March   , 1905

                                 Cham Jones
My commission expires Oct 22-1905   Notary Public.

                                              Choctaw 3972.

                    Muskogee, Indian Territory, April 4, 1905.

Anderson Thomas,
    Owl, Indian Territory.

Dear Sir:

    Receipt is hereby acknowledged of the affidavits of Mollie M. Thomas and J. A. Carmack to the birth of George Thomas, son of Anderson and Mollie M. Thomas, February 10, 1905, and the same have been filed with our records as an application for the enrollment of said child.

Applications for Enrollment of Choctaw Newborn
Act of 1905 Volume V

Respectfully,

Commissioner in Charge.

COMMISSIONERS:
TAMS BIXBY,
THOMAS B. NEEDLES,
C.R. BRECKINBRIDGE.

WM. O. BEALL
Secretary

DEPARTMENT OF THE INTERIOR,
COMMISSIONER TO THE FIVE CIVILIZED TRIBES.

$W^m O.B.$

REFER IN REPLY TO THE FOLLOWING:

N.B. 289.

ADDRESS ONLY THE
COMMISSION TO THE FIVE CIVILIZED TRIBES.

Muskogee, Indian Territory, April 8, 1905.

A. Thomas,
    Ryan, Indian Territory.

Dear Sir:

    There is enclosed you herewith for execution application for the enrollment of your infant child, Maggie Thomas, born January 22, 1903.

    The affidavits heretofore filed with the Commission show the child was living on January 28, 1903. It is necessary, for the child to be enrolled, that she was living on March 4, 1905. You will please insert the age of the mother in the place left blank for that purpose.

    In having these affidavits executed care should be exercised to see that all names are written in full, as they appear in the body of the affidavit, and in the event that either of the persons signing the affidavit are unable to write, signatures by mark must be attested by two witnesses. Each affidavit must be executed before a Notary Public and the notarial seal and signature of the officer must be attached to each separate affidavit.

    Respectfully,
    T.B. Needles
    Commissioner in Charge.

LER 8-5

Applications for Enrollment of Choctaw Newborn
Act of 1905   Volume V

Choctaw 3972.

Muskogee, Indian Territory, April 12, 1905.

Anderson Thomas,
    Owl, Indian Territory.

Dear Sir:

    Receipt is hereby acknowledged of the affidavits of Mollie M. Thomas and S. K. Montgomery to the birth of Maggie Thomas, daughter of Anderson and Mollie M. Thomas, January 22, 1903, and the same have been filed with our records as an application for the enrollment of said child.

        Respectfully,

        Commissioner in Charge.

Choc New Born 290
    William Fenton Hamilton
    (Born Sep. 15, 1904)

BIRTH AFFIDAVIT.

DEPARTMENT OF THE INTERIOR.
COMMISSION TO THE FIVE CIVILIZED TRIBES.

IN RE APPLICATION FOR ENROLLMENT, as a citizen of the Choctaw Nation, of William Fenton Hamilton, born on the 15 day of Sept, 1904

Name of Father: W^m H Hamilton   a citizen of the Choctaw Nation.
Name of Mother: Mamie Hamilton   a citizen of the Choctaw Nation.

        Postoffice   Bee, Ind. Ter.

Applications for Enrollment of Choctaw Newborn
Act of 1905   Volume V

AFFIDAVIT OF MOTHER.

UNITED STATES OF AMERICA, Indian Territory,
Central   DISTRICT.

I, Mamie Hamilton, on oath state that I am twenty four years of age and a citizen by blood, of the Choctaw Nation; that I am the lawful wife of Wm H. Hamilton (deceased), who is a citizen, by intermarriage of the Choctaw Nation; that a male child was born to me on 15th day of September, 1904, that said child has been named William Fenton Hamilton, and is now living.

        Mamie Hamilton

Witnesses To Mark:

 Subscribed and sworn to before me this 18 day of Mar, 1905.

        D.P. Slaughter
         Notary Public.

AFFIDAVIT OF ATTENDING PHYSICIAN OR MID-WIFE.

UNITED STATES OF AMERICA, Indian Territory,
Central   DISTRICT.

I, S.P. Stalcup, a Physician, on oath state that I attended on Mrs. Mamie Hamilton, wife of Wm H. Hamilton (deceased) on the 15" day of Sept., 1904; that there was born to her on said date a male child; that said child is now living and is said to have been named ....

        S.P. Stalcup

Witnesses To Mark:

 Subscribed and sworn to before me this 18 day of Mar, 1905.

        D.P. Slaughter
         Notary Public.

Applications for Enrollment of Choctaw Newborn
Act of 1905 Volume V

Choc New Born 291
    Elias Jackson Ward
    (Born Apr. 22, 1903)
    Maggie Lorene Ward
    (Born Nov. 13, 1904)

BIRTH AFFIDAVIT.

DEPARTMENT OF THE INTERIOR.
COMMISSION TO THE FIVE CIVILIZED TRIBES.

IN RE APPLICATION FOR ENROLLMENT, as a citizen of the Choctaw Nation, of Elias Jackson Ward, born on the 22^d day of April, 1903

Name of Father: Lonnie E. Ward   a citizen of the Choctaw Nation.
Name of Mother: Ada Ward   a citizen of the " Nation.

    Postoffice   Dibble, Ind Ter

AFFIDAVIT OF MOTHER.

UNITED STATES OF AMERICA, Indian Territory,
    Southern   DISTRICT.

    I, Ada Ward daughter of A.J.S.Barnett, on oath state that I am twenty five years of age and a citizen by Blood, of the Choctaw Nation; that I am the lawful wife of Lonnie E. Ward, who is a citizen, by Intermarried of the Choctaw Nation; that a male child was born to me on 22^d day of April, 1903, that said child has been named Elias Jackson Ward, and is now living.

                       Ada Ward

Witnesses To Mark:

    Subscribed and sworn to before me this 5 day of May, 1904

                   Jas M Gordon
                       Notary Public.

My commission expires Mch 1907

Applications for Enrollment of Choctaw Newborn
Act of 1905 Volume V

AFFIDAVIT OF ATTENDING PHYSICIAN OR MID-WIFE.

UNITED STATES OF AMERICA, Indian Territory, }
.... DISTRICT. }

    I, J H Howard , a M.D. , on oath state that I attended on Mrs. Ada Ward , wife of Lonnie E Ward on the 22 day of April , 1903; that there was born to her on said date a male child; that said child is now living and is said to have been named Elias Jackson Ward

                                      J H Howard M.D.

Witnesses To Mark:

    Subscribed and sworn to before me this 5th day of May , 1904

                                Jas M Gordon
                                    Notary Public.

My commission expires Mch 1907

BIRTH AFFIDAVIT.

DEPARTMENT OF THE INTERIOR.
COMMISSION TO THE FIVE CIVILIZED TRIBES.

    IN RE APPLICATION FOR ENROLLMENT, as a citizen of the Choctaw Nation of Elias Jackson Ward , born on the _____ day of _____ , 1_____

Name of Father: Lonnie E. Ward   a citizen of the Intermarried Nation.
Name of Mother: Adah Ward   a citizen of the Choctaw Nation.

                      Postoffice Dibble Ind Ter

AFFIDAVIT OF MOTHER.

UNITED STATES OF AMERICA, INDIAN TERRITORY, }
Southern   DISTRICT. }

    I, Adah Ward , on oath state that I am twenty-five years of age and a citizen by Blood , of the Choctaw Nation; that I am the lawful wife of Lonnie E Ward , who is a citizen, by Intermarried of the Choctaw Nation; that a Male child was born to me on 22^d day of April , 1903, that said child has been named Elias Jackson Ward , and is now living.

                                    Adah Ward

Applications for Enrollment of Choctaw Newborn
Act of 1905   Volume V

WITNESSES TO MARK:

Subscribed and sworn to before me this 29   day of   March   , 1905.

James M Gordon
Notary Public.

My Com Expires March 1907

AFFIDAVIT OF ATTENDING PHYSICIAN OR MID-WIFE.

UNITED STATES OF AMERICA, INDIAN TERRITORY,
Southern   DISTRICT.

I, J H Howard , a Physician , on oath state that I attended on Mrs. Adah Ward , wife of Lonnie E. Ward on the 22 day of April , 190 3; that there was born to her on said date a Male child; that said child is now living and is said to have been named Elias Jackson Ward

WITNESSES TO MARK: J.H. Howard M.D.

Subscribed and sworn to before me this 29   day of   March   , 1905.

James M Gordon
Notary Public.

My Com Expires March 1907

BIRTH AFFIDAVIT.

DEPARTMENT OF THE INTERIOR.
COMMISSION TO THE FIVE CIVILIZED TRIBES.

IN RE APPLICATION FOR ENROLLMENT, as a citizen of the   Choctaw   Nation of   Maggie Lorene Ward , born on the _____ day of _____ , 1_____

Name of Father: Lonnie E. Ward   a citizen of the Intermarried Nation.
Name of Mother: Adah Ward   a citizen of the   Choctaw   Nation.

Postoffice   Dibble Ind Ter

224

Applications for Enrollment of Choctaw Newborn
Act of 1905 Volume V

AFFIDAVIT OF MOTHER.

UNITED STATES OF AMERICA, INDIAN TERRITORY,
Southern DISTRICT.

I, Adah Ward, on oath state that I am twenty-five years of age and a citizen by Blood, of the Choctaw Nation; that I am the lawful wife of Lonnie E Ward, who is a citizen, by Intermarried of the Choctaw Nation; that a Female child was born to me on ~~Nov~~ 13 day of Nov, 1904, that said child has been named Maggie Lorene Ward, and is now living.

WITNESSES TO MARK: Adah Ward

Subscribed and sworn to before me this 29 day of March, 1905.

                         James M Gordon
                               Notary Public.

My Com Expires March 1907

AFFIDAVIT OF ATTENDING PHYSICIAN OR MID-WIFE.

UNITED STATES OF AMERICA, INDIAN TERRITORY,
Southern DISTRICT.

I, W.W. Crenshaw, a Physician, on oath state that I attended on Mrs. Adah Ward, wife of Lonnie E. Ward on the 13 day of Nov, 1904; that there was born to her on said date a Female child; that said child is now living and is said to have been named Maggie Lorene Ward

WITNESSES TO MARK: W.W. Crenshaw M.D.

Subscribed and sworn to before me this 29 day of March, 1905.

                         James M Gordon
                             Notary Public.

My Com Expires March 1907

Applications for Enrollment of Choctaw Newborn
Act of 1905   Volume V

BIRTH AFFIDAVIT.

DEPARTMENT OF THE INTERIOR.
COMMISSION TO THE FIVE CIVILIZED TRIBES.

IN RE APPLICATION FOR ENROLLMENT, as a citizen of the   Choctaw   Nation, of Elias Jackson Ward   , born on the 22   day of   April , 1903

Name of Father: L. E. Ward   a non citizen of the ....Nation.
Name of Mother: Adah Ward   a citizen of the   Choctaw   Nation.

Postoffice   *(Illegible)*

AFFIDAVIT OF MOTHER.

UNITED STATES OF AMERICA, Indian Territory, }
    Southern   DISTRICT. }

I,   Adah Ward   , on oath state that I am   25   years of age and a citizen by blood   , of the   Choctaw   Nation; that I am the lawful wife of   L E Ward   , who is a citizen, by blood   of the   United States Nation; that a   male   child was born to me on   22   day of   April   , 1903; that said child has been named Elias Jackson Ward   , and was living March 4, 1905.

                            Adah Ward

Witnesses To Mark:
{

Subscribed and sworn to before me this   4 day of   April   , 1905

                          J.E. Williams
                              Notary Public.

AFFIDAVIT OF ATTENDING PHYSICIAN OR MID-WIFE.

UNITED STATES OF AMERICA, Indian Territory, }
Southern   DISTRICT. }

I,   J H Howard   , a   M.D.   , on oath state that I attended on Mrs.   Alluh[sic] Ward   , wife of   Lonnie E Ward   on the 22^{d} day of April , 1903; that there was born to her on said date a   Male   child; that said child was living March 4, 1905, and is said to have been named Elias Jackson Ward

                         J.H. Howard M.D.

Witnesses To Mark:
{

Applications for Enrollment of Choctaw Newborn
Act of 1905   Volume V

Subscribed and sworn to before me this 5 day of   April   , 1905

J M Gordon
Notary Public.

My term of office expires Mch 1907

BIRTH AFFIDAVIT.

DEPARTMENT OF THE INTERIOR.
COMMISSION TO THE FIVE CIVILIZED TRIBES.

IN RE APPLICATION FOR ENROLLMENT, as a citizen of the   Choctaw   Nation, of Maggie Lorine[sic] Ward   , born on the 13th day of   November , 1904

Name of Father: L. E. Ward   a citizen of the   U.S.   Nation.
Name of Mother: Adah Ward   a citizen of the   Choctaw   Nation.

Postoffice   Dibble I.T.

AFFIDAVIT OF MOTHER.

UNITED STATES OF AMERICA, Indian Territory, }
    Southern   **DISTRICT.** }

I,   Adah Ward   , on oath state that I am 25   years of age and a citizen by blood   , of the   Choctaw   Nation; that I am the lawful wife of   L E Ward   , who is a citizen, by blood   of the   United States   Nation; that a   female   child was born to me on   13th day of   November   , 1904; that said child has been named Maggie Lorine Ward   , and was living March 4, 1905.

Adah Ward

Witnesses To Mark:
{

Subscribed and sworn to before me this 4 day of   April   , 1905

J.E. Williams
Notary Public.

Applications for Enrollment of Choctaw Newborn
Act of 1905   Volume V

AFFIDAVIT OF ATTENDING PHYSICIAN OR MID-WIFE.

UNITED STATES OF AMERICA, Indian Territory,}
Southern   DISTRICT.

I, W.W. Crenshaw , a M.D. , on oath state that I attended on Mrs. Adah Ward , wife of Lonnie E Ward on the 13th day of Nov , 1904; that there was born to her on said date a Female child; that said child was living March 4, 1905, and is said to have been named Maggie Lorine Ward

Wesley W Crenshaw M.D.

Witnesses To Mark:
{

Subscribed and sworn to before me this 5th day of April , 1905

James M Gordon
Notary Public.
my term of office expires Mch 1907

BIRTH AFFIDAVIT.

DEPARTMENT OF THE INTERIOR.
COMMISSION TO THE FIVE CIVILIZED TRIBES.

IN RE APPLICATION FOR ENROLLMENT, as a citizen of the Choctaw Nation, of Elias Jackson Ward , born on the 22nd day of April , 1903

Name of Father: Lonnie E. Ward   a citizen of the Choctaw Nation.
Name of Mother: Adah Ward   a citizen of the Choctaw Nation.

Postoffice   Dibble Ind Ter

AFFIDAVIT OF MOTHER.

UNITED STATES OF AMERICA, Indian Territory,}
Southern   DISTRICT.

I, Adah Ward , on oath state that I am twenty-five years of age and a citizen by blood , of the Choctaw Nation; that I am the lawful wife of Lonnie E Ward , who is a citizen, by intermarriage of the Choctaw Nation; that a male child was born to me on 22nd day of April , 1903; that said child has been named Elias Jackson Ward , and was living March 4, 1905.

Adah Ward

Applications for Enrollment of Choctaw Newborn
Act of 1905 Volume V

Witnesses To Mark:

{

    Subscribed and sworn to before me this 14 day of   April   , 1905

                              James M Gordon
                              Notary Public.

My term of office expires Mch 1907

AFFIDAVIT OF ATTENDING PHYSICIAN OR MID-WIFE.

UNITED STATES OF AMERICA, Indian Territory, }
   Southern   DISTRICT. }

    I, John H Howard   , a   M.D.   , on oath state that I attended on Mrs. Adah Ward   , wife of   Lonnie E Ward   on the 22nd day of April , 1903; that there was born to her on said date a   Male   child; that said child was living March 4, 1905, and is said to have been named Elias Jackson Ward

                              John H. Howard M.D.

Witnesses To Mark:

{

    Subscribed and sworn to before me this 14th day of   April   , 1905

                              James M Gordon
                              Notary Public.

My term of office expires Mch 1907

                                      7-4163

                      Muskogee, Indian Territory, May 14, 1904.

Lonnie E. Ward,
    Dibble, Indian Territory.

Dear Madam[sic]:

    Receipt is hereby acknowledged of the affidavits of Ada Ward and J. H. Howard, relative to the birth of your infant son, Elias Jackson Ward, April 22, 1903, which it is presumed have been forwarded as an application for enrollment of said child as a citizen by blood of the Choctaw Nation.

    You are informed that under the provisions of the Act of Congress, approved July 1, 1902, the Commission is now without authority to receive or consider the original

Applications for Enrollment of Choctaw Newborn
Act of 1905   Volume V

application for enrollment of any person whomsoever as a citizen of the Choctaw or Chickasaw Nation.

Respectfully,

Chairman.

7-4163

Muskogee, Indian Territory, April 6, 1905.

Lonnie E. Ward,
    Dibble, Indian Territory.

Dear Sir:

    Receipt is hereby acknowledged of the affidavits of Adah Ward and J. H. Howard to the birth of Elias Jackson Ward, son of Lonnie and Adah Ward, April 22, 1903; also affidavits of Adah Ward and W. W. Crenshaw to the birth of Maggie Lorene Ward, daughter of Lonnie Ward and Adah Ward, November 13, 1904, and the same have been filed with our records as applications for the enrollment of said children.

Respectfully,

Commissioner in Charge.

N. B. 291

COPY

Muskogee, Indian Territory, April 10, 1905.

Lonnie E. Ward,
    Dibble, Indian Territory.

Dear Sir:

    There is inclosed you herewith for execution application for the enrollment of your infant child, Elias Jackson Ward, born April 22, 1903.

    The affidavits heretofore filed with the Commission show the child was living on May 5, 1904. It is necessary, for the child to be enrolled, that he was living on March 4, 1905. Please insert the mother's age in space provided for that purpose.

    In having these affidavits executed care should be exercised to see that all names are written in full, as they appear in the body of the affidavit, and in the event that either of the persons signing the affidavit are unable to write, signatures by mark must be

Applications for Enrollment of Choctaw Newborn
Act of 1905   Volume V

attested by two witnesses. Each affidavit must be executed before a Notary Public and the notarial seal and signature of the officer must be attached to each separate affidavit.

Respectfully,
SIGNED
T. B. Needles.
Commissioner in Charge.

LM 10-52

Choctaw 4163.

Muskogee, Indian Territory, April 12, 1905.

L. E. Ward,
    Dibble, Indian Territory.

Dear Sir:

    Receipt is hereby acknowledged of the affidavits of Adah Ward and J. H. Howard to the birth of Elias Jackson Ward; also the affidavits of Adah Ward and Wesley W. Crenshaw to the birth of Maggie Lorine Ward, children of Lonnie E. and Adah Ward, April 22, 1903 and November 13, 1904, respectively, and the same have been filed with our records as applications for the enrollment of said children.

Respectfully,

Commissioner in Charge.

Choctaw N.B. 291

Muskogee, Indian Territory, April 19, 1905.

Lonnie E. Ward,
    Dibble, Indian Territory.

Dear Sir:

    Receipt is hereby acknowledged of the affidavits of Adah Ward and John H. Howard to the birth of Elias Jackson Ward, son of Lonnie E. and Adah Ward, April 22, 1903, and the same have been filed with our records in the matter of the enrollment of the above named child.

Respectfully,

Chairman.

**Applications for Enrollment of Choctaw Newborn
Act of 1905   Volume V**

Choc New Born 292
    Thelma Thyra Selsor
    (Born Feb. 9, 1903)
    Shelby Selsor
    (Born April 12, 1905)

292

NEW BORN
CHOCTAW
ENROLLMENT

Thelma Thyra Selsor
    (Born February 9, 1903)

Shelby Selsor
    (Born April 12, 1905)

Subsequent to March 4, 1905
    No. 2 decision rendered Dec. 29, 1905
        Decline to receive or consider.
    copy of decision forwarded attorneys
    for Choctaw and Chickasaw nations[sic]
                    Dec. 29, 1905
    Copy of decision forwarded
    applicant Dec. 29, 1905
    Record forwarded department Dec. 29, 1905
    Action approved by Secretary of Interior.
                    Feb. 6, 1905

As Citizen of the
Choctaw NATION
Act of Congress
Approved March 3, 1905

Notice of departmental action forwarded attorney for Choctaw and
Chickasaw nations[sic]. Feb. 16, 1906

Notice of departmental actions
mailed applicant Feb. 16, 1906.

                Over

Applications for Enrollment of Choctaw Newborn
Act of 1905   Volume V

Oct. 31, 1906 Dept. requested to return record
as to No. 2 for readjudication under Act of
April 26, 1906. Nov. 30, 1906 Record returned
by Dept.

NEW BORN AFFIDAVIT

No ....

CHOCTAW ENROLLING COMMISSION

IN THE MATTER OF THE APPLICATION FOR ENROLLMENT as a citizen of the Choctaw Nation, of   Thelma Thyra Selsor   born on the 9th day of   Feb   190 3

Name of father   John Selsor   a citizen of   Choctaw   Nation, final enrollment No. 395
Name of mother   Agnes Selsor   a citizen of   Choctaw   Nation, final enrollment No. 11557

Owl I.T.   Postoffice.

AFFIDAVIT OF MOTHER

UNITED STATES OF AMERICA }
   INDIAN TERRITORY
DISTRICT   Central

I   Agnes Selsor   , on oath state that I am .... years of age and a citizen by   Blood   of the   Choctaw   Nation, and as such have been placed upon the final roll of the   Choctaw   Nation, by the Honorable Secretary of the Interior my final enrollment number being   11557 ; that I am the lawful wife of   John Selsor   , who is a citizen of the   Choctaw   Nation, and as such has been placed upon the final roll of said Nation by the Honorable Secretary of the Interior, his final enrollment number being   395   and that a   Female   child was born to me on the   9th   day of   Feb   190 3; that said child has been named   Thelma Thyra Selsor   , and is now living.

WITNESSETH: Agnes Selsor

Must be two witnesses { Frank Williams
who are citizens   { T. W. Jones

Applications for Enrollment of Choctaw Newborn
Act of 1905   Volume V

Subscribed and sworn to before me this, the 25 day of Feb 190 5

John H Cross
Notary Public.

My Commission Expires: Sept 24 1908

Affidavit of Attending Physician or Midwife

UNITED STATES OF AMERICA,
INDIAN TERRITORY,
.... DISTRICT

I, J. M. Settle a Physician on oath state that I attended on Mrs. Agnes Selsor wife of John Selsor on the 9 day of Feb , 190 3, that there was born to her on said date a Female child, that said child is now living, and is said to have been named Thelma Thyra Selsor

J.M. Settle M. D.

Subscribed and sworn to before me this the 21 day of Feb 1905

Minnie Lillard
Notary Public.

WITNESSETH:

Must be two witnesses who are citizens and know the child.
{ Frank Williams
  T. W. Jones

We hereby certify that we are well acquainted with J. M. Settle, M.D. a Physician and know him to be reputable and of good standing in the community.

Must be two citizen witnesses.
{ W F Harrison
  Marvin J Burris

Applications for Enrollment of Choctaw Newborn
Act of 1905   Volume V

BIRTH AFFIDAVIT.

DEPARTMENT OF THE INTERIOR.
COMMISSION TO THE FIVE CIVILIZED TRIBES.

IN RE APPLICATION FOR ENROLLMENT, as a citizen of the Choctaw Nation, of Thelma Thyra Selsor, born on the 9 day of Feb, 1903

Name of Father: John Selsor   a citizen of the Choctaw Nation.
Name of Mother: Agnes Selsor   a citizen of the Choctaw Nation.

Postoffice   Owl I.T.

AFFIDAVIT OF MOTHER.

UNITED STATES OF AMERICA, Indian Territory,
Central DISTRICT.

I, Agnes Selsor, on oath state that I am 34 years of age and a citizen by Blood, of the Choctaw Nation; that I am the lawful wife of John Selsor, who is a citizen, by Intermarriage of the Choctaw Nation; that a Female child was born to me on 9 day of Feb, 1903; that said child has been named Thelma Thyra Selsor, and was living March 4, 1905.

Agnes Selsor

Witnesses To Mark:

Subscribed and sworn to before me this 27 day of March, 1905

John H Cross
Notary Public.

AFFIDAVIT OF ATTENDING PHYSICIAN OR MID-WIFE.

UNITED STATES OF AMERICA, Indian Territory,
Central DISTRICT.

Also Dr. Settle attended with me
I, Susan Johnston, a Midwife, on oath state that I attended on Mrs. Agnes Selsor, wife of John Selsor on the 9 day of Feb, 1903; that there was born to her on said date a Female child; that said child was living March 4, 1905, and is said to have been named Thelma Thyra Selsor

Susan Johnston

Witnesses To Mark:

Applications for Enrollment of Choctaw Newborn
Act of 1905 Volume V

Subscribed and sworn to before me this 27 day of March, 1905

John H Cross
Notary Public.

DEPARTMENT OF THE INTERIOR,
COMMISSIONER TO THE FIVE CIVILIZED TRIBES.

Record in the matter of the application for the enrollment as a citizen by blood of the Choctaw Nation of - - -

Shelby Selsor.

7-N.B.292.

BIRTH AFFIDAVIT.

DEPARTMENT OF THE INTERIOR.
COMMISSION TO THE FIVE CIVILIZED TRIBES.

IN RE APPLICATION FOR ENROLLMENT, as a citizen of the Choctaw Nation, of Shelby Selsor, born on the 12 day of April, 1905

Name of Father: John Selsor   a citizen of the Choctaw Nation.
Name of Mother: Agnes Selsor   a citizen of the Choctaw Nation.

Postoffice   Owl I.T.

AFFIDAVIT OF MOTHER.

UNITED STATES OF AMERICA, Indian Territory,
Central   DISTRICT.

I, Agnes Selsor, on oath state that I am 35 years of age and a citizen by Blood, of the Choctaw Nation; that I am the lawful wife of John Selsor, who is a citizen, by Intermarriage of the Choctaw Nation; that a male child was born to me on 12 day of April, 1905; that said child has been named Shelby Selsor, and was living March 4, 1905.

Agnes Selsor

Witnesses To Mark:

Applications for Enrollment of Choctaw Newborn
Act of 1905 Volume V

Subscribed and sworn to before me this 29 day of   April   , 1905

>John H Cross
>Notary Public.

AFFIDAVIT OF ATTENDING PHYSICIAN OR MID-WIFE.

UNITED STATES OF AMERICA, Indian Territory, }
Central   DISTRICT. }

I, J. A. Carmack, a Physician, on oath state that I attended on Mrs. Agnes Selsor, wife of John Selsor on the 12 day of April, 1905; that there was born to her on said date a male ~~child; that said child was living March 4, 1905~~, said child is now living and is said to have been named Shelby Selsor

>J A Carmack

Witnesses To Mark:
{

Subscribed and sworn to before me this 29 day of   April   , 1905

>John H Cross
>Notary Public.

7-N.B. 292.

DEPARTMENT OF THE INTERIOR,
COMMISSIONER TO THE FIVE CIVILIZED TRIBES.

In the matter of the application for the enrollment of Shelby Selsor as a citizen by blood of the Choctaw Nation.

--:DECISION:--

It appears from the record herein that on May 1, 1905 there was filed with the Commission to the Five Civilized Tribes an application for the enrollment of Shelby Selsor as a citizen by blood of the Choctaw Nation.

It further appears from the record herein, and from the records of the Commission to the Five Civilized Tribes, that the applicant was born April 12, 1905, and is the son of Agnes Selsor, a recognized and enrolled citizen by blood of the Choctaw Nation, whose name appears as No. 11557 upon the final roll of citizens by blood of the Choctaw Nation approved by the Secretary of the Interior the March 10, 1903, and John Selsor, a recognized and enrolled citizen by intermarriage of the Choctaw Nation, whose name appears as No. 395 upon the final roll of citizens by intermarriage of the Choctaw Nation approved by the Secretary of the Interior September 3, 1903.

Applications for Enrollment of Choctaw Newborn
Act of 1905   Volume V

The Act of Congress approved March 3, 1905, (33 Stats., 1060), provides:
"That the Commission to the Five Civilized Tribes is authorized for sixty days after the date of the approval of this act to receive and consider applications for enrollment of children born subsequent to September twenty-fifth, nineteen hundred and two, and prior to March fourth, nineteen hundred and five, and who were living on said latter date, to citizens by blood of the Choctaw and Chickasaw tribes of Indians whose enrollment has been approved by the Secretary of the Interior prior to the date of the approval of this act; and to enroll and make allotments to such children."

I am of the opinion that, inasmuch as the said Shelby Selsor was not born prior to March 4, 1905, I am without authority to receive or consider the application for his enrollment as a citizen by blood of the Choctaw Nation and that therefore, I should decline to receive or consider said application under the provisions of the law above quotes, and it is so ordered.

Tams Bixby Commissioner.

Muskogee, Indian Territory.
DEC 29 1905

7-NB-292

COPY

Muskogee, Indian Territory, December 29, 1905.

John Selsor,
    Owl, Indian Territory.

Dear Sir:

Inclosed herewith you will find a copy of the decision of the Commissioner to the Five Civilized Tribes, rendered December 29, 1905, declining to receive or consider the application for the enrollment of your minor child, Shelby Selsor, as a citizen by blood of the Choctaw Nation.

The decision, with the record of proceedings in the case, is this day transmitted to the Secretary of the Interior for review. The final decision of the Secretary will be made known to you as soon as this office is informed of the same.

Respectfully,
SIGNED   Tams Bixby
Commissioner.

Registered.
Incl. 7-NB-292.

Applications for Enrollment of Choctaw Newborn
Act of 1905   Volume V

7-NB-292   **COPY**

Muskogee, Indian Territory, December 29, 1905.

Mansfield, McMurray & Cornish,
    Attorneys for Choctaw and Chickasaw Nations,
        South McAlester, Indian Territory.

Gentlemen:

    Inclosed herewith you will find a copy of the decision of the Commissioner to the Five Civilized Tribes, rendered December 29, 1905, declining to receive or consider the application for the enrollment of your minor child, Shelby Selsor, as a citizen by blood of the Choctaw Nation.

    The decision, with the record of proceedings in the case, is this day transmitted to the Secretary of the Interior for review. The final decision of the Secretary will be made known to you as soon as this office is informed of the same.

                                              Respectfully,
                                            SIGNED   *Tams Bixby*

Incl. 7-NB-292.   Commissioner.

COPY

Muskogee, Indian Territory, December 29, 1905.

The Honorable,
    The Secretary of the Interior.

Sir:

    There is herewith transmitted the record of proceedings in the matter of the application for the enrollment of Shelby Selsor as a citizen by blood of the Choctaw Nation, including the decision of the Commissioner to the Five Civilized Tribes, dated December 29, 1905, declining to receive or consider said application.

                                              Respectfully,
                                            SIGNED   *Tams Bixby*

2 Incl. 7-NB-292.   Commissioner.

Through the
    Commissioner of Indian Affairs.

Applications for Enrollment of Choctaw Newborn
Act of 1905   Volume V

Land
124-1906   (Copy)

DEPARTMENT OF THE INTERIOR.
Office of Indian Affairs.

WASHINGTON, January 24, 1906.

The Honorable,
   The Secretary of the Interior.

Sir:

I have the honor to enclose a report from the Commissioner to the Five Civilized Tribes, dated December 29, 1905, transmitting the record relative to the application for enrollment as a citizen by blood of Shelby Selsor.

December 29, 1905, the Commissioner decided adversely to the application.

The record shows that Shelby Selsor was born April 12, 1905, and is the son of Agnes Selsor, whose name appears at Number 11557, on the final roll of citizens by blood of the Choctaw Nation approved by the Department March 10, 1903, and John Selsor, whose name appears at Number 395 on the final roll of citizens by intermarriage of the Choctaw Nation approved by the Department September 3, 1903.

In view of the record and of the fact that Shelby Selsor was not born prior to March 4, 1905, as required by the terms of the act of March 3, 1905 (33 Stats., 1071), the approval of the Commissioner's decision adverse to the application is recommended.

Very respectfully,

MMM - C   C. F. LARRABEE, Acting Commissioner.

Applications for Enrollment of Choctaw Newborn
Act of 1905 Volume V

D.C. 5406-1906
I.T.D.1426-1906 (Copy)

CRW
LLB
LRS

Secretary's Office.
DEPARTMENT OF THE INTERIOR,
Washington, D. C.

February 6, 1906.

Commissioner to the Five Civilized Tribes,
Muskogee, Indian Territory.

Sir:

December 29, 1905, you transmitted the record in the matter of the application for the enrollment of Shelby Selsor as a citizen by blood of the Choctaw Nation.

Reporting January 24, 1906, the Indian Office recommended that your decision, adverse to the applicant be approved. A copy of its letter is inclosed.

The Department concure[sic] in said recommendation, and your decision dated December 29, 1905, is hereby affirmed.

Respectfully,

(signed) THOS. RYAN.
First Assistant Secretary.

1 inclosure.

7-NB-292

Muskogee, Indian Territory, February 16, 1906.

John Selsor,
Owl, Indian Territory.

Dear Sir:

You are hereby notified that the Secretary of the Interior the Interior under date of February 6, 1906, affirmed the decision of this office dated December 29, 1905, declining to receive or consider the application for the enrollment of your minor child, Shelby Selsor, as a citizen by blood of the Choctaw Nation.

Respectfully,
Acting Commissioner.

Applications for Enrollment of Choctaw Newborn
Act of 1905   Volume V

7-NB-292

Muskogee, Indian Territory, February 16, 1906.

Mansfield, McMurray & Cornish,
    Attorneys for Choctaw and Chickasaw Nations,
        South McAlester, Indian Territory.

Gentlemen:

    You are hereby notified that the Secretary of the Interior under date of February 6, 1906, affirmed the decision of this office dated December 29, 1905, declining to receive or consider the application for the enrollment of Shelby Selsor as a citizen by blood of the Choctaw Nation.

                Respectfully,

                                  Acting Commissioner.

7-292

Muskogee, Indian Territory, February 23, 1906.

Chief Clerk,
    Choctaw Land Office,
        Atoka, Indian Territory.

Dear Sir:

    Receipt is hereby acknowledged of your letter of February 17, 1906, in which you state that the name of Shelby Selsor does not appear on duplicate Choctaw new born card No. 292 in your possession.

    For your information there is inclosed herewith copy of Choctaw new born card No. 292 and you are directed to make the records of your office conform to the information thereon.

                Respectfully,

KB 2-23.   Acting Commissioner.

Applications for Enrollment of Choctaw Newborn
Act of 1905   Volume V

7-292

Muskogee, Indian Territory, February 23, 1906.

Chief Clerk,
    Chickasaw Land Office,
        Ardmore, Indian Territory.

Dear Sir:

For your information there is inclosed herewith copy of Choctaw new born card No. 292.

You are therefore directed to make duplicate of this card in your possession conform to the information thereon.

Respectfully,

KB 3-23.   Acting Commissioner.

7-NB-292

Muskogee, Indian Territory, May 7, 1906.

John Selsor,
    Owl, Indian Territory.

Dear Sir:

Receipt is hereby acknowledged of your letter of May 3, 1906, making application for the enrollment of your son Shelby Selsor who was born April 12, 1905, and stating that you forwarded affidavits to his enrollment last July.

The communications from this office inclosed with your letter are herewith returned and you are advised that if you desire to make application for the enrollment of your son Shelby Selsor under the act of Congress approved April 26, 1906, you should forward evidence of his birth upon the blank inclosed herewith.

Respectfully,

EB 1-7   Acting Commissioner.
B. C.

Applications for Enrollment of Choctaw Newborn
Act of 1905   Volume V

Muskogee, Indian Territory, October 31, 1906.

The Honorable,
    The Secretary of the Interior.

Sir:

    December 29, 1905, the Commissioner to the Five Civilized Tribes rendered a decision declining to receive or consider the application of Shelby Selsor for enrollment as a citizen of the Choctaw Nation under the Act of Congress approved March 3, 1905 for the reason that said child was born subsequent to March 3, 1905, and on February 4, 1906 (I.T.D. 1426-1906) this acting was approved by the Secretary of the Interior.

    In view of the provision of Section 2 of the Act of Congress approved April 26, 1906, I have the honor to request that the record in this case be returned for readjudication under said act.

    Respectfully,

Through the Commissioner   Commissioner.
    of Indian Affairs.

COPY

DEPARTMENT OF THE INTERIOR,
OFFICE OF INDIAN AFFAIRS,

Land

WASHINGTON.

12386-1906   November 20, 1906.
96982-1906.

The Honorable,
    The Secretary of the Interior.

Sir:

    Referring to Departmental letter of February 6, 1906, (I.T.D. 1426-1906), affirming the decision of the Commissioner to the Five Civilized Tribes, rejecting the application of Shelby Selsor for enrollment as a citizen by blood of the Choctaw Nation, I have the honor to transmit herewith a communication from the Commissioner to the Five Civilized Tribes, dated October 31, 1906, requesting that the record in this case be returned to him for readjudication under the provisions of section 2 of the Act of Congress approved April 26, 1906 (34 Stat., 137).

    The record in this case is also transmitted.

Applications for Enrollment of Choctaw Newborn
Act of 1905   Volume V

Very respectfully,

C. F. Larrabee,

Acting Commissioner.

EWE-EH.

CRW

DEPARTMENT OF THE INTERIOR,   llb

WASHINGTON.

I.T.D. 1426-1906
23254-
D. C. 53176-1906

November 30, 1906.

LRS.

Commissioner to the Five Civilized Tribes,
   Muskogee, Indian Territory.

Sir:

On November 20, 1906 (Land 96982), the Indian Office transmitted the record, together with your communication, dated October 31, 1906, requesting that the record in the matter of the rejected application of Shelby Selsor for enrollment as a citizen by blood of the Choctaw Nation be returned to you for readjudication under the provisions of section 2 of the act of Congress approved Aril 26, 1906, (34 Stat., 137).

In view of said act, the record is returned as requested.

Respectfully,

Thos. Ryan,

First Assistant Secretary.

Through the Commissioner
   of Indian Affairs.

4 inclosures.

Applications for Enrollment of Choctaw Newborn
Act of 1905   Volume V

7NB292.

Muskogee, Indian Territory, December 15, 1906.

John Selsor,
  Owl, Indian Territory.

Dear Sir:

You are hereby advised that on November 30, 1906, the Secretary of the Interior remanded the record in the matter of the application for the enrollment of your child, Shelby Selsor, born April 12, 1905, as a newborn citizen of the Choctaw Nation, under the Act of Congress approved March 3, 1905, for enrollment under the Act of April 26, 1906.

You should therefore forward affidavits to the birth of this child, on the blank enclosed herewith, for the purpose of showing whether or not said child was living March 4, 1906.

Respectfully,

BA   Commissioner.

Choc New Born 293
  Ambrose Henry Ward
  (Born Nov. 3, 1904)

BIRTH AFFIDAVIT.

DEPARTMENT OF THE INTERIOR.
COMMISSION TO THE FIVE CIVILIZED TRIBES.

IN RE APPLICATION FOR ENROLLMENT, as a citizen of the   Choctaw   Nation, of Ambrose Henry Ward   , born on the   3   day of   Nov   , 1904

Name of Father: Benjamin F Ward   a citizen of the   Choctaw   Nation.
Name of Mother: Locey[sic] Ward   a citizen of the   Choctaw   Nation.

Postoffice   Hewitt

Applications for Enrollment of Choctaw Newborn
Act of 1905   Volume V

AFFIDAVIT OF MOTHER.

UNITED STATES OF AMERICA, Indian Territory,
Southern DISTRICT.

I, Lockey Ward, on oath state that I am 20 years of age and a citizen by Marriage, of the Choctaw Nation; that I am the lawful wife of Benjamin F Ward, who is a citizen, by blood of the Choctaw Nation; that a male child was born to me on 3rd day of Nov, 1904, that said child has been named Ambrose Henry Ward, and is now living.

                                            Lockey Ward

Witnesses To Mark:
- E.S. Adde
- A S Patterson

Subscribed and sworn to before me this 28 day of January, 1905.

                                            GR Spencer
                                                  Notary Public.

AFFIDAVIT OF ATTENDING PHYSICIAN OR MID-WIFE.

UNITED STATES OF AMERICA, Indian Territory,
Southern DISTRICT.

I, Ambrose M Davie, a Physician, on oath state that I attended on Mrs. Lockey Ward, wife of Benjamin F Ward on the 3 day of November, 1904; that there was born to her on said date a male child; that said child is now living and is said to have been named Ambrose Henry Ward

                                            AM David MD

Witnesses To Mark:
- E.S. Adde
- A S Patterson

Subscribed and sworn to before me this 28 day of January, 1905.

                                            GR Spencer
                                                 Notary Public.

Applications for Enrollment of Choctaw Newborn
Act of 1905   Volume V

BIRTH AFFIDAVIT.

DEPARTMENT OF THE INTERIOR.
COMMISSION TO THE FIVE CIVILIZED TRIBES.

IN RE APPLICATION FOR ENROLLMENT, as a citizen of the Choctaw Nation, of Ambrose Henry Ward, born on the 3rd day of November, 1904

Name of Father: Benjamin F Ward   a citizen of the Choctaw Nation.
Name of Mother: Lockey Ward   a citizen of the Choctaw Nation.

Postoffice Hewitt

AFFIDAVIT OF MOTHER.

UNITED STATES OF AMERICA, Indian Territory, }
Southern DISTRICT.

I, Lockey Ward, on oath state that I am 20 years of age and a citizen by intermarriage, of the Choctaw Nation; that I am the lawful wife of Benjamin F Ward, who is a citizen, by blood of the Choctaw Nation; that a male child was born to me on 3rd day of November, 1904; that said child has been named Ambrose Henry Ward, and was living March 4, 1905.

Lockey Ward

Witnesses To Mark:
{

Subscribed and sworn to before me this 22 day of April, 1905.

W A Darling
Notary Public.

AFFIDAVIT OF ATTENDING PHYSICIAN OR MID-WIFE.

UNITED STATES OF AMERICA, Indian Territory, }
Southern DISTRICT.

I, A. M. Davie, a Physician, on oath state that I attended on Mrs. Lockey Ward, wife of Benjamin F Ward on the 3rd day of November, 1904; that there was born to her on said date a male child; that said child was living March 4, 1905, and is said to have been named Ambrose Henry Ward

AM Davie M.D.

Witnesses To Mark:
{

Applications for Enrollment of Choctaw Newborn
Act of 1905 Volume V

Subscribed and sworn to before me this 22 day of April , 1905

W A Darling
Notary Public.

7-4134

Muskogee, Indian Territory, February 4, 1905.

Benjamin F. Ward,
    Hewitt, Indian Territory.

Dear Sir:

    Receipt is hereby acknowledged of the affidavits of Lockey Ward and A. M. Davy[sic] to the birth of Ambrose Henry Ward, son of Benjamin F. and Lockey Ward, November 31, 1904, which it is presumed have been forwarded as an application for enrollment of said child.

    You are advised that under the provisions of the act of Congress approved July 1, 1902, no children born to citizens of the Choctaw and Chickasaw Nations subsequent to September 25, 1902, the date of the ratification of said act, are entitled to enrollment and allotment in the Choctaw and Chickasaw Nations.

Respectfully,

Chairman.

7-4134

Muskogee, Indian Territory, February 17, 1905.

Benjamin F. Ward,
    Hewitt, Indian Territory.

Dear Sir:

    Receipt is hereby acknowledged of your letter of February 12, 1905, relative to the affidavits recently forwarded to the birth of your son Ambrose Henry Ward, November 31, 1904, and calling attention to the fact that the date of his death as given in our letter was in error.

    In reply to your letter you are advised that it appears from the affidavits of Lockey Ward and Ambrose M. Davie that said child was born November 3, 1904. You are advised, however, that under the provisions of the act of Congress approved July 1, 1902,

Applications for Enrollment of Choctaw Newborn
Act of 1905 Volume V

no children born to citizens of the Choctaw and Chickasaw Nations subsequent to September 25, 1902, the date of the ratification of said act, are entitled to enrollment and allotment in the Choctaw and Chickasaw Nations.

Respectfully,

Chairman.

N. B. 293

COPY

Muskogee, Indian Territory, April 8, 1905.

Benjamin F. Ward,
  Hewitt, Indian Territory.

Dear Sir:

There is inclosed you herewith for execution application for the enrollment of your infant child, Ambrose Henry Ward, born November 3, 1904.

The affidavits heretofore filed with the Commission show the child was living on January 28, 1905. It is necessary, for the child to be enrolled, that he was living on March 4, 1905. You will please insert the mother's age in space for the purpose.

In having these affidavits executed care should be exercised to see that all names are written in full, as they appear in the body of the affidavit, and in the event that either of the persons signing the affidavit are unable to write, signatures by mark must be attested by two witnesses. Each affidavit must be executed before a Notary Public and the notarial seal and signature of the officer must be attached to each separate affidavit.

Respectfully,
SIGNED
T. B. Needles.
Commissioner in Charge.

Applications for Enrollment of Choctaw Newborn
Act of 1905 Volume V

7 NB 293

Muskogee, Indian Territory, April 26, 1905.

Benjamin F. Ward,
    Hewitt, Indian Territory.

Dear Sir:

    Receipt is hereby acknowledged of the affidavits of Lockey Ward and A. M. Davie to the birth of Ambrose Henry Ward, son of Benjamin F. and Lockey Ward, November 3, 1904, and the same have been filed with the records in the matter of the enrollment of said child.

                Respectfully,

                            Chairman.

Choc New Born 294
    Frances Willis
    (Born Oct. 18, 1904)

BIRTH AFFIDAVIT.

DEPARTMENT OF THE INTERIOR.
COMMISSION TO THE FIVE CIVILIZED TRIBES.

IN RE APPLICATION FOR ENROLLMENT, as a citizen of the Choctaw Nation, of Frances Willis, born on the 18th day of October, 1904

Name of Father: Eastman Willis   a citizen of the Choctaw Nation.
Name of Mother: Bicy "   a citizen of the " Nation.

Postoffice   Atoka I T

AFFIDAVIT OF MOTHER.

UNITED STATES OF AMERICA, Indian Territory,
    Central   DISTRICT.

    I, Bicy Willis, on oath state that I am 28 years of age and a citizen by blood, of the Choctaw Nation; that I am the lawful wife of Eastman Willis, who is a citizen, by blood of the Choctaw Nation; that a female child

Applications for Enrollment of Choctaw Newborn
Act of 1905 Volume V

was born to me on 18th   day of October   , 1904; that said child has been named Frances Willis , and was living March 4, 1905.

                                      Her
                              Bicy x Willis

Witnesses To Mark: mark
{ WH Martin
{ J.D. Ward

Subscribed and sworn to before me this 18th day of   March   , 1905

                                 W.H. Angell
                                   Notary Public.

AFFIDAVIT OF ATTENDING PHYSICIAN OR MID-WIFE.

UNITED STATES OF AMERICA, Indian Territory,
   Central   DISTRICT.

    I,   Eliza Ann Sexton   , a   Mid-wife   , on oath state that I attended on Mrs. Bicy Willis   , wife of   Eastman Willis   on the 18th day of October , 1904; that there was born to her on said date a   female   child; that said child was living March 4, 1905, and is said to have been named   Frances Willis

                                   Her
                           Eliza Ann x Sexton

Witnesses To Mark: mark
{ WH Martin
{ J.D. Ward

Subscribed and sworn to before me this 18th day of   March   , 1905

                                 W.H. Angell
                                   Notary Public.

Applications for Enrollment of Choctaw Newborn
Act of 1905   Volume V

Choc New Born 295
    Carrel[sic] Tucker
    (Born Dec. 21, 1902)
    Grady Tucker
    (Born Dec. 14, 1904)

Indian Territory
Central District.

    Edward T. Tucker being first duly sworn deposes and says that he is a citizen, by marriage, of the Choctaw Nation and that there was born to his wife, Zona Tucker, a male child on the 21st day of December 1902, and that said child is now living [sic] has been named   Carrel Tucker

                              Edward T. Tucker

Subscribed and sworn to before me this the 22nd day of December 1902.

                              CG Adkins
                                  Notary Public.

Indian Territory,
Central District.

    Mrs. Zona Tucker being first duly sworn deposes and says that she is a citizen of the Choctaw Nation by blood; that she is the wife of Edward T. Tucker and that there was born to her on the 21st day of December 1902, a male child; that said child is now living and has been named   Carrel Tucker

                              Zona Tucker

Subscribed and sworn to before me this the 22nd day of December 1902.

                              CG Adkins
                                  Notary Public.

Indian Territory,
Central District.

    I. T. Harbour being first duly sworn deposes and says that he is a practicing physician and that he attended Mrs. E. T. Tucker during confinement on the 21st day of December 1902, and that there was born to her a male child; that said child is living and said to have been named   Carrel Tucker

                              I. T. Harbour M.D.

Applications for Enrollment of Choctaw Newborn
Act of 1905   Volume V

Subscribed and sworn to before me this the 22nd day of December 1902.

         CG Adkins
           Notary Public.

NEW-BORN AFFIDAVIT.

   Number...............

...Choctaw Enrolling Commission...

IN THE MATTER OF THE APPLICATION FOR ENROLLMENT, as a citizen of the Choctaw Nation, of   Carrel Tucker

born on the   21   day of   Dec   190 2

Name of father   Edward T Tucker   a citizen of   Choctaw
Nation final enrollment No.   31
Name of mother   Zona Tucker   a citizen of   Choctaw
Nation final enrollment No.   6665

          Postoffice   Cameron, I.T.

AFFIDAVIT OF MOTHER.

UNITED STATES OF AMERICA
INDIAN TERRITORY
 Central   DISTRICT

    I   Zona Tucker   , on oath state that I am   30   years of age and a citizen by   Blood   of the   Choctaw   Nation, and as such have been placed upon the final roll of the   Choctaw   Nation, by the Honorable Secretary of the Interior my final enrollment number being   6665 ; that I am the lawful wife of   Edward T Tucker   , who is a citizen of the   Choctaw   Nation, and as such has been placed upon the final roll of said Nation by the Honorable Secretary of the Interior, his final enrollment number being   31   and that a   Male   child was born to me on the   21   day of   Dec   190 2; that said child has been named   Carrel Tucker   , and is now living.

Witnesseth.   Zona Tucker

 Must be two
 Witnesses who Clyde McMurtrey
 are Citizens.   Alfred Wade McClure

Applications for Enrollment of Choctaw Newborn
Act of 1905   Volume V

Subscribed and sworn to before me this 11 day of Feb 190 5

(Name Illegible)
Notary Public.

My commission expires:

AFFIDAVIT OF ATTENDING PHYSICIAN OR MIDWIFE

UNITED STATES OF AMERICA
INDIAN TERRITORY
   Central   DISTRICT

I, I.T. Harbour a Physician on oath state that I attended on Mrs. Zona Tucker wife of Edward T Tucker on the 21 day of Dec , 190 2, that there was born to her on said date a male child, that said child is now living, and is said to have been named Carrel Tucker

I.T. Harbour $m.D.$

Subscribed and sworn to before me this, the 11 day of Feb 190 5

(Name Illegible) Notary Public.

WITNESSETH:

Must be two witnesses who are citizens
{ Alfred Wade McClure
  Clyde McMurtrey

We hereby certify that we are well acquainted with I.T. Harbour a Physician and know him to be reputable and of good standing in the community.

Alfred Wade McClure   _____

Clyde McMurtrey   _____

Applications for Enrollment of Choctaw Newborn
Act of 1905   Volume V

NEW-BORN AFFIDAVIT.

Number..................

...Choctaw Enrolling Commission...

IN THE MATTER OF THE APPLICATION FOR ENROLLMENT, as a citizen of the Choctaw Nation, of Grady Tucker

born on the 15 day of __Dec__ 190 4

Name of father   Edward T Tucker   a citizen of   Choctaw Nation final enrollment No. 31
Name of mother   Zona Tucker   a citizen of   Choctaw Nation final enrollment No. 6665

Postoffice   Cameron, I.T.

AFFIDAVIT OF MOTHER.

UNITED STATES OF AMERICA
INDIAN TERRITORY
   Central   DISTRICT

I   Zona Tucker   , on oath state that I am 30 years of age and a citizen by   Blood   of the   Choctaw   Nation, and as such have been placed upon the final roll of the Choctaw Nation, by the Honorable Secretary of the Interior my final enrollment number being   6665 ; that I am the lawful wife of   Edward T Tucker   , who is a citizen of the Choctaw   Nation, and as such has been placed upon the final roll of said Nation by the Honorable Secretary of the Interior, his final enrollment number being   31   and that a   Male   child was born to me on the   15   day of   Dec   190 4; that said child has been named   Grady Tucker   , and is now living.

Witnesseth.   Zona Tucker

Must be two Witnesses who are Citizens.   Clyde McMurtrey
                                          Alfred Wade McClure

Subscribed and sworn to before me this   11   day of   Feb   190 5

                                (Name Illegible)
                                      Notary Public.
My commission expires:

Applications for Enrollment of Choctaw Newborn
Act of 1905 Volume V

AFFIDAVIT OF ATTENDING PHYSICIAN OR MIDWIFE

UNITED STATES OF AMERICA
INDIAN TERRITORY
Central DISTRICT

I, M.W. Harrison a Physician on oath state that I attended on Mrs. Zona Tucker wife of Edward T Tucker on the 15 day of Dec , 190 4, that there was born to her on said date a male child, that said child is now living, and is said to have been named Grady Tucker

M.W. Harrison *M.D.*

Subscribed and sworn to before me this, the 11 day of Feb 190 5

(Name Illegible) Notary Public.

WITNESSETH:
Must be two witnesses who are citizens
 { Alfred Wade McClure

Clyde McMurtrey

We hereby certify that we are well acquainted with M.W. Harrison a Physician and know him to be reputable and of good standing in the community.

Alfred Wade McClure

Clyde McMurtrey

BIRTH AFFIDAVIT.

DEPARTMENT OF THE INTERIOR.
COMMISSION TO THE FIVE CIVILIZED TRIBES.

IN RE APPLICATION FOR ENROLLMENT, as a citizen of the Choctaw Nation, of Grady Tucker , born on the 15 day of Dec , 1904

Name of Father: Edward T Tucker a citizen of the Choctaw Nation.
Name of Mother: Zona Tucker a citizen of the Choctaw Nation.

Postoffice Cameron I.T.

Applications for Enrollment of Choctaw Newborn
Act of 1905 Volume V

AFFIDAVIT OF MOTHER.

UNITED STATES OF AMERICA, Indian Territory,
Central DISTRICT.

I, Zona Tucker, on oath state that I am 33 years of age and a citizen by blood, of the Choctaw Nation; that I am the lawful wife of Edward T. Tucker, who is a citizen, by marriage of the Choctaw Nation; that a male child was born to me on 15th day of December, 1904, that said child has been named Grady Tucker, and is now living.

        Zona Tucker

Witnesses To Mark:

 Subscribed and sworn to before me this 30th day of March, 1905.

        Wirt Franklin
        Notary Public.

AFFIDAVIT OF ATTENDING PHYSICIAN OR MID-WIFE.

UNITED STATES OF AMERICA, Indian Territory,
Central DISTRICT.

I, M.W. Harrison, a Physician, on oath state that I attended on Mrs. Zona Tucker, wife of Edward T Tucker on the 15 day of Dec, 1904; that there was born to her on said date a male child; that said child is now living and is said to have been named Grady Tucker

        M.W. Harrison M.D.

Witnesses To Mark:
 J.B. Pilgrim
 J.P. Nabors

 Subscribed and sworn to before me this 29 day of March, 1905.

       (Name Illegible)
My Com expires Dec 9-07   Notary Public.

Applications for Enrollment of Choctaw Newborn
Act of 1905 Volume V

BIRTH AFFIDAVIT.

DEPARTMENT OF THE INTERIOR.
COMMISSION TO THE FIVE CIVILIZED TRIBES.

IN RE APPLICATION FOR ENROLLMENT, as a citizen of the Choctaw Nation, of Carrell Tucker, born on the 21 day of Dec, 1902

Name of Father: Edward T Tucker   a citizen of the Choctaw Nation.
Name of Mother: Zona Tucker   a citizen of the Choctaw Nation.

Postoffice   Cameron I.T.

AFFIDAVIT OF MOTHER.

UNITED STATES OF AMERICA, Indian Territory,
Central DISTRICT.

I, Zona Tucker, on oath state that I am 33 years of age and a citizen by blood, of the Choctaw Nation; that I am the lawful wife of Edward T. Tucker, who is a citizen, by marriage of the Choctaw Nation; that a male child was born to me on 21st day of December, 1902, that said child has been named Carrell Tucker, and is now living.

Zona Tucker

Witnesses To Mark:

Subscribed and sworn to before me this 30th day of March, 1905.

Wirt Franklin
Notary Public.

AFFIDAVIT OF ATTENDING PHYSICIAN OR MID-WIFE.

UNITED STATES OF AMERICA, Indian Territory,
Central DISTRICT.

I, I.T. Harbour, a Physician, on oath state that I attended on Mrs. Zona Tucker, wife of Edward T Tucker on the 21 day of Dec, 190; that there was born to her on said date a male child; that said child is now living and is said to have been named Carrell Tucker

I.T. Harbour M.D.

Witnesses To Mark:

Applications for Enrollment of Choctaw Newborn
Act of 1905   Volume V

Subscribed and sworn to before me this 30 day of   March   , 1905.

(Name Illegible)
Notary Public.

Choc New Born 296
William Landles Shannon
(Born July 7, 1903)

NEW-BORN AFFIDAVIT.

Number..............

Choctaw Enrolling Commission.

IN THE MATTER OF THE APPLICATION FOR ENROLLMENT, as a citizen of the Choctaw   Nation, of   William Landles Shannon

born on the 7   day of   July   190 3

Name of father   O.L. Shannon   a citizen of   Choctaw
Nation final enrollment No   750
Name of mother   Rennie Shannon   a citizen of   Choctaw
Nation final enrollment No   11054

Postoffice   Durant I.T.

AFFIDAVIT OF MOTHER.

UNITED STATES OF AMERICA,
   INDIAN TERRITORY,
   Central   DISTRICT

I   Rennie Shannon   , on oath state that I am 26   years of age and a citizen by   blood   of the   Choctaw Nation, and as such have been placed upon the final roll of the   Choctaw Nation, by the Honorable Secretary of the Interior my final enrollment number being 11054 ; that I am the lawful wife of   O.L. Shannon   , who is a citizen of the   Choctaw Nation, and as such has been placed upon the final roll of said Nation by the Honorable Secretary of the Interior, his final enrollment number being   750   and that a   male child was born to me on the   7   day of   July   190 3; that said child has been named   William Landles Shannon   , and is now living.

Applications for Enrollment of Choctaw Newborn
Act of 1905 Volume V

Rennie Shannon

WITNESSETH:
Must be two Witnesses who are Citizens. } J.J. Gardner
Rebecca Jackson

Subscribed and sworn to before me this 14 day of January 190 5

J Ernest Bower
Notary Public.

My commission expires Sept 23 - 1907

AFFIDAVIT OF ATTENDING PHYSICIAN OR MIDWIFE

UNITED STATES OF AMERICA
INDIAN TERRITORY
Central DISTRICT

I, William O Shannon a Practicing Physician on oath state that I attended on Mrs. Rennie Shannon wife of O.L. Shannon on the 7 day of July , 190 3, that there was born to her on said date a Male child, that said child is now living, and is said to have been named William Landles Shannon

Wm O Shannon M.D.

Subscribed and sworn to before me this, the 14 day of January 190 5

James Bower
Notary Public.

WITNESSETH:
Must be two witnesses who are citizens and know the child. } J. J. Gardner
Rebecca Jackson

We hereby certify that we are well acquainted with .... a .... and know .... to be reputable and of good standing in the community.

J.J. Gardner
Rebecca Jackson

Applications for Enrollment of Choctaw Newborn
Act of 1905 Volume V

BIRTH AFFIDAVIT.

DEPARTMENT OF THE INTERIOR.
COMMISSION TO THE FIVE CIVILIZED TRIBES.

IN RE APPLICATION FOR ENROLLMENT, as a citizen of the Choctaw Nation, of William Landles Shannon , born on the 7th day of July , 1903

Name of Father: Ober L. Shannon   a citizen of the Choctaw Nation.
Name of Mother: Rennie Shannon   a citizen of the " Nation.

Postoffice ....

AFFIDAVIT OF MOTHER.

UNITED STATES OF AMERICA, Indian Territory,
.... DISTRICT.

I, Rennie Shannon , on oath state that I am 26 years of age and a citizen by Blood , of the Choctaw Nation; that I am the lawful wife of Ober L. Shannon , who is a citizen, by Intermarriage of the Choctaw Nation; that a male child was born to me on Seventh day of July , 1903, that said child has been named William Landles Shannon , and is now living.

Rennie Shannon

Witnesses To Mark:
{

Subscribed and sworn to before me this 21 day of March , 1905.

L.B. Wilkins
Notary Public.

AFFIDAVIT OF ATTENDING PHYSICIAN OR MID-WIFE.

UNITED STATES OF AMERICA, Indian Territory,
.... DISTRICT.

I, W O Shannon , a Physician , on oath state that I attended on Mrs. Rennie Shannon , wife of Ober L. Shannon on the 7th day of July , 1903; that there was born to her on said date a male child; that said child is now living and is said to have been named William Landles Shannon

W.O. Shannon, M.D.

Witnesses To Mark:
{

Applications for Enrollment of Choctaw Newborn
Act of 1905   Volume V

Subscribed and sworn to before me this 21 day of   March   , 1905.

L.B. Wilkins
Notary Public.

7-3937

Muskogee, Indian Territory, March 25, 1905.

Ober L. Shannon,
    Durant, Indian Territory.

Dear Sir:

    Receipt is hereby acknowledged of the affidavits of Rennie Shannon and W. O. Shannon, to the birth of William Landles Shannon, son of Ober L. and Rennie Shannon, July 7, 1903, and the same have been filed with our records as an application for the enrollment of said child.

Respectfully,

Chairman.

Choc New Born 297
    Thomas Vernon Terry
    (Born Nov. 8, 1902)

NEW-BORN AFFIDAVIT.

Number............

...Choctaw Enrolling Commission...

    IN THE MATTER OF THE APPLICATION FOR ENROLLMENT, as a citizen of the Choctaw   Nation, of   Thomas Vernon Terry

born on the 8th day of   November   190 2

Applications for Enrollment of Choctaw Newborn
Act of 1905 Volume V

Name of father   Noah M Terry   a citizen of   Choctaw
Nation final enrollment No.   751
Name of mother   Alice L. Terry   a citizen of   Choctaw
Nation final enrollment No.   11065

Postoffice   Bradley, Ind. Ter.

AFFIDAVIT OF MOTHER.

UNITED STATES OF AMERICA
INDIAN TERRITORY
Southern   DISTRICT

I   Alice L. Terry   , on oath state that I am 27 years of age and a citizen by   birth   of the   Choctaw Nation, and as such have been placed upon the final roll of the   Choctaw Nation, by the Honorable Secretary of the Interior my final enrollment number being   11065; that I am the lawful wife of   Noah M. Terry   , who is a citizen of the Choctaw   Nation, and as such has been placed upon the final roll of said Nation by the Honorable Secretary of the Interior, his final enrollment number being   751   and that a   Male   child was born to me on the   8th day of   November   190 2; that said child has been named   Thomas Vernon Terry   , and is now living.

Witnesseth.   Alice L Terry
Must be two
Witnesses who
are Citizens.

Subscribed and sworn to before me this   16   day of   Mar   190 5

J. R. Armstrong
Notary Public.

My commission expires: Feb 25 - 1909

AFFIDAVIT OF ATTENDING PHYSICIAN OR MIDWIFE

UNITED STATES OF AMERICA
INDIAN TERRITORY
Southern   DISTRICT

I,   Malinda Walker   a   Mid-wife on oath state that I attended on Mrs.   Alice L. Terry   wife of   Noah M. Terry on the   8th day of   November , 190 2, that there was born to her on said date a   male child, that said child is now living, and is said to have been named   Thomas Vernon Terry

Malinda Walker   MiD. *wife*

Subscribed and sworn to before me this, the   16   day of   March   190 5

Applications for Enrollment of Choctaw Newborn
Act of 1905 Volume V

WITNESSETH:
   Must be two witnesses
   who are citizens

J.R. Armstrong   Notary Public.
My commission expires Feb 25 - 1909

    We hereby certify that we are well acquainted with   Noah M Terry
and Alice L. Terry   and know   Them   to be reputable and of good standing in the community.

                                       Kenner B Cobb

                                       J B Hampton

Choc New Born 298
    Cina Adams
    (Born Oct. 4, 1902)

BIRTH AFFIDAVIT.

Department of the Interior,
COMMISSION TO THE FIVE CIVILIZED TRIBES.

    IN RE APPLICATION FOR ENROLLMENT, as a citizen of the   Choctaw   Nation, of   Cina Adams   , born on the   4   day of   Oct   , 190 2

Name of Father: Lee Adams   a citizen of the   Choctaw   Nation.
Name of Mother: Willie Adams   a citizen of the   Choctaw   Nation.

                   Post-Office: Mayhew I.T.

AFFIDAVIT OF MOTHER.

UNITED STATES OF AMERICA,
    INDIAN TERRITORY,
  Cent   District.

    I,   Willie Adams   , on oath state that I am   24   years of age and a citizen by   Blood   , of the   Choctaw   Nation; that I am the lawful wife of   Lee Adams   , who is a citizen, by Marriage   of the   Choctaw   Nation; that a   Female   child was born to me on   4 day of   ~~March~~   Oct   , 190 2, that said child has been named   Cina Adams   , and is now living.

Applications for Enrollment of Choctaw Newborn
Act of 1905 Volume V

                    her
                    Willie x Adams

WITNESSES TO MARK: mark

{ J.E. Ruffin
{ Chas A. Hopkins

Subscribed and sworn to before me this 4 *day of* Dec , 190 2

                  Perry M Clark
                  Notary Public.

AFFIDAVIT OF ATTENDING PHYSICIAN OR MID-WIFE.

UNITED STATES OF AMERICA,
   INDIAN TERRITORY,
Cent   District.

I, Lulu Adams , a midwife , on oath state that I attended on Mrs. Willie Adams , wife of Lee Adams on the 4 day of Oct , 190 2; that there was born to her on said date a Female child; that said child is now living and is said to have been named Cina Adams

                  her
                  Lulu x Adams

WITNESSES TO MARK: mark

{ J.E. Ruffin
{ Chas A. Hopkins

Subscribed and sworn to before me this 4 *day of* Dec , 190 2

                  Perry M Clark
                  Notary Public.

NEW-BORN AFFIDAVIT.

        Number..................

...Choctaw Enrolling Commission...

IN THE MATTER OF THE APPLICATION FOR ENROLLMENT, as a citizen of the Choctaw Nation, of Sinie[sic] Adams

born on the 4 day of October 190 2

Applications for Enrollment of Choctaw Newborn
Act of 1905 Volume V

Name of father   Lee Adams   non a^citizen of   Choctaw
Nation final enrollment No.   ~~11072~~
Name of mother   Willie Adams   a citizen of   Choctaw
Nation final enrollment No.   11072

Postoffice   Boswell

AFFIDAVIT OF MOTHER.

UNITED STATES OF AMERICA
INDIAN TERRITORY
Central   DISTRICT

I   Willie Adams   , on oath state that I am 28 years of age and a citizen by blood of the Choctaw Nation, and as such have been placed upon the final roll of the Choctaw Nation, by the Honorable Secretary of the Interior my final enrollment number being 11072; that I am the lawful wife of   Lee Adams   , who is a non citizen of the Choctaw Nation, ~~and as such has been placed upon the final roll of said Nation by the Honorable Secretary of the Interior, his final enrollment number being 11072~~ and that a Female child was born to me on the 4 day of October 190 2; that said child has been named   Sinie Adams   , and is now living.

Witnesseth.   Willie Adams

Must be two Witnesses who are Citizens.   T W Hunter
W.E. Anderson

Subscribed and sworn to before me this 27 day of Feb 190 5

SH Downing
Notary Public.

My commission expires: March 14th 1908

AFFIDAVIT OF ATTENDING PHYSICIAN OR MIDWIFE

UNITED STATES OF AMERICA
INDIAN TERRITORY
Central   DISTRICT

I,   Lula Adams   a   Midwife   on oath state that I attended on Mrs.   Willie Adams   wife of   Lee Adams   on the 4 day of October , 190 2, that there was born to her on said date a Female child, that said child is now living, and is said to have been named   Sinie Adams

Lula Adams   M.D.

Applications for Enrollment of Choctaw Newborn
Act of 1905 Volume V

WITNESSETH:

Must be two witnesses who are citizens and know the child.

TW Hunter

W.E. Anderson

Subscribed and sworn to before me this, the 27 day of February 190 5

S H Downing   Notary Public.

We hereby certify that we are well acquainted with Lula Adams a Midwife and know her to be reputable and of good standing in the community.

TW Hunter

W.E. Anderson

BIRTH AFFIDAVIT.

DEPARTMENT OF THE INTERIOR.
COMMISSION TO THE FIVE CIVILIZED TRIBES.

IN RE APPLICATION FOR ENROLLMENT, as a citizen of the Choctaw Nation, of Sinie Adams, born on the 3rd[sic] day of October, 1902

Name of Father: Lee Adams   a citizen of the U.S. Nation.
Name of Mother: Willie Adams   a citizen of the Choctaw Nation.

Postoffice Boswell I.T.

AFFIDAVIT OF MOTHER.

UNITED STATES OF AMERICA, Indian Territory, Central DISTRICT.

I, Willie Adams, on oath state that I am 28 years of age and a citizen by blood, of the Choctaw Nation; that I am the lawful wife of Lee Adams, who is a citizen, by .... of the U.S. Nation; that a female child was born to me on 4th day of October, 1902; that said child has been named Sinie Adams, and was living March 4, 1905.

Willie Adams

Witnesses To Mark:

Applications for Enrollment of Choctaw Newborn
Act of 1905   Volume V

Subscribed and sworn to before me this 12th day of April , 1905

(seal)

        J.R. Armstrong
         Notary Public.

AFFIDAVIT OF ATTENDING PHYSICIAN OR MID-WIFE.

UNITED STATES OF AMERICA, Indian Territory,
 Central   DISTRICT.

 I, Lula Adams , a midwife , on oath state that I attended on Mrs. Willie Adams , wife of Lee Adams on the 4th day of October , 1902; that there was born to her on said date a female child; that said child was living March 4, 1905, and is said to have been named Sinie Adams

         Lular Adams

Witnesses To Mark:

{

 Subscribed and sworn to before me this 12th day of April , 1905

(seal)

        J.R. Armstrong
         Notary Public.

            7-3944
            17- 636

      Muskogee, Indian Territory, December 16, 1902.

Perry M. Clark,
 Mayhew, Indian Territory.

Dear Sir:

 Receipt is hereby acknowledged of your letter of the 4th inst., enclosing the application for enrollment as a Choctaw freedman of Viola Hunter, minor daughter of Ward and Addie Hunter, born January 23, 1898; also the application for enrollment as a Choctaw freedman of Charles Hunter, infant son of Ward and Addie Hunter, born August 23, 1900; and the same being in proper form have been duly filed with the records of the Commission, and these children listed for enrollment as Choctaw freedmen.

 Receipt is also acknowledged of the certificate of G. N. Belvin, County and Probate Judge of Jackson County, Choctaw Nation, to the marriage of Walter Hunter and Ida Burris on March 28, 1898; and the same has been filed with the record in this case.

Applications for Enrollment of Choctaw Newborn
Act of 1905 Volume V

You also enclose the application for enrollment as a citizen of the Choctaw Nation of Cina Adams, infant daughter of Lee and Willie Adams, born October 4, 1902.

You are advised that the Commission is without authority to enroll this child as a citizen of the Choctaw Nation, it appearing that said child was born October 4, 1902, subsequent to the ratification by the citizens of the Choctaw and Chickasaw Nations on September 25, 1902, of an act of Congress approved July 1, 1902 (32 Stats., 641).

Section twenty-eight thereof provides as follows:

"The names of all persons living on the date of the final ratification of this agreement entitled to be enrolled as provided in section 27 hereof shall be placed upon the rolls made by said Commission; and no child born thereafter to a citizen or freedman and no person intermarried thereafter to a citizen shall be entitled to enrollment or to participate in the distribution of the tribal property of the Choctaws and Chickasaws."

Respectfully,

Acting Commissioner.

N. B. 298
COPY
Muskogee, Indian Territory, April 8, 1905.

Lee Adams,
    Mayhew, Indian Territory.

Dear Sir:

There is inclosed you herewith for execution application for the enrollment of your infant child, Cina Adams, born October 4, 1902.

The affidavits heretofore filed with the Commission show the child was living on December 4, 1902. It is necessary, for the child to be enrolled, that she was living on March 4, 1905. You will please insert the age of the mother in the space left blank for that purpose.

In having these affidavits executed care should be exercised to see that all names are written in full, as they appear in the body of the affidavit, and in the event that either of the persons signing the affidavit are unable to write, signatures by mark must be attested by two witnesses. Each affidavit must be executed before a Notary Public and the notarial seal and signature of the officer must be attached to each separate affidavit.

Applications for Enrollment of Choctaw Newborn
Act of 1905 Volume V

Respectfully,
SIGNED
T. B. Needles.
Commissioner in Charge.

LM 8-2

7-4684

Muskogee, Indian Territory, April 17, 1905.

William W. Pusley,
McAlester, Indian Territory.

Dear Sir:

Receipt is hereby acknowledged of the affidavits of Willie Adams and Lular Adams to the birth of Sinie Adams, daughter of you and Willie Adams, October 3, 1902 and the same have been filed with our records as an application for the enrollment of said child.

Respectfully,

Chairman.

7-NB-298.

Muskogee, Indian Territory, May 18, 1905.

Lee Adams,
Boswell, Indian Territory.

Dear Sir:

There are enclosed you herewith affidavits of Willie Adams, mother, and Lula Adams, mid-wife to the birth of your infant child, Sinie Adams, to which the notary public, before whom they were executed, failed to affix his seal.

Before his matter can be finally determined it will be necessary for you to return the enclosed application with the seal, which must be an impression and not a scrool[sic], affixed.

Respectfully,

Chairman.

Applications for Enrollment of Choctaw Newborn
Act of 1905 Volume V

7-N.B.298.

Muskogee, Indian Territory, May 25, 1905.

Lee Adams,
    Boswell, Indian Territory.

Dear Sir:

    Receipt is hereby acknowledged of the affidavits of Willie and Lula Adams to the birth of your child, Sinie Adams, which have been corrected by having the seal of the notary affixed thereto, and the same have been filed with our records in the matter of the enrollment of the above named child.

        Respectfully,

                Chairman.

Muskogee, Indian Territory, July 25, 1905.

Chief Clerk,
    Choctaw Land Office,
        Atoka, Indian Territory.

Dear Sir:

    Refer to duplicate Choctaw New Born Roll Card No. 298, in the possession of your office and change the name of the applicant thereon to read "Sinie Adams" instead of "Cina Adams."

        Respectfully,

                Commissioner.

Muskogee, Indian Territory, July 25, 1905.

Chief Clerk,
    Chickasaw Land Office,
        Ardmore, Indian Territory.

    Refer to duplicate Choctaw New Born Roll Card No. 298, in the possession of your office and change the name of the applicant thereon to read "Sinie Adams" instead of "Cina Adams."

        Respectfully,

                Commissioner.

Applications for Enrollment of Choctaw Newborn
Act of 1905 Volume V

Choc New Born 299
    Alfred Lorraine Freeny
    (Born Oct. 10, 1902)
    Wilson R. Freeny
    (Born July 26, 1904)

BIRTH AFFIDAVIT.

DEPARTMENT OF THE INTERIOR,
COMMISSION TO THE FIVE CIVILIZED TRIBES.

IN RE APPLICATION FOR ENROLLMENT, as a citizen of the Choctaw Nation, of Alfred Lorraine Freeny, born on the 10 day of October, 1902

Name of Father: Jasper D. Freeny   a citizen of the Choctaw Nation.
Name of Mother: Grace Freeny   a citizen of the Choctaw Nation.

Post-Office: Caddo, I.T.

AFFIDAVIT OF MOTHER.

UNITED STATES OF AMERICA,
   INDIAN TERRITORY,
   Central District.

   I, Grace Freeny, on oath state that I am 19 years of age and a citizen by adoption, of the Choctaw Nation; that I am the lawful wife of Jasper D. Freeny, who is a citizen, by blood of the Choctaw Nation; that a male child was born to me on the 10 day of October, 190 2, that said child has been named Alfred Lorraine Freeny, and is now living.

                              Grace Freeny

WITNESSES TO MARK:

Subscribed and sworn to before me this 21 day of November, 1902

                              D.N. Linebaugh
                                  NOTARY PUBLIC.

Applications for Enrollment of Choctaw Newborn
Act of 1905   Volume V

AFFIDAVIT OF ATTENDING PHYSICIAN OR MID-WIFE.

UNITED STATES OF AMERICA,
  INDIAN TERRITORY,
  Central   District.

I, W.J. Melton, a physician, on oath state that I attended on Mrs. Grace Freeny, wife of Jasper D Freeny on the 10 day of October, 1902; that there was born to her on said date a male child; that said child is now living and is said to have been named Alfred Lorraine Freeny.

W.J. Melton, M.D.

WITNESSES TO MARK:

Subscribed and sworn to before me this 21 day of November, 1902.

JL Rappolee
NOTARY PUBLIC.

NEW BORN AFFIDAVIT

No ....

CHOCTAW ENROLLING COMMISSION

IN THE MATTER OF THE APPLICATION FOR ENROLLMENT as a citizen of the Choctaw Nation, of Alfred Lorraine Freeny born on the 10th day of October 1902

Name of father Jasper D. Freeny   a citizen of Choctaw Nation, final enrollment No. 11076

Name of mother Grace Freeny   a citizen of Choctaw Nation, final enrollment No. 672

Caddo I.T.   Postoffice.

Applications for Enrollment of Choctaw Newborn
Act of 1905   Volume V

AFFIDAVIT OF MOTHER

UNITED STATES OF AMERICA }
INDIAN TERRITORY
DISTRICT   Central

I   Grace Freeny   , on oath state that I am   21   years of age and a citizen by   Marriage   of the   Choctaw   Nation, and as such have been placed upon the final roll of the   Choctaw   Nation, by the Honorable Secretary of the Interior my final enrollment number being   672   ; that I am the lawful wife of   Jasper D. Freeny   , who is a citizen of the   Choctaw   Nation, and as such has been placed upon the final roll of said Nation by the Honorable Secretary of the Interior, his final enrollment number being   11076   and that a   male   child was born to me on the   10"   day of   October   190 2; that said child has been named   Alfred L. Freeny   , and is now living.

WITNESSETH: Grace Freeny

Must be two witnesses { *(Name Illegible)*
who are citizens   { F. Manning

Subscribed and sworn to before me this, the   16ᵗʰ   day of   February   , 190 5

A E Folsom
Notary Public.

My Commission Expires:
Jan 9 - 1909

Affidavit of Attending Physician or Midwife

UNITED STATES OF AMERICA, }
INDIAN TERRITORY,
Central   DISTRICT

I,   W.J. Melton   a   Practicing Physician on oath state that I attended on Mrs. Grace Freeny   wife of   Jasper D Freeny on the   10ᵗʰ   day of October   , 190 2, that there was born to her on said date a   male child, that said child is now living, and is said to have been named   Alfred L. Freeny

W.J. Melton   M. D.

Subscribed and sworn to before me this the   21ˢᵗ   day of   Feb.   1905

J.H. Cossart
Notary Public.

Applications for Enrollment of Choctaw Newborn
Act of 1905   Volume V

WITNESSETH:

Must be two witnesses who are citizens and know the child. { *(Name Illegible)*
F Manning

We hereby certify that we are well acquainted with   Dr W.J. Melton a   Physician   and know   him   to be reputable and of good standing in the community.

Must be two citizen witnesses. { *(Name Illegible)*
F. Manning

NEW BORN AFFIDAVIT

No ....

CHOCTAW ENROLLING COMMISSION

IN THE MATTER OF THE APPLICATION FOR ENROLLMENT as a citizen of the Choctaw Nation, of   Wilson R. Freeny   born on the   26th day of   July   190 4

Name of father   Jasper D. Freeny   a citizen of   Choctaw   Nation, final enrollment No.   11076

Name of mother   Grace Freeny   a citizen of   Choctaw   Nation, final enrollment No.   672

Caddo I.T.   Postoffice.

AFFIDAVIT OF MOTHER

UNITED STATES OF AMERICA
INDIAN TERRITORY
DISTRICT   Central

I   Grace Freeny   , on oath state that I am   21   years of age and a citizen by   Marriage   of the   Choctaw   Nation, and as such have been placed upon the final roll of the   Choctaw   Nation, by the Honorable Secretary of the Interior my final enrollment number being   672   ; that I am the lawful wife of   Jasper D. Freeny   , who is a citizen of the   Choctaw   Nation, and as such has been placed upon the final roll of said Nation by the Honorable Secretary of the Interior, his final enrollment number being   11076   and that a   male   child

Applications for Enrollment of Choctaw Newborn
Act of 1905 Volume V

was born to me on the 26th day of July 190 4; that said child has been named Wilson R. Freeny , and is now living.

WITNESSETH: Grace Freeny

Must be two witnesses { *(Name Illegible)*
who are citizens   F. Manning

Subscribed and sworn to before me this, the 16th day of February , 190 5

A E Folsom
Notary Public.

My Commission Expires:
Jan 9 - 1909

Affidavit of Attending Physician or Midwife

UNITED STATES OF AMERICA,
   INDIAN TERRITORY,
Central   DISTRICT

I, W.J. Melton a Practicing Physician on oath state that I attended on Mrs. Grace Freeny wife of Jasper D Freeny on the 26th day of July , 190 4, that there was born to her on said date a male child, that said child is now living, and is said to have been named Wilson R. Freeny

W.J. Melton   M. D.

Subscribed and sworn to before me this the 21st day of Feb. 1905

J.H. Cossart
Notary Public.

WITNESSETH:

Must be two witnesses { *(Name Illegible)*
who are citizens and
know the child.   F Manning

We hereby certify that we are well acquainted with Dr W.J. Melton a Physician and know him to be reputable and of good standing in the community.

Must be two citizen { *(Name Illegible)*
witnesses.   F. Manning

Applications for Enrollment of Choctaw Newborn
Act of 1905   Volume V

BIRTH AFFIDAVIT.

DEPARTMENT OF THE INTERIOR.
COMMISSION TO THE FIVE CIVILIZED TRIBES.

IN RE APPLICATION FOR ENROLLMENT, as a citizen of the   Choctaw   Nation, of Alfred L Freeny   , born on the   10   day of   Oct   , 1902

Name of Father: Jasper D Freeny   a citizen of the   Choctaw   Nation.
Name of Mother: Grace Freeny   a citizen of the   Choctaw   Nation.

Postoffice   Caddo Ind Ter

AFFIDAVIT OF MOTHER.

UNITED STATES OF AMERICA, Indian Territory, }
    Central   DISTRICT.   }

I,   Grace Freeny   , on oath state that I am   22   years of age and a citizen by Marriage   , of the   Choctaw   Nation; that I am the lawful wife of   Jasper D Freeny   , who is a citizen, by   blood   of the   Choctaw   Nation; that a   male   child was born to me on the 10th day of   Oct   , 1902; that said child has been named   Alfred L Freeny   , and was living March 4, 1905.

Grace Freeny

Witnesses To Mark:
{ Peter Maytubby Jr

Subscribed and sworn to before me this 31st day of   March   , 1905

J F Belote
Notary Public.

AFFIDAVIT OF ATTENDING PHYSICIAN OR MID-WIFE.

UNITED STATES OF AMERICA, Indian Territory, }
    Central   DISTRICT.   }

I,   W J Melton   , a   Physician   , on oath state that I attended on Mrs.   Grace Freeny   , wife of   Jasper D Freeny   on the 10th day of   Oct   , 1902; that there was born to her on said date a   male   child; that said child was living March 4, 1905, and is said to have been named Alfred L Freeny

W.J. Melton

Applications for Enrollment of Choctaw Newborn
Act of 1905   Volume V

Witnesses To Mark:
   { Peter Maytubby Jr

    Subscribed and sworn to before me this   31   day of   March   , 1905

                          J F Belote
                                Notary Public.

BIRTH AFFIDAVIT.

DEPARTMENT OF THE INTERIOR.
COMMISSION TO THE FIVE CIVILIZED TRIBES.

IN RE APPLICATION FOR ENROLLMENT, as a citizen of the   Choctaw   Nation, of   Wilson F Freeny   , born on the   26   day of   July   , 1904

Name of Father: Jasper D Freeny   a citizen of the   Choctaw   Nation.
Name of Mother: Grace Freeny   a citizen of the   Choctaw   Nation.

                  Postoffice   Caddo Ind Ter

AFFIDAVIT OF MOTHER.

UNITED STATES OF AMERICA, Indian Territory, }
    Central   DISTRICT. }

    I,   Grace Freeny   , on oath state that I am   22   years of age and a citizen by Marriage   , of the   Choctaw   Nation; that I am the lawful wife of   Jasper D Freeny   , who is a citizen, by blood   of the   Choctaw   Nation; that a male   child was born to me on   the 26th day of   July   , 1904; that said child has been named   Wilson R Freeny   , and was living March 4, 1905.

                          Grace Freeny

Witnesses To Mark:
   { Peter Maytubby Jr

    Subscribed and sworn to before me this   31   day of   March   , 1905

                          J F Belote
                          Notary Public.

Applications for Enrollment of Choctaw Newborn
Act of 1905   Volume V

AFFIDAVIT OF ATTENDING PHYSICIAN OR MID-WIFE.

UNITED STATES OF AMERICA, Indian Territory,
Central   DISTRICT.

I, D^r W J Melton, a Physician, on oath state that I attended on Mrs. Grace Freeny, wife of Jasper D Freeny on the 26 day of July, 1904; that there was born to her on said date a male child; that said child was living March 4, 1905, and is said to have been named Wilson R Freeny

                                   W.J. Melton

Witnesses To Mark:
  Peter Maytubby Jr

Subscribed and sworn to before me this 31 day of March, 1905

                             J F Belote
                                  Notary Public.

BIRTH AFFIDAVIT.

DEPARTMENT OF THE INTERIOR.
COMMISSION TO THE FIVE CIVILIZED TRIBES.

IN RE APPLICATION FOR ENROLLMENT, as a citizen of the Choctaw Nation, of Alfred Lorraine Freeny, born on the 10th day of October, 1902

Name of Father: Jasper D Freeny   a citizen of the Choctaw Nation.
Name of Mother: Grace Freeny   a citizen of the Choctaw Nation.

                    Postoffice   Caddo I.T.

AFFIDAVIT OF MOTHER.

UNITED STATES OF AMERICA, Indian Territory,
.... DISTRICT.

I, Grace Freeny, on oath state that I am 22 years of age and a citizen by intermarriage, of the Choctaw Nation; that I am the lawful wife of Jasper D Freeny, who is a citizen, by blood of the Choctaw Nation; that a male child was born to me on the 10th day of October, 1902; that said child has been named Alfred Lorraine Freeny, and was living March 4, 1905.

                              Grace Freeny

Applications for Enrollment of Choctaw Newborn
Act of 1905   Volume V

Witnesses To Mark:
{

      Subscribed and sworn to before me this   12   day of   April   , 1905

                              J F Belote
                              Notary Public.

AFFIDAVIT OF ATTENDING PHYSICIAN OR MID-WIFE.

UNITED STATES OF AMERICA, Indian Territory, }
   Central   DISTRICT.   }

    I,   W J Melton   , a   Physician   , on oath state that I attended on Mrs.   Grace Freeny   , wife of   Jasper D Freeny   on the 10th day of October, 1902; that there was born to her on said date a   male   child; that said child was living March 4, 1905, and is said to have been named Alfred Lorraine Freeny

                              W.J. Melton

Witnesses To Mark:
{

      Subscribed and sworn to before me this   12   day of   April   , 1905

                              J F Belote
                              Notary Public.

                                            7-3947.

                Muskogee, Indian Territory, December 5, 1902.

Jasper D. Freeny,
      Caddo, Indian Territory.

Dear Sir:

    Receipt is hereby acknowledged of the application for enrollment as a citizen of the Choctaw Nation of Alfred Lorraine Freeny, infant son of Jasper D. and Grace Freeny, born October 10, 1902.

    You are advised that the Commission is without authority to enroll this child as a citizen of the Choctaw Nation, it appearing that said child was born October 10, 1902, subsequent to the ratification by the citizens of the Choctaw an Chickasaw Nations on September 25, 1902, of an act of Congress approved July 1, 1902 (32 Stats., 641).

Applications for Enrollment of Choctaw Newborn
Act of 1905   Volume V

Section twenty-eight thereof provides as follows:

"The names of all persons living on the date of the final ratification of this agreement entitled to be enrolled as provided in section 27 hereof shall be placed upon the rolls made by said Commission; and no child born thereafter to a citizen or freedman and no person intermarried thereafter to a citizen shall be entitled to enrollment or to participate in the distribution of the tribal property of the Choctaws and Chickasaws."

Respectfully,

Acting Chairman.

N. B. 299

COPY

Muskogee, Indian Territory, April 8, 1905.

Jasper D. Freeny,
Caddo, Indian Territory.

Dear Sir:

There is inclosed you herewith for execution application for the enrollment of your infant child, Alfred Lorraine Freeny, born October 10, 1902.

The affidavits heretofore filed with the Commission show the child was living on November 21, 1902. It is necessary, for the child to be enrolled, that he was living on March 4, 1905. Please insert the age of the mother in space provided for the purpose.

In having these affidavits executed care should be exercised to see that all names are written in full, as they appear in the body of the affidavit, and in the event that either of the persons signing the affidavit are unable to write, signatures by mark must be attested by two witnesses. Each affidavit must be executed before a Notary Public and the notarial seal and signature of the officer must be attached to each separate affidavit.

Respectfully,
SIGNED

T. B. Needles.

LM 8-1   Commissioner in Charge.

Applications for Enrollment of Choctaw Newborn
Act of 1905 Volume V

7 NB 299

Muskogee, Indian Territory, April 19, 1905.

Jasper D. Freeny,
    Caddo, Indian Territory.

Dear Sir:

    Receipt is hereby acknowledged of your letter of April 12, 1905, transmitting affidavits of Grace Freeny and W. J. Melton to the birth of Alfred Lorraine Freeny, son of Jasper D. and Grace Freeny, October 10, 1902, and the same have been filed with our records as an application for the enrollment of said child.

    It is stated that you recently forwarded application for the enrollment of two children and as only one of them was returned for correction, you wish to know if the application of Wilson R. Freeny was in proper form, and in reply you are informed that the affidavits heretofore forwarded to the birth of Wilson R. Freeny have been filed with our records as an application for the enrollment of said child and in event further evidence is necessary to enable the Commission to determine his right to enrollment you will be duly notified.

    Respectfully,

Chairman.

Choctaw N.B. 299.

Muskogee, Indian Territory, April 28, 1905.

Jasper D. Freeny,
    Caddo, Indian Territory.

Dear Sir:

    Receipt is hereby acknowledged of your letter of April 18, asking if the applications for the enrollment of Alfred L. Freeny and Wilson R. Freeny have been received.

    In reply to your letter you are advised that the affidavits heretofore forwarded to the birth of Alfred Lorane[sic] Freeny and Wilson R. Freeny have been filed with our records as applications for the enrollment of said children.

    Respectfully,

Chairman.

Applications for Enrollment of Choctaw Newborn
Act of 1905   Volume V

Choc New Born 300
   Zona King
   (Born Nov. 19, 1902)

BIRTH AFFIDAVIT.

Department of the Interior,
COMMISSION TO THE FIVE CIVILIZED TRIBES.

IN RE APPLICATION FOR ENROLLMENT, as a citizen of the Choctaw Nation, of Zona King, born on the 19 day of November, 190 2

Name of Father: Mitchell King   a citizen of the Choctaw Nation.
Name of Mother: Emma King   a citizen of the Choctaw Nation.

Post-Office: Legal, Ind. Ter

AFFIDAVIT OF MOTHER.

UNITED STATES OF AMERICA,
   INDIAN TERRITORY,
   Central District.

I, Emma King, on oath state that I am 24 years of age and a citizen by blood, of the Choctaw Nation; that I am the lawful wife of Mitchell King, who is a citizen, by blood of the Choctaw Nation; that a girl child was born to me on 19 day of Nov, 190 2, that said child has been named Zona King, and is now living.

                   her mark
              x Emma King

WITNESSES TO MARK:
  { Henry E Turner
    Anderson King

Subscribed and sworn to before me this 18 day of Dec, 190 2.

            John D Grubbs
              Notary Public.

Applications for Enrollment of Choctaw Newborn
Act of 1905   Volume V

AFFIDAVIT OF ATTENDING PHYSICIAN OR MID-WIFE.

UNITED STATES OF AMERICA,
   INDIAN TERRITORY,
   Central   District.

  I, Pika Lawrance , a midwife , on oath state that I attended on Mrs. Emma King , wife of Mitchell King   on the 19 day of Nov , 190 2; that there was born to her on said date a   Girl   child; that said child is now living and is said to have been named Zona King

her mark
x Pika Lawrance

WITNESSES TO MARK:
{ Henry E Turner
{ Anderson King

Subscribed and sworn to before me this 18 day of Dec , 190 2.

John D Grubbs
Notary Public.

NEW BORN AFFIDAVIT

No ....

CHOCTAW ENROLLING COMMISSION

IN THE MATTER OF THE APPLICATION FOR ENROLLMENT as a citizen of the Choctaw Nation, of   Zona King   born on the 19th   day of   November   190 2

  Name of father   Mitchell King   a citizen of   Choctaw   Nation, final enrollment No.   11104
  Name of mother   Emma King   a citizen of   Choctaw   Nation, final enrollment No.   11105

Legal, Ind. Ter.   Postoffice.

Applications for Enrollment of Choctaw Newborn
Act of 1905   Volume V

AFFIDAVIT OF MOTHER

UNITED STATES OF AMERICA
   INDIAN TERRITORY
DISTRICT   Central

I   Emma King   , on oath state that I am   years of age and a citizen by   Blood   of the   Choctaw   Nation, and as such have been placed upon the final roll of the   Choctaw   Nation, by the Honorable Secretary of the Interior my final enrollment number being   11105   ; that I am the lawful wife of   Mitchell King   , who is a citizen of the   Choctaw Nation, and as such has been placed upon the final roll of said Nation by the Honorable Secretary of the Interior, his final enrollment number being   11104   and that a   Female   child was born to me on the   19th day of   November   190 2; that said child has been named   Zona King   , and is now living.

WITNESSETH: Emma King

Must be two witnesses   D A Lawrance
who are citizens   Joseph Summers
McGee King

Subscribed and sworn to before me this, the   3   day of   February   , 190 5

Richard E Kemp
Notary Public.

My Commission Expires: Dec. 19 - 1908

Affidavit of Attending Physician or Midwife

UNITED STATES OF AMERICA,
   INDIAN TERRITORY,
Central   DISTRICT

I,   Siney Riddle   a   Midwife   on oath state that I attended on Mrs.   Emma King   wife of   Mitchell King   on the   19th   day of   November   , 190 2, that there was born to her on said date a   a   Female   child, that said child is now living, and is said to have been named   Zona King

Siney Riddle   *Midwife*

Subscribed and sworn to before me this the   3   day of   February   1905

Richard E Kemp
Notary Public.

My Commission Expires 12/17/1908

Applications for Enrollment of Choctaw Newborn
Act of 1905   Volume V

WITNESSETH:

Must be two witnesses who are citizens and know the child.
{ DA Lawrence
Joseph Summers
McGee King }

We hereby certify that we are well acquainted with Siney Riddle a Midwife and know her to be reputable and of good standing in the community.

Must be two citizen witnesses.
{ DA Lawrence
Joseph Summers
McGee King }

BIRTH AFFIDAVIT.

DEPARTMENT OF THE INTERIOR.
COMMISSION TO THE FIVE CIVILIZED TRIBES.

IN RE APPLICATION FOR ENROLLMENT, as a citizen of the Choctaw Nation, of Zona King, born on the 19 day of November, 1902

Name of Father: Mitchell King   a citizen of the Choctaw Nation.
Name of Mother: Emma King   a citizen of the Choctaw Nation.

Postoffice   Legal, Ind. Ter.

AFFIDAVIT OF MOTHER.

UNITED STATES OF AMERICA, Indian Territory, Central DISTRICT.

I, Emma King, on oath state that I am 27 years of age and a citizen by Blood, of the Choctaw Nation; that I am the lawful wife of Mitchell King, who is a citizen, by Blood of the Choctaw Nation; that a Female child was born to me on 19 day of November, 1902; that said child has been named Zona King, and was living March 4, 1905.

           her
         Emma King x
           mark

Witnesses To Mark:
{ Joe Summers
Osborne S Lawrence }

Applications for Enrollment of Choctaw Newborn
Act of 1905 Volume V

Subscribed and sworn to before me this 27 day of March, 1905

Richard E Kemp
Notary Public.
My Commission exp. Dec. 17 - 1908

AFFIDAVIT OF ATTENDING PHYSICIAN OR MID-WIFE.

UNITED STATES OF AMERICA, Indian Territory, }
Central DISTRICT. }

I, Sina Riddle, a mid-wife, on oath state that I attended on Mrs. Emma King, wife of Mitchell King on the 19 day of November, 1902; that there was born to her on said date a Female child; that said child was living March 4, 1905, and is said to have been named Zona King

                                      her
                            Sina Riddle x

Witnesses To Mark: mark
  { Joe Summers
    Osborne S Lawrence

Subscribed and sworn to before me this 27 day of March, 1905

Richard E Kemp
Notary Public.
My Com Ex. 12/17/1908

Choctaw 3965.

Muskogee, Indian Territory, April 4, 1905.

Mitchell King,
    Legal, Indian Territory.

Dear Sir:

    Receipt is hereby acknowledged of the affidavits of Emma King and Sina Riddle to the birth of Zona King, daughter of Mitchell and Emma King, November 19, 1902, and the same have been filed with our records as an application for the enrollment of said child.

                            Respectfully,

                                    Commissioner in Charge.

Applications for Enrollment of Choctaw Newborn
Act of 1905   Volume V

<u>Choc New Born 301</u>
    Henry Russel[sic] Davis
    (Born Sep. 20, 1903)

BIRTH AFFIDAVIT.

DEPARTMENT OF THE INTERIOR.
COMMISSION TO THE FIVE CIVILIZED TRIBES.

IN RE APPLICATION FOR ENROLLMENT, as a citizen of the Choctaw Nation, of Henry Russell Davis , born on the 20 day of Sept , 1903

Name of Father: Henry Carl Davis   a citizen of the Choctaw Nation.
Name of Mother: Mary Davis   a citizen of the U. States Nation.

        Postoffice   Lehigh, I.T.

AFFIDAVIT OF MOTHER.

UNITED STATES OF AMERICA, Indian Territory,
    Central   DISTRICT.

    I, Mary Davis , on oath state that I am 25 years of age and a citizen by Intermarriage , of the Choctaw Nation; that I am the lawful wife of Henry Carl Davis , who is a citizen, by blood of the Choctaw Nation; that a male child was born to me on 20th day of September , 1904[sic], that said child has been named Henry Russell Davis , and is now living.

        Mary Davis

Witnesses To Mark:

    Subscribed and sworn to before me this 19 day of Dec. , 1904.

        Dwight Brown
           Notary Public.

AFFIDAVIT OF ATTENDING PHYSICIAN OR MID-WIFE.

UNITED STATES OF AMERICA, Indian Territory,
    Central   DISTRICT.

    I, David Gardner , a physician , on oath state that I attended on Mrs. Mary Davis , wife of Henry Carl Davis on the 20 day of Sept , 1903;

Applications for Enrollment of Choctaw Newborn
Act of 1905   Volume V

that there was born to her on said date a   male   child; that said child is now living and is said to have been named   Henry Russell Davis

David Gardner M.D.

Witnesses To Mark:
{

Subscribed and sworn to before me this   21st   day of   December   , 1904

Dwight Brown
Notary Public.

NEW-BORN AFFIDAVIT.

Number..............

Choctaw Enrolling Commission.

IN THE MATTER OF THE APPLICATION FOR ENROLLMENT, as a citizen of the   Choctaw   Nation, of   Henry Russell Davis

born on the   20   day of   September   190 3

Name of father   Henry Carl Davis   a citizen of   Choctaw
Nation final enrollment No   12004
Name of mother   Mary T Davis   a citizen of   Choctaw
Nation final enrollment No   407

Postoffice   Lehigh I.T.

AFFIDAVIT OF MOTHER.

UNITED STATES OF AMERICA,
   INDIAN TERRITORY,
   Central   DISTRICT

I   Mary T Davis   , on oath state that I am   25   years of age and a citizen by   Intermarriage of the   Choctaw   Nation, and as such have been placed upon the final roll of the   Choctaw   Nation, by the Honorable Secretary of the Interior my final enrollment number being   407   ; that I am the lawful wife of   Henry Carl Davis   , who is a citizen of the   Choctaw   Nation, and as such has been placed upon the final roll of said Nation by the Honorable Secretary of the Interior, his final enrollment number being   12004   and that a   male   child was born to me on the   20   day of   September   190 3; that said child has been named   Henry Russell Davis   , and is now living.

Mary T Davis

Applications for Enrollment of Choctaw Newborn
Act of 1905   Volume V

WITNESSETH:

Must be two Witnesses who are Citizens.
- Etta R Davis
- Carl Davis

Subscribed and sworn to before me this 16 day of January 190 5

Dwight Brown
Notary Public.

My commission expires Dec 2 1908

Affidavit of Attending Physician or Midwife

UNITED STATES OF AMERICA,
INDIAN TERRITORY,
Central   DISTRICT

I, David Gardner a Physician on oath state that I attended on Mrs. Mary T Davis wife of Carl Davis on the 20th day of September , 190 3, that there was born to her on said date a male child, that said child is now living, and is said to have been named Henry Russell Davis

David Gardner   M. D.

Subscribed and sworn to before me this the 22 day of Feb 1905

Dwight Brown
Notary Public.

WITNESSETH:

Must be two witnesses who are citizens and know the child.
- Etta R Davis
- Carl Davis

We hereby certify that we are well acquainted with David Gardner a physician and know him to be reputable and of good standing in the community.

Must be two citizen witnesses.
- Etta R Davis
- Carl Davis

Applications for Enrollment of Choctaw Newborn
Act of 1905 Volume V

BIRTH AFFIDAVIT.

DEPARTMENT OF THE INTERIOR.
COMMISSION TO THE FIVE CIVILIZED TRIBES.

IN RE APPLICATION FOR ENROLLMENT, as a citizen of the Choctaw Nation, of Henry Russell Davis , born on the 20 day of Sept , 1903

Name of Father: Henry Carl Davis   a citizen of the Choctaw Nation.
Name of Mother: Mary J. Davis   a citizen of the Choctaw Nation.

Postoffice Lehigh Ind Ter

AFFIDAVIT OF MOTHER.

UNITED STATES OF AMERICA, Indian Territory,
Central   DISTRICT.

I, Mary T Davis , on oath state that I am 25 years of age and a citizen by Intermarriage , of the Choctaw Nation; that I am the lawful wife of Henry Carl Davis , who is a citizen, by Blood of the Choctaw Nation; that a Male child was born to me on 20th day of September , 1903; that said child has been named Henry Russell Davis , and was living March 4, 1905.

Mary T Davis

Witnesses To Mark:
{

Subscribed and sworn to before me this 25 day of May , 190....

Dwight Brown
Notary Public.

AFFIDAVIT OF ATTENDING PHYSICIAN OR MID-WIFE.

UNITED STATES OF AMERICA, Indian Territory,
Central   DISTRICT.

I, David Gardner , a physician , on oath state that I attended on Mrs. Mary T Davis , wife of Henry Carl Davis on the 20 day of September , 1903; that there was born to her on said date a Male child; that said child was living March 4, 1905, and is said to have been named Henry Russell Davis

David Gardner MD

Witnesses To Mark:
{

Applications for Enrollment of Choctaw Newborn
Act of 1905 Volume V

Subscribed and sworn to before me this 25 day of May , 190....

                                   Dwight Brown
                                   Notary Public.

BIRTH AFFIDAVIT.

DEPARTMENT OF THE INTERIOR.
COMMISSION TO THE FIVE CIVILIZED TRIBES.

IN RE APPLICATION FOR ENROLLMENT, as a citizen of the Choctaw Nation, of Henry Russell Davis , born on the 20 day of September , 1903

Name of Father: Henry Carl Davis   a citizen of the Choctaw Nation.
Name of Mother: Mary J. Davis   a citizen of the Choctaw Nation.

                     Postoffice   Lehigh IT

AFFIDAVIT OF MOTHER.

UNITED STATES OF AMERICA, Indian Territory, }
     Central   **DISTRICT.** }

I, Mary T Davis , on oath state that I am 25 years of age and a citizen by intermarriage , of the Choctaw Nation; that I am the lawful wife of Henry Carl Davis , who is a citizen, by blood of the Choctaw Nation; that a male child was born to me on 20 day of September , 1905[sic]; that said child has been named Henry Russell Davis , and was living March 4, 1905.

                               Mary T Davis

Witnesses To Mark:
{

Subscribed and sworn to before me this 18 day of March , 1905

                               CH Ewing
                                   Notary Public.

AFFIDAVIT OF ATTENDING PHYSICIAN OR MID-WIFE.

UNITED STATES OF AMERICA, Indian Territory, }
     Central   **DISTRICT.** }

I, David Gardner , a Physician , on oath state that I attended on Mrs. Mary T Davis , wife of Henry Carl Davis on the 20 day of

Applications for Enrollment of Choctaw Newborn
Act of 1905   Volume V

September   , 1903; that there was born to her on said date a ~~fem~~   male   child; that said child was living March 4, 1905, and is said to have been named Henry Russell Davis

David Gardner

Witnesses To Mark:
{

Subscribed and sworn to before me this 18 day of   Mch   , 1905

CH Ewing
Notary Public.

7-4296

Muskogee, Indian Territory, March 22, 1905.

Henry Carl Davis,
    Lehigh, Indian Territory.

Dear Sir:

    Receipt is hereby acknowledged of the affidavits of Mary T. Davis and David Gardner to the birth of Henry Russell Davis, son of Henry Carl and Mary T. Davis, September 20, 1903, and the same have been filed with our records as an application for the enrollment of said child.

Respectfully,

Chairman.

7-NB-301.

Muskogee, Indian Territory, May 22, 1905.

Henry Carl Davis,
    Lehigh, Indian Territory.

Dear Sir:

    There is enclosed you herewith for execution application for the enrollment of your infant child, Henry Russell Davis.

    In the mothers[sic] affidavit of December 19, 1904, the date of the childs[sic] birth is given as September 10, 1904, the physicians[sic] affidavit of December 21, 1904, gives the date of birth as September 20, 1903, while the affidavits executed by the same parties on March 18, 1905, the date of birth is given as September 20, 1905, and

Applications for Enrollment of Choctaw Newborn
Act of 1905 Volume V

September 20, 1903. Please insert the correct date and return the application to this office.

In having these affidavits executed care should be exercised to see that all names are written in full, as they appear in the body of the affidavit, and in the event that either of the persons signing the affidavit are unable to write, signatures by mark must be attested by two witnesses. Each affidavit must be executed before a Notary Public and the notarial seal and signature of the officer must be attached to each separate affidavit.

Respectfully,

VR 22-12.

Chairman.

7-N.B. 301.

Muskogee, Indian Territory, May 31, 1905.

Henry Carl Davis,
    Lehigh, Indian Territory.

Dear Sir:

Receipt is hereby acknowledged of the affidavits of Mary T. Davis and David Gardner, M.D. to the birth of Henry Russell Davis, son of Henry Carl and Mary T. Davis, September 20, 1903, and the same have been filed with our records as an application for the enrollment of said child.

Respectfully,

Chairman.

Applications for Enrollment of Choctaw Newborn
Act of 1905 Volume V

Choc New Born 302
    Vernon Clay McCarty
    (Born April 14, 1903)

BIRTH AFFIDAVIT.

DEPARTMENT OF THE INTERIOR,
COMMISSION TO THE FIVE CIVILIZED TRIBES.

In Re Application for Enrollment, as a citizen of the Choctaw Nation, of Vernon Clay McCarty , born on the 14th day of April , 1903

Name of Father: Carl C. McCarty   a citizen of the Choctaw Nation.
Name of Mother: Etta Regena McCarty   a citizen of the Choctaw Nation.

        Post-office   Coalgate, Ind Terr

AFFIDAVIT OF MOTHER.

UNITED STATES OF AMERICA, }
    INDIAN TERRITORY,
    Central   District.

    I, Etta Regena McCarty , on oath state that I am sixteen years of age and a citizen by blood , of the Choctaw Nation; that I am the lawful wife of Carl C. McCarty , who is a citizen, by blood of the Choctaw Nation; that a male child was born to me on 14th day of April , 1903 , that said child has been named Vernon Clay McCarty , and is now living.

                      Etta Regena McCarty

WITNESSES TO MARK:

    Subscribed and sworn to before me this 5 day of April , 1904.

                      Dwight Brown
                          NOTARY PUBLIC.

Applications for Enrollment of Choctaw Newborn
Act of 1905 Volume V

AFFIDAVIT OF ATTENDING PHYSICIAN OR MID-WIFE.

UNITED STATES OF AMERICA, }
  INDIAN TERRITORY,
  Central   District.

    I,   David Gardner , a   Physician , on oath state that I attended on Mrs. Etta E[sic] McCarty , wife of   Carl C. McCarty   on the 14th day of April , 1903 ; that there was born to her on said date a   male   child; that said child is now living and is said to have been named   Vernon Clay McCarty

                          David Gardner M.D.

WITNESSES TO MARK:
{

    Subscribed and sworn to before me this 5 day of   April , 1904.

                          Dwight Brown
                               NOTARY PUBLIC.

NEW-BORN AFFIDAVIT.

            Number..............

Choctaw Enrolling Commission.

    IN THE MATTER OF THE APPLICATION FOR ENROLLMENT, as a citizen of the ~~Vernon Clay McCarty~~ Choctaw   Nation, of ~~Choctaw~~   Vernon Clay McCarty

born on the 14   day of April   190 3

Name of father   Carl Clay McCarty   a citizen of   United States
Nation final enrollment No ....
Name of mother Etta R McCarty (nee Davis)   a citizen of   Choctaw
Nation final enrollment No   12005

                    Postoffice   Lehigh, I.T.

AFFIDAVIT OF MOTHER.

UNITED STATES OF AMERICA, }
  INDIAN TERRITORY,
  Central   DISTRICT

    I   Etta R. McCarty (nee Davis)   on oath state that I am 17 years of age and a citizen by   blood   of the Choctaw   Nation, and as such have been placed upon the final roll of the   Choctaw   Nation, by the Honorable Secretary of the Interior my final enrollment number being   12005   ; that I am the lawful

Applications for Enrollment of Choctaw Newborn
Act of 1905 Volume V

wife of   Carl Clay McCarty   , who is a citizen of the   United States   Nation, and as such has been placed upon the final roll of said Nation by the Honorable Secretary of the Interior, his final enrollment number being ——and that a   male   child was born to me on the   14   day of   April   190 3; that said child has been named   Vernon Clay McCarty , and is now living.

Etta R McCarty (nee Davis)

WITNESSETH:

Must be two Witnesses who are Citizens.
- Mary Davis
- Carl Davis

Subscribed and sworn to before me this   16"   day of   January   190 5

Dwight Brown
Notary Public.

My commission expires   Dec 2 1908

AFFIDAVIT OF ATTENDING PHYSICIAN OR MIDWIFE

UNITED STATES OF AMERICA
INDIAN TERRITORY
   Central   DISTRICT

I,   Dr David Gardner & H.G. Goben   Physicians on oath state that I attended on Mrs.   Etta R McCarty (nee Davis)   wife of   Carl McCarty on the   14th day of   April   , 190 3, that there was born to her on said date a   male   child, that said child is now living, and is said to have been named   Vernon Clay McCarty

David Gardner   M.D.

Subscribed and sworn to before me this, the   25 day of   Jan   190 5

Dwight Brown
Notary Public.

WITNESSETH:

Must be two witnesses who are citizens and know the child.
- Mary Davis
- RW Harrison

We hereby certify that we are well acquainted with   David Gardner   a   physician   and know   him   to be reputable and of good standing in the community.

- Mary Davis
- R W Harrison

Applications for Enrollment of Choctaw Newborn
Act of 1905 Volume V

BIRTH AFFIDAVIT.

DEPARTMENT OF THE INTERIOR.
COMMISSION TO THE FIVE CIVILIZED TRIBES.

IN RE APPLICATION FOR ENROLLMENT, as a citizen of the Choctaw Nation, of Vernon Clay McCarty , born on the 14 day of April , 1903

Name of Father: Carl Clay McCarty non citizen of the .... Nation.
Name of Mother: Etta R Davis McCarty a citizen of the Choctaw Nation.

Postoffice Lehigh I.T.

AFFIDAVIT OF MOTHER.

UNITED STATES OF AMERICA, Indian Territory,
Central DISTRICT.

I, Etta R Davis McCarty , on oath state that I am 17 years of age and a citizen by blood , of the Choctaw Nation; that I am the lawful wife of Carl Clay McCarty , who is a non citizen, by .... of the .... Nation; that a male child was born to me on 14 day of April , 1903; that said child has been named Vernon Clay McCarty , and was living March 4, 1905.

Etta R Davis McCarty

Witnesses To Mark:

Subscribed and sworn to before me this 18 day of March , 1905

C.H. *(Illegible)*
Notary Public.

AFFIDAVIT OF ATTENDING PHYSICIAN OR MID-WIFE.

UNITED STATES OF AMERICA, Indian Territory,
Central DISTRICT.

I, David Gardner , a Physician , on oath state that I attended on Mrs. Etta R. David McCarty , wife of Carl Clay McCarty on the 14 day of April , 1903; that there was born to her on said date a male child; that said child was living March 4, 1905, and is said to have been named Vernon Clay McCarty

David Gardner M.D.

Witnesses To Mark:

Applications for Enrollment of Choctaw Newborn
Act of 1905 Volume V

Subscribed and sworn to before me this 18 day of March , 1905

C.H. *(Illegible)*
Notary Public.

7-4296

Muskogee, Indian Territory, March 22, 1905.

Etta R Davis McCarty,
    Lehigh, Indian Territory.

Dear Madam:

Receipt is hereby acknowledged of your affidavit and the affidavit of David Gardner to the birth of Vernon Clay McCarty, son of Carl Clay and Etta R. Davis McCarty, April 14, 1903, and the same have been filed with our records as an application for the enrollment of said child.

Respectfully,

Chairman.

---

7 NB 302

Muskogee, Indian Territory, April 11, 1905.

C. C. McCarty,
    P. O. Box 102,
        Durant, Indian Territory.

Dear Sir:

Receipt is hereby acknowledged of your letter of April 4th, asking if the name of your child, Vernon Clay McCarty, is all right on the record.

In reply to your letter, you are informed that the affidavits heretofore forwarded to the birth of your child, Vernon Clay McCarty, have been filed with our records as an application for the enrollment of said child, and in the event further evidence is necessary to enable the Commission to determine his right to enrollment, you will be duly notified.

Respectfully,

Commissioner in Charge.

Applications for Enrollment of Choctaw Newborn
Act of 1905   Volume V

7- N.B. 302

COPY

Muskogee, Indian Territory, April 11, 1905.

C. C. McCarty,
    Durant, Indian Territory.

Dear Sir:

    Receipt is hereby acknowledged of your letter of April 2, 1905, asking if land May be set aside for your child, Vernon Clay McCarty, for whom birth affidavit has been recently filed with the Commission.

    In reply to your letter you are advised that no reservation of land or selection of allotment can be made for children for whom application has been made under the provisions of the act of Congress approved March 3, 1905, until their enrollment has been approved by the Secretary of the Interior.

    Respectfully,
    SIGNED
    T. B. Needles.
    Commissioner in Charge.

---

7 NB 302

Muskogee, Indian Territory April 27, 1905.

Carl C. McCarty,
    Durant, Indian Territory.

Dear Sir:

    Receipt is hereby acknowledged of your letter of April 7, 1905, stating that you have been appointed guardian of your child Vernon Clay McCarty by the United States Court and you protest against any other person selecting allotment for said child.

    This information has been made a matter of record.

    Respectfully,

    Chairman.

Applications for Enrollment of Choctaw Newborn
Act of 1905   Volume V

7-NB-202[sic]

Muskogee, Indian Territory, July 10, 1905.

C. C. McCarty,
    Durant, Indian Territory.

Dear Sir:

    Receipt is hereby acknowledged of your letter of July 5, 1905, asking if the application for the enrollment of your minor child Vernon Clay McCarty has been received; you also ask relative to the enrollment of intermarried citizens who were married before the ratification of the Supplemental Treaty on September 25, 1902.

    In reply to your letter you are advised that the name of your child Vernon Clay McCarty has been placed upon a schedule of citizens by blood of the Choctaw Nation which has been forwarded the Secretary of the Interior, but as you do not state the name of the intermarried citizen to whom you refer it is impracticable to give you any information as to whether or not any application has been made for the enrollment of said person as an intermarried citizen of the Choctaw or Chickasaw Nation.

    You are further advised that no action has yet been taken on your application for enrollment as an intermarried citizen of the Choctaw Nation, but when a decision is reached you will be notified of the action taken therein.

    Respectfully,

Commissioner.

7-NB-302

Muskogee, Indian Territory, July 12, 1905.

C. C. McCarty,
    Durant, Indian Territory.

Dear Sir:

    Receipt is hereby acknowledged of your letter of June 2, 1905, which was received at this office July 10, 1905, asking if the enrollment of your child Vernon Clay McCarty has been approved.

    In reply to your letter you are advised that the name of your child Vernon Clay McCarty has been placed upon a schedule of citizens by blood of the Choctaw Nation which has been forwarded the Secretary of the Interior and you will be notified when his enrollment is approved by the Department.

Applications for Enrollment of Choctaw Newborn
Act of 1905   Volume V

Respectfully,

Commissioner.

7-NB-302

Muskogee, Indian Territory, August 3, 1905.

C. C. McCarty,
    McGee, Indian Territory.

Dear Sir:

    Receipt is hereby acknowledged of your letter of July 22, 1905, asking if your child has been approved by the Secretary of the Interior.

    In reply to your letter you are advised that on July 22, 1905, the Secretary of the Interior approved the enrollment of Vernon Clay McCarty as a citizen by blood of the Choctaw Nation and selection of allotment May now be made in his behalf in accordance with the rules and regulations governing the selection of allotments and the designation of homesteads in the Choctaw and Chickasaw Nations.

Respectfully,

Commissioner.

(The letter below does not belong with the current applicant.)

7-D-302

Muskogee, Indian Territory, August 10, 1905.

J. H. Bristo,
    Gowen, Indian Territory.

Dear Sir:

    Receipt is hereby acknowledged of your letter of August 5, 1905, enclosing affidavit of Culverson Thompson which you offer in support of the application of Morris Battiest as a citizen by blood of the Choctaw Nation and the same has been filed with the record in this case.

Respectfully,

Acting Commissioner.

Applications for Enrollment of Choctaw Newborn
Act of 1905   Volume V

Choc New Born 303
    Bennie Jones
    (Born Aug. 24, 1903)

BIRTH AFFIDAVIT.

DEPARTMENT OF THE INTERIOR,
COMMISSION TO THE FIVE CIVILIZED TRIBES.

In Re Application for Enrollment, as a citizen of the Choctaw Nation, of Bennie Jones, born on the 24th day of Aug, 1903

Name of Father: Jonas Jones   a citizen of the Choctaw Nation.
Name of Mother: Sophia Jones   a citizen of the Choctaw Nation.

          Post-office   Stringtown, IT

AFFIDAVIT OF MOTHER.

UNITED STATES OF AMERICA, }
   INDIAN TERRITORY,
  Central Judicial   District.

    I, Sophia Jones, on oath state that I am 39 years of age and a citizen by blood, of the Choctaw Nation; that I am the lawful wife of Jonas Jones, who is a citizen, by blood of the Choctaw Nation; that a male child was born to me on 24th day of Aug, 1903, that said child has been named Bennie Jones, and is now living.

                                    her
                              Sophia + Jones
WITNESSES TO MARK: mark
  { T.H. Kennedy
    Chas Collins

    Subscribed and sworn to before me this 28th day of Nov, 1903

                              D.S. Kennedy
                                 NOTARY PUBLIC.

Applications for Enrollment of Choctaw Newborn
Act of 1905   Volume V

AFFIDAVIT OF ATTENDING PHYSICIAN OR MID-WIFE.

UNITED STATES OF AMERICA,
   INDIAN TERRITORY,
Central Judicial District.

I, Jonas Jones, a ...., on oath state that I ~~attended on Mrs.~~ was the only one present and attended Sophia Jones, wife of my wife on the 24th day of Aug, 1903; that there was born to her on said date a male child; that said child is now living and is said to have been named Bennie Jones

his
Bennie + Jones
mark

WITNESSES TO MARK:
{ T.H. Kennedy
{ Chas Collins

Subscribed and sworn to before me this 28th day of Nov, 1903

D.S. Kennedy
NOTARY PUBLIC.

NEW-BORN AFFIDAVIT.

Number............

...Choctaw Enrolling Commission...

IN THE MATTER OF THE APPLICATION FOR ENROLLMENT, as a citizen of the Choctaw Nation, of Bennie Jones

born on the 22nd [sic] day of Aug 1903

Name of father Jonas Jones	a citizen of	Choctaw
Nation final enrollment No. 12025		
Name of mother Sophia Jones	a citizen of	Choctaw
Nation final enrollment No. 12026		
	Postoffice	Stringtown, IT

Applications for Enrollment of Choctaw Newborn
Act of 1905 Volume V

AFFIDAVIT OF MOTHER.

UNITED STATES OF AMERICA
INDIAN TERRITORY
Central Judicial DISTRICT

I Sophia Jones , on oath state that I am 38 years of age and a citizen by blood of the Choctaw Nation, and as such have been placed upon the final roll of the Choctaw Nation, by the Honorable Secretary of the Interior my final enrollment number being 12026; that I am the lawful wife of Jonas Jones , who is a citizen of the Choctaw Nation, and as such has been placed upon the final roll of said Nation by the Honorable Secretary of the Interior, his final enrollment number being 12025 and that a male child was born to me on the 22nd[sic] day of Aug 190 3; that said child has been named Bennie Jones , and is now living.

Witnesseth.

Sophia x Jones

her

mark

Must be two Witnesses who are Citizens. (Name Illegible)

(Name Illegible)

Subscribed and sworn to before me this 10th day of Feby 190 5

D.S. Kennedy
Notary Public.

My commission expires: Nov 1st 1905

AFFIDAVIT OF ATTENDING PHYSICIAN OR MIDWIFE

UNITED STATES OF AMERICA
INDIAN TERRITORY
Central Judicial DISTRICT

I, Jonas Jones ~~a~~ attendant on oath state that I attended on Mrs. Sophia Jones wife of Jonas Jones on the 22nd[sic] day of Aug. , 190 3, that there was born to her on said date a male child, that said child is now living, and is said to have been named Bennie Jones

Witness

John Kennedy
J F Miller

Jonas Jones +

his

mark

~~M.D~~.

WITNESSETH:

Must be two witnesses who are citizens and know the child. JE Tucker

James Baker

Applications for Enrollment of Choctaw Newborn
Act of 1905 Volume V

Subscribed and sworn to before me this, the 10th day of Feby 190 5

D.S. Kennedy   Notary Public.

We hereby certify that we are well acquainted with Jonas Jones a Attendant and know him to be reputable and of good standing in the community.

{ D.S. Kennedy

{ *(Name Illegible)*

BIRTH AFFIDAVIT.

DEPARTMENT OF THE INTERIOR.
COMMISSION TO THE FIVE CIVILIZED TRIBES.

IN RE APPLICATION FOR ENROLLMENT, as a citizen of the Choctaw Nation, of Bennie Jones , born on the 22nd[sic] day of August , 1903

Name of Father: Jonas Jones   a citizen of the Choctaw Nation.
Name of Mother: Sophia Jones   a citizen of the Choctaw Nation.

Postoffice   Stringtown, I.T.

AFFIDAVIT OF MOTHER.

UNITED STATES OF AMERICA, Indian Territory, }
    Central   DISTRICT. }

I, Sophia Jones , on oath state that I am 38 years of age and a citizen by blood , of the Choctaw Nation; that I am the lawful wife of Jonas Jones , who is a citizen, by blood of the Choctaw Nation; that a male child was born to me on 22nd[sic] day of August , 1903; that said child has been named Bennie Jones , and was living March 4, 1905.

                         her
                  Sophia x Jones
                        mark

Witnesses To Mark:
   { JW Jones
   { Richard Shanafelt

Subscribed and sworn to before me this 3rd day of April , 1905

                   W.H. Angell
                      Notary Public.

Applications for Enrollment of Choctaw Newborn
Act of 1905   Volume V

Husband
AFFIDAVIT OF ~~ATTENDING PHYSICIAN OR MID-WIFE~~.

UNITED STATES OF AMERICA, Indian Territory, }
Central   DISTRICT.

    I, Jonas Jones , a ——————— , on oath state that I attended on Mrs. Sophia Jones my , wife of ——————— on the 22nd[sic] day of August, 1903; that there was born to her on said date a   male   child; that said child was living March 4, 1905, and is said to have been named Bennie Jones and that there was no one present on the date of the birth of said child except my said wife and myself

                                                his
                                   Jones x Jones
Witnesses To Mark: mark
  { JW Jones
    Richard Shanafelt

    Subscribed and sworn to before me this 3rd day of   April   , 1905

                                     W.H. Angell
                                          Notary Public.

BIRTH AFFIDAVIT.

DEPARTMENT OF THE INTERIOR.
COMMISSION TO THE FIVE CIVILIZED TRIBES.

    IN RE APPLICATION FOR ENROLLMENT, as a citizen of the   Choctaw   Nation, of Bennie Jones   , born on the 24   day of August   , 1903

Name of Father: Jonas Jones   a citizen of the   Choctaw   Nation.
Name of Mother: Sophia Jones   a citizen of the   Choctaw   Nation.

                            Postoffice   Stringtown, I.T.

                          AFFIDAVIT OF MOTHER.

UNITED STATES OF AMERICA, Indian Territory, }
Central Judicial   DISTRICT.

    I,   Sophia Jones   , on oath state that I am   28[sic]   years of age and a citizen by   blood   , of the   Choctaw   Nation; that I am the lawful wife of Jonas Jones   , who is a citizen, by blood   of the   Choctaw   Nation; that a male   child was born to me on   24   day of August   , 1903; that said child has been named   Bennie Jones   , and was living March 4, 1905.

Applications for Enrollment of Choctaw Newborn
Act of 1905   Volume V

                                                her
                                       Sophia + Jones

Witnesses To Mark: mark
  { Geo W Bartlett
  { W H *(Illegible)*

Subscribed and sworn to before me this 12th day of   April   , 1905

                                  D.S. Kennedy
                                         Notary Public.

AFFIDAVIT OF ATTENDING PHYSICIAN OR MID-WIFE.

UNITED STATES OF AMERICA, Indian Territory, }
   Central Judicial   DISTRICT. }

     I,   Jonas Jones   , a ...., on oath state that I attended on Mrs.   Sophia Jones   my , wife of ——————— on the 24 day of August, 1903; that there was born to her on said date a   male   child; that said child was living March 4, 1905, and is said to have been named Bennie Jones

                                         his
                                   Jones x Jones

Witnesses To Mark: mark
  Geo W Bartlett
  W H *(Illegible)*

Subscribed and sworn to before me this 12th day of   April   , 1905

                                  D.S. Kennedy
                                         Notary Public.

                                   COPY   N.B. 203[sic]

                     Muskogee, Indian Territory, April 7, 1905.

Jonas Jones,
     Stringtown, Indian Territory.

Dear Sir:

     There is inclosed you herewith for execution application for the enrollment of your infant child, Bennie Jones, born August 24, 1903.

     The affidavits heretofore filed with the Commission show the child was living on November 28, 1903. It is necessary, for the child to be enrolled, that he was living on

Applications for Enrollment of Choctaw Newborn
Act of 1905   Volume V

March 4, 1905. You will please insert the mother's age in the place left blank for that purpose.

In having these affidavits executed care should be exercised to see that all names are written in full, as they appear in the body of the affidavit, and in the event that either of the persons signing the affidavit are unable to write, signatures by mark must be attested by two witnesses. Each affidavit must be executed before a Notary Public and the notarial seal and signature of the officer must be attached to each separate affidavit.

In case there was no physician or midwife in attendance upon your wife at the time of the birth of the applicant, it will be necessary that you submit the affidavits of two persons who know the child was born, stating date of birth, that he was living on March 4, 1905 and that Sophia Jones is his mother.

                                  Respectfully,
                                  SIGNED
                                T. B. Needles.

SEV 1-7.   Commissioner in Charge.

                                                Choctaw N.B. 303.

                    Muskogee, Indian Territory, April 16, 1905.

Jonas Jones,
      Stringtown, Indian Territory.

Dear Sir:

      Receipt is hereby acknowledged of the affidavits of Sophia Jones and Jonas Jones to the birth of Bennie Jones, son of Jonas and Sophia Jones, August 24, 1903, and the same have been filed with our records in the matter of the enrollment of said child.

                                Respectfully,

                                               Chairman.

Applications for Enrollment of Choctaw Newborn
Act of 1905   Volume V

7-NB-303.

Muskogee, Indian Territory, May 22, 1905.

Jonas Jones,
    Stringtown, Indian Territory.

Dear Sir:

    Referring to the application for the enrollment of your infant child, Bennie Jones, born August 24, 1903, it is noted from The affidavits heretofore filed in this office that there was no physician or midwife in attendance upon your wife at the time of birth of the applicant.

    In[sic] this is correct it will be necessary for you to file in this office the affidavits of two disinterested parties who have actual knowledge of the facts that the child was born, the date of his birth; that he was living on March 4, 1905, and that Sophia Jones is his mother.

    Respectfully,

Chairman.

7-N.B. 303.

Muskogee, Indian Territory, June 10, 1905.

Jonas Jones,
    Stringtown, Indian Territory.

Dear Sir:

    Receipt is hereby acknowledged of your letter of May 30, transmitting the affidavits of Reason Bond and Christopher D. Moore to the birth of Bennie Jones, son of Jonas and Sophia Jones, August 24, 1903, and the same have been filed with our records in the matter of the enrollment of said child.

    Respectfully,

Chairman.

Applications for Enrollment of Choctaw Newborn
Act of 1905   Volume V

United States of America
Ind Ter Central District

I Reason Bond do solemly[sic] swear that I know Bennie Jones that he was born Aug the 24 1903 and is now living and that Sophia Jones is his mother.

Reason Bond

Subscribed and sworn to before me this day the 30 day of May 1905

Lark Sadler
Notary Public

My commission expires
    Jan the 10 1905[sic]

United States of America
Ind Ter Central District

I Christopher D Moore do solemly[sic] swear that I do know Bennie Jones, that he was born Aug the 24 1903 and is now living and that Sophia Jones is his mother

Christopher D Moore

Subscribed and sworn to before me this the 30 day of May 1905

Lark Sadler
Notry[sic] Public

My commission expires
    Jan the 10 1905[sic]

Applications for Enrollment of Choctaw Newborn
Act of 1905 Volume V

Choc New Born 304
    Ronald Tucker
    (Born Aug. 25, 1904)

Choc NB
Card 304

DEPARTMENT OF THE INTERIOR,
COMMISSION TO THE FIVE CIVILIZED TRIBES.
FILED

MAR 30 1905
    Tams Bixby CHAIRMAN.

Please return these[sic] *marriage license.*

No. 1904

Certificate of Record of Marriages.

UNITED STATES OF AMERICA,
  INDIAN TERRITORY, } SCT:
  Central   DISTRICT.

I,   E.J. Fannin   , Clerk of the United States Court in the Indian Territory and District aforesaid, do hereby CERTIFY, that the License for and Certificate of the Marriage of

Mr. Lewis Tucker   and

Miss Ida Sanders   was

filed in my office in said Territory and District the 2 day of November A.D., 190 3 and duly recorded in Book 2 of Marriage Record, Page 334

    WITNESS my hand and seal of said Court, at Atoka , this 3 day of November , A.D. 190 3

E. J. Fannin
    Clerk.

By J.D. Catlin *Deputy.*

**Applications for Enrollment of Choctaw Newborn
Act of 1905   Volume V**

No. 1904

FORM NO. 598.

MARRIAGE LICENSE.

UNITED STATES OF AMERICA,
   THE INDIAN TERRITORY, } ss:
   Central   DISTRICT.

To any Person Authorized by Law to Solemnize Marriage—Greeting:

You are hereby commanded to solemnize the Rite and publish the Banns of Matrimony between Mr.   Lewis Tucker   of   Phillips   in the Indian Territory, aged 27 years, and Miss Ida Sanders   of   Phillips   in the Indian Territory, aged 20 years, according to law, and do you officially sign and return this License to the parties therein named.

WITNESS my hand and official seal, this 5 day of September A. D. 190 3

E. J. Fannin

Clerk of the United States Court.

JD Catlin   *Deputy*

CERTIFICATE OF MARRIAGE.

UNITED STATES OF AMERICA,
   THE INDIAN TERRITORY, } ss:
   .... DISTRICT.

I,   Frank M Colville   a Licensed M.E. Preacher

do hereby CERTIFY, that on the 6th day of September A, D. 190 3 ; I did duly and according to law, as commanded in the foregoing License, solemnize the Rite and publish the BANNS OF MATRIMONY between the parties therein named.

Witness my hand this .... day of ...., A. D. 190......

My credentials are recorded in the office of the Clerk of the United States Court in the Indian Territory, Central District, Book C Page 159   Northern District I.T.

Frank M Colville

a Licensed M.E. Preacher

Applications for Enrollment of Choctaw Newborn
Act of 1905 Volume V

NOTE. -The License and Certificate of Marriage must be returned to the Office of the Clerk of the United States Court of the Indian Territory, from whence it was issued, within sixty days from the date thereof, or the party to whom the License was issued will be liable in the amount of One Hundred Dollars ($100.00).

BIRTH AFFIDAVIT.

DEPARTMENT OF THE INTERIOR.
COMMISSION TO THE FIVE CIVILIZED TRIBES.

IN RE APPLICATION FOR ENROLLMENT, as a citizen of the Choctaw Nation, of Ronald Tucker, born on the 25 day of Aug, 1904.

Name of Father: Louis Tucker   a citizen of the Choctaw Nation.
Name of Mother: Ida Tucker   a citizen of the .... Nation.

Postoffice Phillips IT

AFFIDAVIT OF MOTHER.

UNITED STATES OF AMERICA, Indian Territory,
Central DISTRICT.

I, Ida Tucker, on oath state that I am 20 years of age and a citizen by ...., of the .... Nation; that I am the lawful wife of Louis Tucker, who is a citizen, by blood of the Choctaw Nation; that a male child was born to me on 25 day of Aug, 1904; that said child has been named Ronald Tucker, and was living March 4, 1905.

                             Ida Tucker

Witnesses To Mark:

Subscribed and sworn to before me this 24 day of Mch, 1905.

                             AT West
                             Notary Public.

AFFIDAVIT OF ATTENDING PHYSICIAN OR MID-WIFE.

UNITED STATES OF AMERICA, Indian Territory,
Central DISTRICT.

I, Martha Allen, a midwife, on oath state that I attended on Mrs. Ida Tucker, wife of Louis Tucker on the 25 day of Aug, 1904; that there was born to her on said date a male child; that said child was living March 4, 1905, and is said to have been named Ronald Tucker

Applications for Enrollment of Choctaw Newborn
Act of 1905 Volume V

Martha Allen

Witnesses To Mark:
{

Subscribed and sworn to before me this 24 day of Mch , 1905

AT West

Notary Public.

Choc New Born 305
John Hampton Tucker, Jr.
(Born Dec. 26, 1902)

BIRTH AFFIDAVIT.

DEPARTMENT OF THE INTERIOR.
COMMISSION TO THE FIVE CIVILIZED TRIBES.

IN RE APPLICATION FOR ENROLLMENT, as a citizen of the Choctaw Nation, of Jon Hampton Tucker Jr. , born on the 26th day of December , 1902

Name of Father: John Hampton Tucker   a citizen of the Choctaw Nation.
Name of Mother: Ella May Tucker   a citizen of the Choctaw Nation.

Postoffice South McAlester, Indian Territory

AFFIDAVIT OF MOTHER.

UNITED STATES OF AMERICA, Indian Territory,
Central   DISTRICT.

I, Ella May Tucker , on oath state that I am 28 years of age and a citizen by marriage , of the Choctaw Nation; that I am the lawful wife of John Hampton Tucker , who is a citizen, by blood of the Choctaw Nation; that a Male child was born to me on 26th day of December , 1902; that said child has been named John Hampton Tucker Jr , and was living March 4, 1905.

Ella May Tucker

Witnesses To Mark:
{

Applications for Enrollment of Choctaw Newborn
Act of 1905   Volume V

Subscribed and sworn to before me this 15th day of   March   , 1905

          G Rosewinkel
My commission expires   Notary Public.
 April 6, 1907

AFFIDAVIT OF ATTENDING PHYSICIAN OR MID-WIFE.

UNITED STATES OF AMERICA, ~~Indian Territory~~,
.... ~~DISTRICT~~.

  I,   J.R. Pollock   , a   Physician   , on oath state that I attended on Mrs. Ella May Tucker , wife of John Hampton Tucker   on the 26th day of December   , 1902; that there was born to her on said date a   Male   child; that said child was living March 4, 1905, and is said to have been named John Hampton Tucker Jr.

          J. R. Pollock M.D.

Witnesses To Mark:
 { Edith Brown Casey
   Pearle Hinckle Brown

Subscribed and sworn to before me this 18 day of   March   , 1905

          B J Houston
My commission expires   Notary Public.
  June 1st 1905.   Tarrant Co Texas

              7-NB-305.

      Muskogee, Indian Territory, June 10, 1905.

John Hampton Tucker,
  South McAlester, Indian Territory.

Dear Sir:

  Receipt is hereby acknowledged of your letter of June 6, asking whether the enrollment of your child, John Hampton Tucker, Jr.,,,[sic] has been approved.

  In reply to your letter you are advised that the name of your son, John Hampton Tucker, Jr., has been placed upon a schedule of citizens by blood of the Choctaw Nation prepared for forwarding to the Secretary of the Interior, and you will be informed when his enrollment is approved.

       Respectfully,

            Chairman.

Applications for Enrollment of Choctaw Newborn
Act of 1905 Volume V

<u>Choc New Born 306</u>
    Claud Crofford Marlow
    (Born Jan. 23, 1905)

(The Marriage License below typed as given.)

              Marriage Liscense.

Chocktaw Nation
    Atoka County.

    To any person authorized to solemnize marriages- Greeting:

You are hereby commanded to solemnize the rite and publish the banns of matrimony between Mr. Reuben Marlow of Lehigh, in the Indian Territory. age 23 years, a citizen of the Chocktaw Nation, and Miss Carry Mc Cown of Lehigh, a citizen of the United States in the Indian Territory, aged 18 yrs. to the parties therein named.
Witness my hand and official seal,This 31st day of Dec.A.D. 1903.

                    (Signed (W.R. Harrison
                                  Clerk of the County Court
                          By Zadoo Harrison,
                                Deputy,

              Certificate of Marriage.
              ....

Chocktaw Nation,
                    I, A.T. Wen   a Mayor of the
    Atoka County.

Incorporated town of Lehigh, I.T. Do hereby certify, that on the 3rd day of Jan. A.D.1904. ,I did duly, and according to law,as commanded in the foregoing license, solemnize the Rite and publish the Banns of Matrimony between the parties therein named.
    Witness my hand this 4th day of Jan. A.D.1904.
                                A.T. Wen
                                a Mayor.

I,hereby certify that the within marriage license is duly recorded in my office in Vol. no. 1. page 188 Atoka County ,Records , this Jan. 20th, A.D. 1904.

                              R.W.Harrison,
                                County Clerk
                              Atoka County, C.N.

Applications for Enrollment of Choctaw Newborn
Act of 1905 Volume V

I.E.C.Olds, A notary public,in and for the Southern District,Indian Territory,duly commissioned and acting,do hereby certify that the above is a true and correct copy of the original.

                I certify that the *(illegible)*   EC Olds
                of the mayor is illegible.
                              Notary Public, So. Dis. I.T

CoM, Exp. Feb, 5, 1908.

BIRTH AFFIDAVIT.

DEPARTMENT OF THE INTERIOR.
COMMISSION TO THE FIVE CIVILIZED TRIBES.

IN RE APPLICATION FOR ENROLLMENT, as a citizen of the   Choctaw   Nation, of Claud Crofford Marlow   , born on the 23 day of January , 1905

Name of Father: Reuben F Marlow   a citizen of the Choctaw   Nation.
Name of Mother: Carrie Marlow   not a citizen of the   Nation.

                    Postoffice   Hickory, Indian Territory

AFFIDAVIT OF MOTHER.

UNITED STATES OF AMERICA, Indian Territory,
    Southern   DISTRICT.

    I, Carrie Marlow , on oath state that I am 19 years of age and ~~a citizen by~~ I am not a citizen , of the .... Nation; that I am the lawful wife of Reuben F Marlow   , who is a citizen, by Blood of the   Choctaw Nation; that a male child was born to me on 23rd day of January   , 1905; that said child has been named Claud Crofford Marlow , and was living March 4, 1905.

                                        Carrie Marlow

Witnesses To Mark:

    Subscribed and sworn to before me this 14th day of March   , 1905

                                    A D Goodenough
                                        Notary Public.

Applications for Enrollment of Choctaw Newborn
Act of 1905   Volume V

AFFIDAVIT OF ATTENDING PHYSICIAN OR MID-WIFE.

UNITED STATES OF AMERICA, Indian Territory, }
Southern   DISTRICT. }

I, Thos B Laumann, a Physician, on oath state that I attended on Mrs. Carrie Marlow, wife of Reuben F Marlow on the 23rd day of January, 1905; that there was born to her on said date a male child; that said child was living March 4, 1905, and is said to have been named Claud Crofford Marlow

Thos B Laumann M.D.

Witnesses To Mark:
{

Subscribed and sworn to before me this 14th day of March, 1905

A D Goodenough
Notary Public.

7-4337

Muskogee, Indian Territory, March 18, 1905.

A. D. Goodenough,
    Sulphur, Indian Territory.

Dear Sir:

Receipt is hereby acknowledged of your letter of March 14, 1905, enclosing the affidavits of Carrie Marlow and Thomas B. Laumann to the birth of Claud Crawford[sic] Marlow, infant son of Reuben F. and Carrie Marlow, January 23, 1905, and the same have been filed with our records as an application for the enrollment of said child.

Respectfully,

Chairman.

Applications for Enrollment of Choctaw Newborn
Act of 1905   Volume V

N. B. 306
COPY
Muskogee, Indian Territory, April 7, 1905.

Reuben F. Marlow,
    Hickory, Indian Territory.

Dear Sir:

    You are hereby advised that before the application for the enrollment of your infant child, Claud Crofford Marlow, can be finally disposed of, it will be necessary for you to furnish the Commission with either the original or a certified copy of the license and certificate of marriage of yourself and Carrie Marlow.

    This should have your immediate attention.

Respectfully,
SIGNED
T. B. Needles.
Commissioner in Charge.

---

7 NB 306

Muskogee, Indian Territory, April 26, 1905.

Reuben F. Marlow,
    Hickory, Indian Territory.

Dear Sir:

    Receipt is hereby acknowledged of your letter of April 17, 1905, inclosing a certified copy of the marriage license and certificate between Reuben F. Marlow and Carrie McCarren[sic], and the same has been filed with the record in the matter of the enrollment of your child, Claud Crawford[sic] Marlow.

Respectfully,

Chairman.

Applications for Enrollment of Choctaw Newborn
Act of 1905   Volume V

7 NB 306

Muskogee, Indian Territory, April 27, 1905.

Reuben F. Marlow,
    Hickory, Indian Territory.

Dear Sir:

    Receipt is hereby acknowledged of your letter of April 17, 1905, inclosing a certified copy of the marriage license and certificate between Reuben F. Marlow and Carrie McCarren[sic], and the same has been filed with the record in the matter of the enrollment of your child, Claud Crawford[sic] Marlow.

                      Respectfully,

                                    Chairman.

Choc New Born 307
    Preston Harrol[sic] Rose
    (Born May 15, 1904)

NEW-BORN AFFIDAVIT.

            Number..................

Choctaw Enrolling Commission.

    IN THE MATTER OF THE APPLICATION FOR ENROLLMENT, as a citizen of the Choctaw   Nation, of   Preston Harrol Rose

born on the   12th[sic]   day of   May   190 4

Name of father   Christopher C Rose   a citizen of   Choctaw
Nation final enrollment No   413
Name of mother   Nettie Rose   a citizen of   Choctaw
Nation final enrollment No   12143

                        Postoffice   Atoka, Indian Territory

Applications for Enrollment of Choctaw Newborn
Act of 1905   Volume V

AFFIDAVIT OF MOTHER.

UNITED STATES OF AMERICA,
INDIAN TERRITORY,
Central   DISTRICT

I   Nettie Rose   on oath state that I am 33 years of age and a citizen by blood   of the Choctaw   Nation, and as such have been placed upon the final roll of the   Choctaw   Nation, by the Honorable Secretary of the Interior my final enrollment number being   12143 ; that I am the lawful wife of Christopher C. Rose   , who is a citizen of the   Choctaw   Nation, and as such has been placed upon the final roll of said Nation by the Honorable Secretary of the Interior, his final enrollment number being 413 and that a   male   child was born to me on the 12th[sic] day of May   190 4 ; that said child has been named Preston Harrol Rose   , and is now living.

                                                   her
                                        Nettie x Rose

WITNESSETH: mark

Must be two Witnesses who are Citizens.   Robert *(Illegible)*
                           Tom McDaniel

Subscribed and sworn to before me this   20th   day of January   190 5

                                      R. M. Rainey
                                             Notary Public.

My commission expires   Dec. 17th 1908

AFFIDAVIT OF ATTENDING PHYSICIAN OR MIDWIFE

UNITED STATES OF AMERICA
INDIAN TERRITORY
Central   DISTRICT

I,   J. S. Fulton   a   Practicing Physician on oath state that I attended on Mrs. Nettie Rose   wife of   Christopher C Rose on the 12[sic]   day of May   , 190 4, that there was born to her on said date a   Male child, that said child is now living, and is said to have been named Preston Harrol Rose

                                J. S. Fulton   M.D.

Subscribed and sworn to before me this, the 12th day of   January   190 5

                                    W A Shoney
                                        Notary Public.

WITNESSETH:

Must be two witnesses who are citizens and know the child.   C.P. Standley
                                 W.C. James

Applications for Enrollment of Choctaw Newborn
Act of 1905 Volume V

We hereby certify that we are well acquainted with .... a .... and know .... to be reputable and of good standing in the community.

         { C. P. Standley

         { W. H. Marshall

BIRTH AFFIDAVIT.

DEPARTMENT OF THE INTERIOR.
COMMISSION TO THE FIVE CIVILIZED TRIBES.

IN RE APPLICATION FOR ENROLLMENT, as a citizen of the Choctaw Nation, of Preston Harrol Rose, born on the 15 day of May, 1904

Name of Father: C C Rose   a citizen of the Choctaw Nation.
Name of Mother: Nettie Rose   a citizen of the Choctaw Nation.

         Postoffice   Atoka I.T.

AFFIDAVIT OF MOTHER.

UNITED STATES OF AMERICA, Indian Territory, }
    Central   DISTRICT. }

I, Nettie Rose, on oath state that I am 33 years of age and a citizen by blood, of the Choctaw Nation; that I am the lawful wife of Christopher C Rose, who is a citizen, by intermarriage of the Choctaw Nation; that a male child was born to me on 15 day of May, 1904; that said child has been named Preston Harrol Rose, and was living March 4, 1905.

                       her
                       Nettie x Rose
Witnesses To Mark: mark
    { Jno H Linebaugh
    { D N Linebaugh

Subscribed and sworn to before me this 23 day of March, 1905

                       Jno H Linebaugh
                          Notary Public.

Applications for Enrollment of Choctaw Newborn
Act of 1905 Volume V

AFFIDAVIT OF ATTENDING PHYSICIAN OR MID-WIFE.

UNITED STATES OF AMERICA, Indian Territory, }
Central DISTRICT. }

I, J. S. Fulton, a physician, on oath state that I attended on Mrs. Nettie Rose, wife of Christopher C Rose on the 15 day of May, 1904; that there was born to her on said date a male child; that said child was living March 4, 1905, and is said to have been named Preston Harrol Rose

J.S. Fulton

Witnesses To Mark:
{

Subscribed and sworn to before me this 24 day of March, 1905

Jno H Linebaugh
Notary Public.

BIRTH AFFIDAVIT.

DEPARTMENT OF THE INTERIOR.
COMMISSION TO THE FIVE CIVILIZED TRIBES.

IN RE APPLICATION FOR ENROLLMENT, as a citizen of the Choctaw Nation, of Preston Harral[sic] Rose, born on the 15 day of May, 1904

Name of Father: C C Rose   a citizen of the Choctaw Nation.
Name of Mother: Nettie Rose   a citizen of the Choctaw Nation.

Postoffice Atoka Ind. Ter.

AFFIDAVIT OF MOTHER.

UNITED STATES OF AMERICA, Indian Territory, }
Central DISTRICT. }

I, Nettie Rose, on oath state that I am 33 years of age and a citizen by Blood, of the Choctaw Nation; that I am the lawful wife of C C Rose, who is a citizen, by Intermarriage of the Choctaw Nation; that a male child was born to me on 15 day of May, 1904; that said child has been named Preston Harral Rose, and was living March 4, 1905.

her
Nettie x Rose
mark

Applications for Enrollment of Choctaw Newborn
Act of 1905   Volume V

Witnesses To Mark:
{ Jno H Linebaugh
{ R.M. Ramey

 Subscribed and sworn to before me this 29 day of   May   , 1905

        Jno H Linebaugh
         Notary Public.

AFFIDAVIT OF ATTENDING PHYSICIAN OR MID-WIFE.

UNITED STATES OF AMERICA, Indian Territory, }
 Central   DISTRICT. }

 I,   J. S. Fulton   , a   Physician   , on oath state that I attended on Mrs.   Nettie Rose   , wife of   C C Rose   on the 15 day of May   , 1904; that there was born to her on said date a   male   child; that said child was living March 4, 1905, and is said to have been named Preston Harral Rose

        J.S. Fulton

Witnesses To Mark:
{

 Subscribed and sworn to before me this 29 day of   May   , 1905

        Jno H Linebaugh
         Notary Public.

---

           7 NB 307

    Muskogee, Indian Territory, April 21, 1905.

Linebaugh Brothers,
  Attorneys at Law,
    Atoka, Indian Territory.

Gentlemen:

 Receipt is hereby acknowledged of your letter of April 15, 1905, asking if the affidavits to the birth of Preston Rose child of Columbus[sic] C. and Nettie Rose have been received and if the same are in proper form.

 In reply to your letter you are informed that the affidavits of Nettie Rose and J. S. Fulton to the birth of Preston Harral Rose, son of C. C. and Nettie Rose May 15, 1904, have been filed with our records as an application for the enrollment of said child.

Applications for Enrollment of Choctaw Newborn
Act of 1905   Volume V

In event further evidence is necessary to enable the Commission to determine the right of this child to enrollment Mr. Rose will be duly advised.

                    Respectfully,

                                      Chairman.

                                      7-NB-307.

                  Muskogee, Indian Territory, May 22, 1905.

C. C. Rose,
    Atoka, Indian Territory.

Dear Sir:

There is enclosed you herewith for execution application for the enrollment of your infant child, Preston Harral Rose.

The affidavits filed with the Commission on March 25, 1905, give the date of the applicants[sic] birth as May 15, 1904, while those filed on the 26th ultimo give it as May 12, 1904. In the enclosed application the date of birth if left blank. Please insert the correct date before having the affidavits executed.

In having these affidavits executed care should be exercised to see that all names are written in full, as they appear in the body of the affidavit, and in the event that either of the persons signing the affidavit are unable to write, signatures by mark must be attested by two witnesses. Each affidavit must be executed before a Notary Public and the notarial seal and signature of the officer must be attached to each separate affidavit.

                    Respectfully,

                                      Chairman.

VR 22-10.

Applications for Enrollment of Choctaw Newborn
Act of 1905   Volume V

7-N.B. 307.

Muskogee, Indian Territory, June 5, 1905.

C. C. Rose,
    Atoka, Indian Territory.

Dear Sir:

Receipt is hereby acknowledged of the affidavits of Nettie Rose and J. S. Fulton to the birth of Preston Harral Rose, son of C. C. and Nettie Rose, May 15, 1904, and the same have been filed with our records in the matter of the enrollment of said child.

Respectfully,

Commissioner in Charge.

Index

ADAMS
   Cina 265,266,270,272
   Dr J A 184
   J A 177,178,183,185
   J A, MD 177,183
   Lee 265,266,267,268,269,270,272
   Lula 268,269,271,272
   Lular 269,271
   Lulu 266,267
   Sinie 266,268,269,271,272
   Willie 265,266,267,268,269, 270,271,272
ADDE
   E S 247
ADKINS
   C G 253,254
AKESON
   N H 119
ALISON
   Sarah 186
ALLEN
   Martha 315,316
ANDERSON
   2 3 268
   Elsie 38,39,40
   Frank 38,39,40
   Perry 38,39,40
   Robinson D 39
   Robnson 38
   W E 267
ANGELL
   W H 29,30,40,85,86,111,130, 131,132,168,169,170,173,174,175,252, 307,308
ANSLEY
   Gilbert 179,180
ARCHER
   Arthur O 170
ARMSTRONG
   Anna 170
   Dr 90,104
   Eliza 166,167,168,169,170,171
   Ellis 175
   J H 88,91,92,93,102,104,105,106
   J H, MD 88,89,91,104,105
   J R 9,10,62,63,64,65,72,75, 94,95,264,265,269

   Jain 166,167
   Jane 166,168,169,170
   Lewis 168,169,170,172,173
   Louis 166,167,168
   Morrow 169
ARNOLD
   Dr J H 57,58,59
   J H 58,59,60
   R J H 61
ASHFORD
   J W 155
BAKER
   James 306
BALL
   E J 150
BANISTER
   J N 87
BARNES
   Robert J 78,79
BARNETT
   E A 129
   A J S 222
BARTLETT
   Geo W 309
BARUTHERS
   J H 80
BATTIEST
   Morris 303
BAXTER
   Alta 42,43,44
   Opal 41,43,44
   Walter W 42,43,44
   Willie O 42
BAYLES
   T H 64
BELL
   F M 122,123
BELOTE
   J F 279,280,281
   J R 278
BELVIN
   G N 269
   Margaret 190
BENCH
   Margaret 190
   Sam 190

Index

BIXBY
    Tams 11,16,17,27,36,69,74,81, 113,114,115,116,128,238,239,313
BLANCHE
    Osborne 203,204,205,206,212
BOBO
    Lacey P 51,52,53,75
BOLAND
    James 22,23,136
BOLING
    Hazel Belle 181
BOLLING
    Hayzell Belle 176
    Hazel Bell 176,177
    Hazel Belle 177,178,179,180,182, 183,184,185
    Hazell Bell 180
    Mrs Walter C 177
    Octavia B 184
    Octavia Belle 176,178,179,182, 183,185
    Octovia Belle 177
    Theodore Dickson 176,179,180
    Theodore Dixon 183
    W C 183
    Walter 183
    Walter C ...176,177,178,179,180,182, 183,184,185
BOLLINT
    Hazell Belle 181
    Theodore Dickson 181
    Walter C 181
BOND
    Reason 311,312
BOSWELL
    S C 97,98,99
BOWER
    J Ernest 261
    James 261
BOWMAN
    W R 41,49
    W R, MD 41
BOYDSTON
    J F 41
BOYDSTUN
    J F 42
BOYSTUN

    J F 41
BRANAUGH
    V 67
BRANUAGH
    V 68
BREAKER
    J J 22,23,25,26
    J J, MD 25
    J T, MD 22
BREEDLANE
    R T 57
BRIDGES
    D A 96
BRISTO
    J H 303
BROWDER
    J C 178
    J D 177
BROWN
    Dwight 289,290,291,292,293, 296,297,298
    Henrietta 108
    Pearle Hinckle 317
BRUNSON
    D D 192,193
BURRIS
    Ida 269
    Marvin J 234
BYRD
    L A 198

CAIN
    P L 40
    P L, MD 38
CALDWELL
    A A 154
CAMPBELL
    C M 128,129
    J B 15
CANE
    P L 38
CARMACK
    J A 216,217,218,237
    J A, MD 217
CARNES
    Cerena 204
    Ellis 186,187,188,189,190,

191,204,205,206
Rebecca 187,188,189,190
S B 205,206
Serane 200
Serena 206
Siney 187,191
Sinie 186,187,188,190,191
Sinnie 186,189
CARNEY
Ellis 212
CART
Bettie 155
J L 155,156
CASEY
Edith Brown 317
CATLIN
J D 27,28,313,314
James D 117
CAUDILL
W C 135,136,137,138,139
CHATEAU
Martin 27,28,29,30
Media Magdalene 29
Medie Magdalene 29
Rosa Angelina 27,29,30
CLARK
Perry M 201,266,269
COBB
Kenner B 265
COCHNAEUR
Bettie 94,95
Henry Clay 94,95
N H 94,95
COCHNAUER
Bettie 95,96,99,101
Betty 96,97,98,100
Henry Clay ...94,95,96,97,99,100,101
N H 99
Nicholas 95,96,97,98,100,101
Nicholas Alexander 94,98,100
CODY
R D 108,109,110,218
R D, MD 108,110
COLBERT
Aaron 189,204,205,206
Cerena 202,204,205,208
Cerina 209

Sam 189
Serena 189,201,206,208,209
COLEMAN
N C 35
COLLINS
Chas 304,305
J D 116
COLVILL
Frank M 314
COSSART
J H 275
COTTON
J D 117
COVINGTON
W P 53
CREECY
Douglas D 17,18,19,20
Ula A 20
Ula L 17,18,19
W C 17,18,19,20
CRENSHAW
W W 225,228,230
W W, MD 225
Wesley W 231
Wesley W, MD 228
CROSS
John H 58,59,108,110,160,161,
162,164,165,166,216,217,218,234,235,
236,237
M E 162,166,216,218
CROWDER
Louis 190
Robert 190

DABBOR
J C 22
DAMRON
Amanda 11,12
Ethel 11,12
W R 11,12
DANDRIDGE
W E 172,173
DARLING
W A 248,249
DAVIE
Ambrose M 247,249
A M 248,251

Index

A M, MD 247,248
DAVIS
   Carl 291,298
   Etta R 291,297,298
   Henry Carl 289,290,292,293, 294,295
   Henry Russel 289
   Henry Russell 289,290,291,292, 293,294,295
   Mary 289,298
   Mary J 292
   Mary T 290,291,292,293,294,295
DAVY
   A M 249
DAWRON
   Ethel 11
DICKEY
   Alton H 125,126,127
   Mary 125,126,127
   Mary McLellan 126,127
   R P 126
   Steward E 125,126,127
DOWLAND
   Myrtle Lee 191
DOWNING
   S H 96,97,98,99,267,268
DUER
   Isaac 1,2
DUNCAN
   G D 71,202,206
   J H 199,200
DUNLAP
   Novie 116,117,120
DUNNIGAN
   Susan 158
DURANT
   Joseph S 81
   Martha 81
   Vicy 186
   Wilson 186
DWIGHT
   E T 94
   Edwin 7,8,9,10,11
   Emma 7,8,9,10,11
   Hunter 7,8,9,10,11

ENGLAND
   George 196
ENNIS
   C H 196
EWING
   C H 293,294

FANNIN
   E J 27,28,116,117,313,314
FARMER
   N S 51
FAULK
   A A 143
FERRANTA
   Isabina 148,149
FERRANTE
   Carolen 145
   Charley 145,146,147,148,149
   Isabina 146,148,149
   Isabinda 146,147
   Isi binda 145,146
   Isibinda 145
   Sante 145,146,147,148,149
FERRAUTE
   Charley 145
FLEMING
   Geo N 180,181
   Geo N, MD 180,181
   George N, MD 183
FOLSOM
   Amos Earl 88,89,90,91,93
   Anus Earl 87,88,91,92,93
   A E 32,47,84,89,103,104, 167,275,277
   Jacb 87
   Jacob 87,88,89,90,91,92,93
   John N 103,104
   Mary 87,88,89,90,91,92,93
   A R 172
FOOSHE & BRONSON 198
FOOSHEE
   Geo A 194
FRANKLIN
   Wirt 258,259
FRAZIER
   Ella 61,62,63,64,65,66
   John 61,62,63,64,65,66,94
   Mary 61,62,63,64,65,66

Index

Ross 80
Solomon 164,165
FREENEY
  Ella B 123
  Reuben 149
FREENY
  Alfred L 275,278,283
  Alfred Larraine 280
  Alfred Lorane 283
  Alfred Lorraine 273,274,281, 282,283
  Grace 273,274,275,276,277,278, 279,280,281,283
  Jasper 280
  Jasper D 273,274,275,276,278,279, 280,281,282,283
  Lee 149,150,151
  Martha 149,150,151
  Reuben 150,151
  Wilson F 279
  Wilson R 273,276,277,280,283
FRONTERHOUSE
  Wm 28
FULSOM
  Amos Earl 92
  Anus Earl 91
  Jacob 92
  Mary 87,89,90,92
FULTON
  J S 323,325,326,328
  J S, MD 323

GALLAHAN
  John 123
GARDNER
  A C 22,23
  David 289,291,292,293,294, 297,299,300
  David, MD 290,291,292,295,297, 298,299
  Dr David 298
  J J 38,39,261
  J T 18,19,20
GENTRY
  I L 190
GOBEN
  H G 196,197,298

GOINS
  Elizabeth 161,162,164,165,166
GOODENOUGH
  A D 319,320
GORDON
  J M 227
  James M 224,225,228,229
  Jas M 222,223
GRUBBS
  John D 284,285
GUYRE
  Sarah J 22

HAMILTON
  Dr N J 136
  Mamie 220,221
  N J 136,137,138,139,140
  N J, MD 136,137,138
  William Fenton 220,221
  Wm H 220,221
HAMPTON
  Bixby 81
  Ellen 79,80,81,82
  Isaac 78,79,80,81,82
  J B 265
  J H 192,193
  Martha 78,79,80,81,82
  Mitchell 78,79,80,81,82
HARBOUR
  I T 253,255,259
  I T, MD 253,255,259
HARGRAVE
  J W 73
HARKINS
  Claud H 57,58,61
  Claud Hassel 56,57,60
  G W 57
  George W 56,57,58,59,60,61
  Hattie 56,57,58,59,60,61
  Mable 56,58,59,61
HARRIS
  Amelia 46,47
HARRISON
  M W 257,258
  M W, MD 257,258
  R W 298,318
  W F 234

Index

W R 318
Zadoo.. 318
HOKUBBI
  Frances 110,111,112,113,114,115
  Peter................ 110,111,112,113,114
  Sisley 110,111,113
HOMER
  D A 72,75
  Jacob.. 52
  S J 46,47
  Sisley 70
HOMES
  Jacob.. 51
HOOVER
  J T 14,15
HOPARKENTUBBI
  David 69,70,71,72
  Isabel 75
  Isabelle 69,70,71,73
  Maggie.........69,70,71,72,73,74,75,77
HOPKENTUBBY
  Maggie.. 76
HOPKINS
  Chas A 266
  D W 179,180,181,182
HORTON
  L B 209
  L D 67,68,187,188,189,190,
  191,202,203,204,205,206,208,210,211,
  212,213
HOUSTON
  B J 317
HOWARD
  J H 223,224,226,229,230,231
  J H, MD 223,224,226
  John H 229,231
  John H, MD 229
HUNTER
  Addie 269
  Charles.. 269
  George 10
  Minnie 10
  T W 267,268
  Thos W 8
  Viola 269
  Walter 269
  Ward 269

IZARD
  John C 13,14,15,16
  Tommie 14,15,16,17
  Tommie J................................ 13,14
  Valley Ester 13
  Valley Esther..............13,14,15,16,17
  Vallie Esther............................ 16,17
JACKSON
  Rebecca 261
JACOB
  Eastman...........167,168,171,172,173,
  174,175
  Nelson 174
  Reason..............171,172,173,174,175
  Sina............171,172,173,174,175,176
  Sinnie 167,168
JAMES
  Betsy.........199,200,201,202,203,204,
  205,206,207,208,209,210,211,212,213
  Lena......................201,202,208,209
  Lorena B...................................... 212
  Moses 199,200,201,202,203,204,
  205,206,207,208,209
  Silas 197
  W C 196,197,323
JENNINGS
  E M... 147
JOHNSON
  Agnes 50,51,52,53,54,55
  Francis 52
  Jas M 70
JOHNSTON
  Susan 235
JONES
  Bennie 304,305,306,307,308,309,
  310,311,312
  Cham 218
  Elbert M 141,142
  G M 71
  Isaac 8
  Isabell 69
  Isabelle 73
  Isreal 90
  J W 108,112,307,308
  Jonas...............304,305,306,307,308,

309,310,311
Sophia.......304,305,306,307,308,309,
310,311,312
T W 108,109,233,234

KEMP
   Richard E 286,288
KENNEDY
   D S 304,305,306,307,309
   John 306
   T H 304,305
KING
   Anderson 284,285
   Emma 284,285,286,287,288
   McGee 286,287
   Mitchell 284,285,286,287,288
   R F 193
   Richard F 193,194,195
   Richard F, MD 194
   Zona 284,285,286,287,288
KINKADE
   Fred V 73
KREBBS
   Amanda 151,158
   Benjamin 152,153,154,155,156,
157,158,159
   Mary Etter Emelina 159
   May Etta Emaline .. 152,153,154,155,
156,157,158,159
   May Etta Emeline 151,156
   Susie B 157
   Susie Bell 154,155,156,157,158
   Sussie B 152,153,156

LABOR
   W M 135,136
LARRABEE
   C F 240,245
LAUMANN
   Thomas B 320
   Thos B 320
   Thos B, MD 320
LAWRANCE
   D A 286,287
   Pika 285
LAWRENCE
   Frank T 44,45

   Ida V 44,45
   Osborne S 287,288
   Ruth 44,45
LEADER
   Francis 50,51,53,54,55
   Icey 51,53
   Joel 50
   Silas 50,52,54
LEFLORE
   Joshua 67,68
LEFLORE
   Joshua 78,79
LEFLORE
   Lita 68
   Litie 67,68
   Sam 67,68
LEFLORE
   Sophie 96
LEWIS
   Culberson 51
   Eliza 33,34
   Joslih 52
   Joslin 52
LILLARD
   Minnie 234
LINDSEY
   Dr W T 107
LINEBAUGH
   D H 45,109
   D N 273,324
   Jno H 324,325,326
LONG
   Le Roy 47
   LeRoy 48,49
   LeRoy, MD 47
   R J, MD 86
   T J 85,86
   T J, MD 84,85
   Thomas 84
LUCKEN
   W B 18
LUVIG
   John 90

MCARTHUR
   Claire L 124
MCCARREN

Carrie 321,322
MCCARTER
   Andrew L 160,161,162,163
   Elberta G 160,161,162,163
   Mattie 160,161,162
MCCARTY
   C C 300,301,302,303
   Carl 298
   Carl C 296,297,301
   Carl Clay 297,298,299,300
   Erra R 298
   Etta E 297
   Etta R 297,298
   Etta R Davis 299,300
   Etta Regena 296
   Vernon Clay 296,297,298,299,300, 301,302,303
MCCLARD
   C C 70,79,80
MCCLELLAN
   Clare D 127,133
   Joseph M 133
   Samuel J 133,134
MCCLELLAND
   Clara D 133
   J M 133
   Samuel J 133
MCCLURE
   Alfred Wade 254,255,256,257
   Betsy 204,211
   D C 199,200
   Douglas 203,204,206
   Douglas C 201,204,211
   Leurena B 203
   Lorena B 199,200,201,203,204, 205,206,207,208,209,210,211,212
   Lourena B 204
   Napoleon B 75,76,77
MCCOWN
   Carry 318
MCDANIEL
   Tom 323
MCKINNEY
   W H 186
   William H 191
   Wm H 186
MCLELAN
   Joseph M 128,129
MCLELLAN
   Ada 130,131,132
   Clara D 130
   Joseph M 130,131,132
   Kittie 130,132
   Mary 125
   Samuel J 127,131,132
MCLELLAND
   Joseph M 134
   Samuel J 134
MCMURTREY
   Clyde 255,256,257
MCMURTRY
   Clyde 254
MCREYNOLDS
   Thomas V 199,200
MANNING
   F 41,42,49,275,276,277
   Forbis 46,47,48,49
   Laura 46,47,48,49
   Lloyd O 46,47,48,49
   Vera 49
MANSFIELD, MCMURRAY &
   CORNISH 115,239,242
MANUS
   Martha 96,97,98,99,100,101
MARLOW
   Carrie 319,320,321
   Claud Crawford 320,321,322
   Claud Crofford 318,319,320,321
   Reuben 318
   Reuben F 319,320,321,322
MARR
   Fred T 73
MARSHALL
   W H 324
MARTIN
   M F 29,30
   W H 252
   W J 170
MATHEWS
   Sarah E 107,109
MATOY
   Ora 103,104,105,106
MAYTUBBY
   Peter, Jr 278,279,280

Index

MELTON
  Dr W J 276,277,280
  W J 12,45,274,275,277, 278,281,283
  W J, MD 274,275,277
MENDS
  Oda 163
MERRILL
  J J 118
  T J 119
MILLER
  J F 306
MONDS
  Richard 160,161,164,165
MONTGOMERY
  S K 215,218,220
  S K, MD 216,218
MOODY
  H A 105
MOON
  R F 21,22
MOORE
  Christopher D 311,312
  J M 24,25
  R F 24
  Rosa 22,23
MORAN
  D S 13,14,15
MOREMAN
  B F 2,3,4
MORGAN
  Lenora M 13,14,15
  Stella 193,194,195
  Stella S 192,193
  T M 15,16
  T M, MD 15
  Theone 192,193,194,195
  Thos M 14
  W K 192,193
  William Kelley 193,194
  William Kelly 195
  Wm K 197,198
MORRESS
  Martha A 95
MORRIS
  E E 215,216
  Martha A 99

NABORS
  J P 258
NALE
  J J 97,98,99
NEEDLES
  T B 11,25,54,66,68,72,82,100, 106,119,148,157,171,176,190,207,219, 231,250,271,282,301,310,321

OAKES
  Daniel W 125
  Mary A 125
  Mary Margariet 125
OLDS
  E C 319
OSHTA
  H 191
  Loker 187
OVERSTREET
  Siner 43,44

PADDICK
  John 117,120
PADDOCK
  John 116
  John Clinton 116,118,119,120,121
  John Quinton 119
  John S 118,119,120,121
  Marie Novie 119
  Novie 118,119,120,121
PARK
  Dr J F 4
  J F 2,4,7
  J F, MD 2,4,5,6
PARKER
  J C 96
PATTERSON
  A S 247
PERKINS
  John A 84
  Noah 84
PHILLIPS
  Charles A 5,6,7
  A D 33,34,102
  A Denton 33,34,35,87,88,90, 91,102,105

Index

PICKENS
  Austin 32
PIKE
  Ella B 123
  Ella B Freeney 124
  Ella Belle Freeney 122,123,124
  F E 122,123,124
  Fred E 123,124
  Mary P 123
  Mary Patricia 122,123,124
PILGRIM
  J B 258
PITCHLYNN
  Edward E 89,90
PLUMMER
  Mike Mayers 195,196,197,198
  Minnie 195,196,197,198
  W G 192,193
  Wallace G 108
  Walter G 195,196,197,198
POLLOCK
  J R 317
  J R, MD 317
PUSLEY
  William W 271
PYKE
  Ella B 124

RAINEY
  R M 323
RALSTON
  C J 92
RAMEY
  R M 326
RAMSEY
  Lena 83,84,85,86
RAPPOLEE
  J L 12,45,274
REASOR
  J M 40
REDSOR
  J M 38
REED
  J W 154
REEDED
  J G 126
REEDER
  J G 126
RENFROW
  C E 18,19
REYNOLDS
  Isabell 125
RICE
  F E 118,120
RICHARDS
  Clara E 142,143,144
  Clare E 141
  E T 179,180
  Samuel Allen 140,142,143,144
  Samuel Allen Wright 141,142
  W 141
  W L 144
  William L 141,142,143,144
RIDDLE
  Clem 21,22,23,24,25,26
  J T 21,22,23,24,25,26
  Mary 23
  Mary A 21,22,24,25,26
  Sina 288
  Siney 286,287
ROBERTS
  Laymon 186,188,189
  Ramsey 112,113
  Rebecca 186,189,191
  Susan 189
  Thomas 189
  Vicey 189
ROBINSON
  Aellie May 140
  Allie M 135,136
  Allie May 136,137,138,139,140
  David 135,136,137,138,139,140
  Morley 134,135,136,137,138, 139,140
ROEBUCK
  Ed 8
ROSE
  C C 324,325,326,327,328
  Christopher C 322,323,324,325
  Columbus C 326
  Mr 327
  Nettie 322,323,324,325,326,328
  Preston 326
  Preston Harral 325,326,327,328

Preston Harrol......... 322,323,324,325
ROSEWINKEL
   G... 317
ROSS
   A Frank.. 2
   S P 146,147,148,149
   S P, MD 146,147
RUFFIN
   J E... 266
RYAN
   Thos...................................... 241,245

SADLER
   Lark 312
SANDERS
   Ida.. 313,314
SCOTT
   J A 62
SEELEY
   Birdie.............................. 1,2,3,4,5,6,7
   George W 1,2,3,4,5,6,7
   May Sofina 1,2
   May Sophina.......................... 1,4,5,7
   Ralph W.. 3,4
   Ralph Whitfield 1,6,7
SELF
   Sam... 166
SELSOR
   Agnes.........233,234,235,236,237,240
   John 233,234,235,236,237,238,
   240,241,243,246
   Shelby.......232,236,237,238,239,240,
   241,242,243,244,245,246
   Thelma Thyra 232,233,234,235
SETTLE
   Dr.. 235
   J M.. 234
   J M, MD 234
SEXTON
   Eliza Ann...................................... 252
SHANAFELT
   Richard 168,307,308
SHANNON
   O L 260,261
   Ober L 262,263
   Rennie..................... 260,261,262,263
   W O 262,263
   W O, MD..................................... 262
   William Landles 260,261,262,263
   William O 261
   Wm O, MD.................................. 261
SHELON
   D.. 168
SHIRKY
   Louisa... 32
SHONEY
   W A 39,323
SKAGGS
   Ada.. 128,129
SKEEN
   M P......................... 142,143,150,151
   M P, MD 142
   N P 144
SKILLERN
   F W.. 18,20
   F W, MD 19
SLAUGHTER
   D P 221
SMITH
   Clora...................................... 107,108
   Clorie............................107,109,110
   R C 109,110
   R L 70
   Rice 107,108
   Sarah.. 108
   Sarah E 107,108,109,110
   W T 89,90
SONEY
   W B 153
SPENCER
   G R 247
STALCUP
   S P 221
STANDLEY
   C P... 323,324
SUMMERS
   Joe 287,288
   Joseph................................... 286,287
SUMTER
   Lena...............................83,84,85,86
   Lena T Ramsey.............................. 84
   Robert O............................. 83,85,86
   Robert O, Jr 83,85,86
   Robert O, Sr 83

Index

Robert O. 84
Robert Osborn, Jr. 83,84
TALBERT
  N H 104
  N J 103
TERRY
  Alice L 264,265
  Noah M 264,265
  Thomas Vernon 263,264
THOMAS
  A 213,214,215,219
  Anderson 216,217,218,220
  George 213,216,217,218
  Maggie 213,214,215,217,218, 219,220
  Mollie M 213,214,215,216, 217,218,220
THOMPSON
  C B 19
  Culverson 303
THRELKELD
  W C 154,156,158
  W C, MD 154,156
  Waller C 153
  Waller C, MD 153
  Walter C 156
TINER
  Andrew J 148
TOMOKINS
  J J 187
TOMPKINS
  J J 187,191
TREADWELL
  S P 218
TROUT
  J L 96
TUCKER
  Carrel 253,254,255
  Carrell 259
  Edward T 253,254,255,256,257, 258,259
  Ella May 316,317
  Grady 253,256,257,258
  Ida 315
  J E 306
  John Hampton 316,317

John Hampton, Jr. 316,317
Lewis 313,314
Louis 315
Mrs E T 253
Ronald 313,315
Zona ... 253,254,255,256,257,258,259
TURNER
  Andrew J 147,149
  Henry E 284,285
  A J 147
VEACH
  C 3,4
  Sophina 1
VINSO
  Belle 10
VINSON
  Belle 8,9,11
WACHUBBIE
  Ellen 62
WAICHUBBIE
  Ellen 63
WALHUBBIE
  Ellen 62
WALKER
  Malinda 264
WALLACE
  Geo O 183
  John 163,164,165,166
  Leona 163,165,166
  Leona G 163,164
  Minerva J ... 160,161,163,164,165,166
WARCHUBBIE
  Ellen 65
WARD
  Ada 222,223,229
  Adah 223,224,225,226,227, 228,229,230,231
  Alluh 226
  Ambrose Henry 246,247,248, 249,250,251
  Banjamin F 250
  Benjamin F 246,247,248,249,251
  Elias Jackson 222,223,224,226, 228,229,230,231
  J D 111,252

L E 226,227,231
Locey 246
Lockey 247,248,249,251
Lonnie 230
Lonnie E 222,223,224,225,226, 228,229,230,231
Maggie Lorene 222,224,225,230
Maggie Lorine 227,231

WEN
A T 318

WESLEY
E D 186
Simeon 186

WEST
A T 315,316

WHITLER
Annie B 201

WILBORNE
L W 122

WILKINS
L B 262,263

WILLIAMS
Frank 233,234
J E 226,227

WILLIS
Bicy 251,252
Eastman 251,252
Frances 251,252
Francis 252

WILSON
Abel 31,32,33,34,35,36
Besie 68
Bessie 33,35,36
Lida 31,32,35
Lida Bessie 31,34,35,36,37
Mary 31,32,33,34,35,36
S W 123,124
S W, MD 123,124
Sarah 33,36

WOLF
Ben 108,109

WOODS
McGee 145

WRIGHT
J Brooks 141,142

YORK

Meda 27
Media 28,30
Rosa 29

YOUNG
M C 178

ZION
Cleo 101,102,103,104,105,106
Floyd 107
H W 103
Henry W 101,102,104,105,106
Ora 101,102,103,104,105,106
Ray 107
Susan 107
A W 104
W E 107

341

www.ingramcontent.com/pod-product-compliance
Lightning Source LLC
Chambersburg PA
CBHW020241030426
42336CB00010B/573